Classic Carousel Carving

From ⅛ Scale to Full-Size
The Dentzel Patterns

H. LeRoy Marlow

 Sterling Publishing Co., Inc. New York

Photos of Armored Horse and Military Horse on color page G and of Orange Blanket Stander on page H taken by Daniel L. Feicht at Cedar Point Amusement Park, Sandusky, Ohio. All other photographs taken by Dave Shelly, University Park, Pennsylvania.

Library of Congress Cataloging-in-Publication Data

Marlow, H. LeRoy.
    Classic carousel carving / H. LeRoy Marlow.
       p. cm.
    Includes index.
    ISBN 0-8069-8252-7
    1. Wood-carving. 2. Merry-go-round art. 3. Animals in art.
I. Title.
TT199.7.M366 1992
731'.832—dc20   92-23217
                                                  CIP

10 9 8 7 6 5 4 3 2 1

Published by Sterling Publishing Company, Inc.
387 Park Avenue South, New York, N.Y. 10016
© 1992 by H. LeRoy Marlow
Distributed in Canada by Sterling Publishing
% Canadian Manda Group, P.O. Box 920, Station U
Toronto, Ontario, Canada M8Z 5P9
Distributed in Great Britain and Europe by Cassell PLC
Villiers House, 41/47 Strand, London WC2N 5JE, England
Distributed in Australia by Capricorn Link Ltd.
P.O. Box 665, Lane Cove, NSW 2066
Manufactured in the United States of America
All rights reserved

Sterling ISBN 0-8069-8252-7

Props for cover photography supplied by Earl Shriver, Dewey, Oklahoma. Tools for carving carousel animals supplied courtesy of Wood Carvers Supply, Inc., Attn: Catalog Mail Order Sales, P. O. Box 7500, Englewood, Florida 34295-7500, USA, Phone 1-800-284-6229.

Note from the Publisher

It is with great regret that I note the passing of LeRoy Marlow, who has been the Sterling author of two fine books, *Carving Carousel Animals* and the book you hold in your hands. LeRoy worked very hard to complete this work before his death, and his effort has been rewarded by a superb book, which reflects his fine craftsmanship, writing and teaching skill and his attention to detail. As you enjoy the wonderful and varied projects compiled here, you will begin to understand and appreciate his devotion to, and skill in, the craft of carving. This book is dedicated to his memory.

—*Charles Nurnberg*

Contents

Color Section opposite page 32

Preface

The carousel, sometimes referred to as the merry-go-round or the flying horses, has been around for centuries. It has delighted the young and the young at heart and has provided many happy family memories. It helped establish the streetcar industry (having a carousel at the end of the line was a means of attracting riders), has seen its demise as a hand-carving industry, and is now experiencing a strong revival. Carousel figures are now recognized as objects of art. Today, carousel animals are produced commercially from aluminum and Fiberglas. There are a few carousel woodcarvers plying their trade today, and their work generally ends up in museums or private homes as collector's items. The Empire Carousel Project, initiated by the State of New York, will make the first all-wooden carousel to be produced in the last 60 years or so.

The cost of authentic antique carousel figures is getting out of reach for most people. In 1990, one Dentzel menagerie animal sold for $148,000. Carving a replica, or having one carved, may be the only option left to many carousel lovers.

This publication is designed to assist the woodcarver to create miniature or full-sized reproductions of the carousel horses and menagerie animals produced by the G. A. Dentzel Company. The Dentzel Company operated for approximately seventy years and produced its last carousel in the mid 1920s. Dentzel carousel animals are perhaps some of the better-known carousel carvings. Often the name of the actual carver has been lost in time and only the company producing the carousel is known. With the Dentzel carvings, there are at least two known carvers, in addition to Gustave and William Dentzel. Daniel C. Muller and Salvatore Cernigliaro each influenced the final product; their creative efforts have been documented. Muller tended to design and carve rugged horses with strong characteristics. The armored and military horses (projects 3 and 5 in this book) illustrate his contribution. Cernigliaro had a more gentle touch, as shown in Project 8 (Cerni's Figure). He is also believed to have introduced the menagerie animals to the carvings produced by the Dentzel Company.

Dentzel animals can be recognized for the repeated pattern of the animals' leg and head positions. For example, a review of the enclosed plans will show the decided similarity of the positions of the standing horses. The changes in trappings and decorations on the romance (outer) side (in the United States this is the right side of the animals) are relied upon to provide variety to the carvings, while at the same time clearly identifying the carving as a Dentzel creation.

Horses with carved and horsehair tails are included among the 25 horse plans. The eagle saddle and the carved tails are examples of work done during the final phase of the Dentzel Company. The earlier carvings had much simpler saddles and horsehair tails.

This book provides all the information necessary for the woodcarver to carve a ⅛-scale model, a full-size animal, or anything in between. As space is limited in apartments, homes, and condos, the ability to produce small-scale animals becomes very important. An estimate of the time needed to carve and paint each figure is provided as a guide in many cases. This is only an estimate; the speed of each carver will vary depending upon his/her experience and ability.

This book introduces 35 Dentzel-style carvings, which are designed to be fun to produce and worthy of being cherished. It is a sequel to *Carving Carousel Animals* (Sterling Publications, 1989), which provided instruction in carving Herschell–Spillman carousel animals. I hope that you—the carver—enjoy working on the projects as much as I enjoyed producing them.

Acknowledgment

Appreciation is expressed to Nancy E. Yoder for the professional manner in which she handled the word-processing duties and to Dave Shelly of University Park, Pennsylvania, and Daniel L. Feicht of Cedar Point Amusement Park, Sandusky, Ohio, for the excellent photographs.

CHAPTER I

Getting Started

The hobby of classic carousel carving can be started with a very minimal cash outlay and little equipment. You do not have to make major commitment of time or money to equipment or training in order to learn if carousel carving is the hobby for you.

Very few tools and supplies are required to carve the ⅛th-scale miniature carousel animals shown in this book. A coping saw to rough out the carving block and a good penknife, X-acto knife, or carving knife is all that is required. A scroll saw and some gouges would be helpful and would make the carving faster and easier, but are not required. I would suggest that you resist the temptation to buy a whole set of gouges. Buy each gouge only when you have a specific need for it, and buy the one with which you are comfortable. The choice is personal. For example, some carvers use a macaroni gouge for almost everything they do; others don't even own one. Throughout this book, references are made to specific gouges; these are only suggestions. I have found they make the work easier or faster, but they are not required to complete the carving successfully.

The only supplies needed are basswood (also called linden or *Tilia*), or some other easily carved wood; glue; sandpaper; and finishing materials (paint, stain, and varnish). More specific information on these items is provided later in this chapter and in Chapter VI, "Finishing Touches."

DEVELOPING THE PLAN

There are some carvers who like to take a block of wood and start carving to see what comes out. If this is your style, you should skip this section. I'm from the school of thought that says in order to end up with a pleasing carving you need a detailed plan. I adhere to this principle religiously and can assure you that a quality carving can be produced if you plan ahead.

If you want to adopt one of the line drawings provided in Chapters III, IV, or V, you already have a plan for the romance[1] side and the

---

[1]On an American carousel the romance side (the outside) is the right side of the horse or animal, because the carousel is rotating in a counterclockwise direction. It is the side that the rider sees first when approaching the carousel.

inside view of each animal, together with the critical dimensions needed. Special instructions for large-scale animals are given in chapters VII and VIII. If you want to develop your own plan, you have three choices: (1) create one from your own imagination; (2) modify one of the existing sketches, or (3) make a replica of an original carousel carving from a photograph or from an actual visit to a carousel or museum.

If you choose to work from an actual carving, I would suggest that you begin by taking a series of 2″ × 2″ color slides. With the slides you will be able to make a plan of the desired size more easily than if you work from prints. Your first slide should be of the romance slide. Your camera should be placed perpendicular to the side of the animal, at about the midpoint of the animal's height and length. You should include the entire animal in the range-finder. This position will minimize parallax. Try to do the same thing for the inside view. This may be more difficult, since other animals on the carousel will probably be in the way. Do the best you can and take additional inside photographs from the front and rear positions if necessary. Be certain to take at least one slide from the front and rear anyway. These do not have to be at any particular angle; they may show the inside or romance side as well as the front and rear. The slides will be very valuable when you do the actual carving. It also is a good idea to take many color photographs or slides at this time to give you information about the carving details of the head, saddle, tail, trappings, body muscles, etc. These will not only help in the carving, but will be helpful in showing what colors to use when it comes time to paint.

Next, decide on the size that you want for the finished carving. The critical dimensions tables provided in Chapters III, IV, and V can serve as a general guide to you. In my experience, if you reduce an animal smaller than the ⅛th scale given in the tables, you will have to sacrifice some of the details. When you determine the length of the animal, mark this distance on a piece of plain white paper by drawing two vertical parallel lines. For example, the ⅛th scale Stander with Bells (Illus. 10) measures 10¹³⁄₁₆″ from the tail to front left knee. Vertical parallel lines 10¹³⁄₁₆″ apart are drawn on white paper. The paper is taped on the wall so that the image from the slide projector can fall on the paper. The slide of the complete romance side is placed in a projector and it is focused so that the tail just touches the left-hand line and the left knee touches the right-hand line. Trace the complete outline of the horse and all of the trappings onto the white paper. You now have a working plan of the romance side.

The simplest way to develop the plan for the inside of the animal is to work from the just-completed romance plan. Using a light table, place the first (romance side) plan *face down* and tape a fresh piece of paper over it. Trace the outline of the horse. While looking at the slides of the inside view of the same horse, draw in the simpler trappings of the inside view on your new paper, based on the slides. If you do not have access to a light table, you can improvise. A small sheet of glass (or a picture frame of the appropriate size) supported at each end by blocks of wood, bricks, or books under which a lamp or extension cord is placed will work nicely. Be careful that the surface will not be damaged by the heat of the bulb and that there is nothing nearby that can catch on fire. Never leave such an improvised light table lit and unattended. You can also tape the first (romance) drawing face down to a clean windowpane on a sunny day. The sunlight will illuminate the drawing. Tape the blank sheet over it and trace the outline.

If you are working from a photograph rather than from a slide, a plan of the proper size can be made by the "square" method, as explained in Chapter VII in the section on "Enlarging the Plan." To start this process, cover your photograph with a piece of translucent paper, like tracing paper. In the event that translucent paper is not available, you can improvise by taking a sheet of typing paper and lightly covering it with vegetable oil. This will make the paper translucent. Blot up the excess oil with a paper towel to minimize any damage to the photograph. I would not recommend this method of improvisation if the photograph is a valuable one, however.

Draw a series of parallel lines, both vertically and horizontally, covering the entire body of the animal, at evenly spaced intervals (for example, every ½"). A drawing board, T-square, and triangle will make this task easier, but if these are not available, the grid can be made with just a ruler and careful measuring. You are now ready to enlarge or reduce the carousel animal photograph to produce your actual working plan, as you now have a plan divided into square units. In order to enlarge it, decide what approximate size you want the animal to be. See the section in Chapter VII, on "Enlarging the Plan" for details of how to proceed.

DIRECTION OF THE WOOD GRAIN

After the plan is developed, you will need to decide how many parts or pieces will be needed to complete the carving block. If you will again refer to Stander with Bells (Illus. 10), you will see that there are nine parts: head, body, right front leg, left front leg (2 sections), right hind leg (2 sections), left hind leg, and tail.[2] Nine pieces are necessary to be sure the finished carving is strong. The wood grain should run horizontally in the body, but if it ran horizontally in the legs, it would produce a very weak leg structure. There-

---

[2]For larger animals, special procedures are necessary. See chapters VII and VIII for details.

fore, each part is laid out so that the part length is parallel with the wood grain. This concept is explained more thoroughly in Chapter II. Large lines across animal drawings on the plans indicate where carving block divisions occur.

After you have divided your plan into the proper number of parts and have made a pattern for each part, you are ready to adhere these patterns to the wood.

CEMENTING THE PATTERN TO THE WOOD

Select wood of the proper thickness for each part. Again referring to Illus. 10 and Table 7 for the Stander with Bells, you will see that the wood for the head is ⅞″ thick; the wood for the body is 1½″ thick; the wood for the front and hind legs is ½″ thick; and the wood for the hind thighs and tail is ¾″ thick.

Cut each pattern from your plan. It is a good idea to make a photocopy of your plan and to use that for your patterns. Be certain to check and see that your photocopy is exactly the same size as your original plan. Not all copiers copy at exactly 100%; with some copying machines it is necessary to make some size adjustments to ensure accurate copies.

Using rubber cement, adhere each pattern to the wood of the proper thickness. If rubber cement is not available, you can use thinned white glue to adhere the pattern. Be certain that the length of the part parallels the grain of the wood. Cut out each part using a coping or scroll saw.

GLUING

Based upon experience, each craftsman has his or her own preference as to which is the best glue to use. I recommend yellow carpenter's glue. It is convenient to use, is formulated especially for wood, and "grabs" faster than the white glue. However, the choice is yours.

For the smaller carvings, all joints are butt joints. In the larger animals, mortise and tenon joints will be used. As any woodworker knows, butt joints are the weakest of all wood joints. They can be made to work very satisfactorily if a few precautions are followed, however. Make certain that the joint areas are flat and smooth. Where end grain is involved, "butter" or "size" the part prior to final gluing. To "butter" the part, place a thin film of glue on both surfaces to be glued and wipe off the excess. When dry, sand them both smooth. This procedure will permit the end grain to soak up the initial glue and thus absorption will not take any strength from the permanent joint. When you are ready to glue, place a thin film of glue on each part to be glued, let the parts sit for about 10 minutes, and then join them. Press the parts together, slide them back and forth until they are permanently seated in the desired position, and set them aside to dry. See chapters VII and VIII for gluing instructions for larger animals.

One additional word of caution: since the yellow glue binds by molecular action, the air, the wood to be joined, and the glue should all be at a temperature of at least 65°F (18°C). Under colder conditions, a good bond may not occur. Where possible, the parts should be clamped during the drying process. For the smaller parts this may be done by using a rubber band or twine. For the larger parts, C clamps, hand screws, or furniture clamps may be used. For softwood, approximately 30 minutes at 70°F (22°C) is the desired clamping time, and for hardwood this time is increased to 45–60 minutes. An increase in the temperature will reduce the time required for the glue to set. When the glue is thoroughly dry, you are ready to begin the actual carving.

CHAPTER II

Enlarged Views of Individual Parts

One characteristic of the horses produced by the G. A. Dentzel Company is the tendency to use the same position of legs, tails, and heads over and over. This becomes quite clear when one reviews the plans in this book. The original carvers relied upon color, trappings, and other embellishments to make each animal look different.

Each carver will have his or her own way to start the carving process. There is no one best way. With that idea in mind, I suggest that the following steps might be helpful to the beginning carver in making a ⅛th-scale carving:

1. Place the carving block in a vise, bench dog, or some other type of hold-down and with a gouge, such as a Number 7 18-mm gouge, remove the excess wood from the larger areas. This could be done on a portion of the front leg, the taper of the hind thighs, the thickness of the neck, and the rounding of the flank, for example. Using a gouge is faster than using a knife, although if you don't have a gouge the knife will work perfectly well.

2. Use a Number 11 3-mm gouge to cut the impressions of the fetlock into the legs.

3. With a knife, reduce the thickness of all four legs between the knee and the ankle to ¼″ (for ⅛-scale animal).

4. Using the point of a knife—an X-acto knife with a Number 11 blade works well—outline the saddle and other trappings on the body with a stop cut. Make a stop cut with the knife held perpendicular to the animal's body. Then remove a chip by making an angular cut into and stopping at the first cut, hence the name *stop cut*.

5. Now proceed to round the animal to its desired finished form, using the critical dimensions, plans, and photographs given in the book as guides.

To aid you, this chapter provides drawings of the component parts, illustrating the details that are common to more than one horse. The basic information contained in this section can be applied to each of the twenty-five horse plans presented in the book. Review the narrative and drawings in this section to see the shape and details of the legs, neck and head, body, and tail. Although there will be minor differences among the horses, this closeup information will help you to visualize the details and will augment the plan drawings.

HEAD AND NECK

In the horse projects given in the book, the head is generally facing down or straight ahead. On some steeds, the eyes may be wide open, denoting speed or spirit, on others they appear more subdued. The mouth may be wide open, showing excitement, or it may be more relaxed. As a horse ages, its teeth are pushed outward, so you will notice that the front edge of the teeth is not perpendicular to the jaw, but has an outward slope.

In most cases the neck is part of the body carving block for the small-scale animals, as noted in the plans. If you do not see a dividing line on the illustration between the head and neck, it means they are both carved from one block. The neck is always wider at the body end than at the head end. The front of the animal's chest has a breastbone, which runs vertically from the pelvic area to the neck. It is wider at the bottom than it is at the top.

Horses with flowing manes generally have most of the mane on the romance (right) side, with only the overlapping hair showing on the inside. Roached (trimmed) manes are identical on the romance side and the inside.

The animal's head may or may not be at an angle to the vertical or longitudinal center line. Of those heads at an angle, some are tilted at only a single angle to the center line—either longitudinally or vertically (Illus. 1, top). Other animals' heads are tilted with respect to both the longitudinal and the vertical center lines. For those horses where there is a single angle, there will be only one vertical or horizontal line on the plan between the head and neck. This line defines both the edge of the neck block as well as the base of the head. (For examples of vertical tilt, see illus. 6, 10, and 14.) For examples of horizontal tilt, see illus. 24, 56, and 65.) Where no lines appear on the head plan, it indicates that the head is facing forward with no sideways tilt. (For examples of no tilt see illus. 4, 8, and 12.) For the single-angle horses, mark the vertical and horizontal center lines on both the neck and the head. Reduce the neck block to its proper thickness, if you have not already done so. For the ⅛-scale horse, cut the head off of a ½″ number 20 brad and insert one end of the brad into the horse's head and the other end into the horse's neck at the point where the center lines cross. Rotate the horse's head on the brad until the proper degree of tilt is achieved, and glue the horse's head in place.

Where a compound angle occurs, the second angle is achieved by having the front surface of the neck block at an angle to the longitudinal center line with the surface sloping towards the romance (right) side (Illus. 1, bottom). In those plans where the double angle occurs (Illus. 42, for example) two parallel lines appear on the plan

SINGLE ANGLE

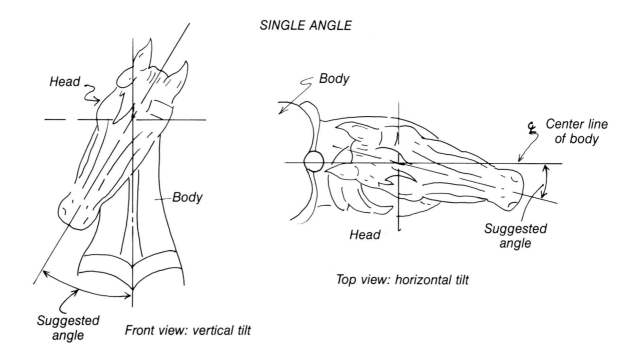

Front view: vertical tilt

Top view: horizontal tilt

COMPOUND ANGLE

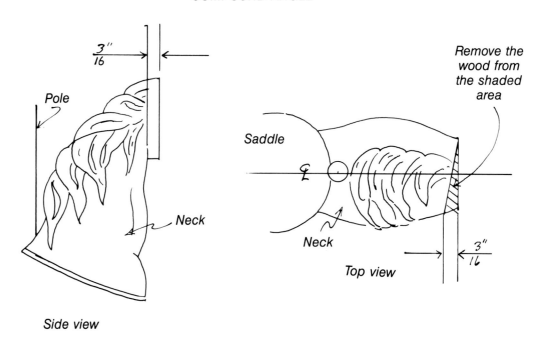

Side view

Illus. 1. Top left and right: single angle of head tilt to center line. Bottom left and right: compound angle.

within the head/neck area. The line to the left is the base of the head block. The line to the right indicates an extension of the neck block. When the neck carving block is prepared for a ⅛-scale horse, an additional ³⁄₁₆″ is added to the front of the neck pattern. When carving, reduce the neck thickness to its rough dimension (usually ¾″ or ⅞″ for a ⅛th-scale horse). Measure ³⁄₁₆″ in from the front edge of the neck on the romance side and draw a line parallel to the front edge (Illus. 1, bottom left). On the top of the block draw a line from the line just drawn on the romance side to the inside front edge. This will outline a triangular area with the wide part at the romance side (Illus. 1, bottom right). Remove the wood from this area. Mark the vertical and horizontal center lines on both the neck and the head. Cut the head off of a ½″ Number 20 brad and insert one end of the brad into the animal's head and the other end into the animal's neck at the point where the two center lines cross. Rotate the head on the brad until the proper degree of tilt is achieved and glue the animal's head in place.

LEGS

Although there are several variations, the legs are of two basic types—straight and bent. The bent leg is made up of at least two separate pieces. Gluing of end-grain wood will be involved, so be certain to "butter" the joints, as explained in the previous chapter. Illustrations 2 and 3 show the shapes of the cross sections of legs at various levels. A Number 1 3-mm gouge is helpful in carving the fetlock areas in the rear of the leg.

TAIL

The majority of the horses included in this book have carved tails. During the 1920s the G. A. Dentzel Company horses had carved wooden tails rather than the horsehair tails of their predecessors. The swirl pattern of the hair varies, but the general carving pro-

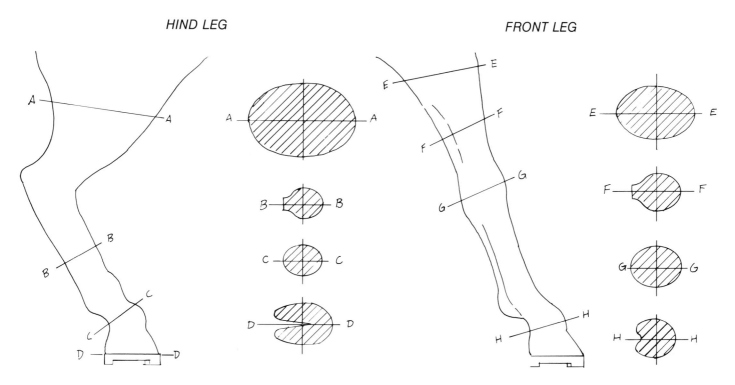

Illus. 2. Side view and cross sections of hind leg (left) and front leg (right) at various heights (not drawn to scale).

cedure is the same. The grain runs lengthwise in all cases. The carved tails are generally in one of three positions—suspended between the hind legs, against the inside of the right hind leg, or overlapping and on top of the right hind leg. For the ⅛-scale horse, there is a ¼″ dowel carved at the top of the tail to fit the hole made in the body.

To make the carved tail that overlaps the right hind leg, start with the tail pattern, just as you would for the straight carved tail. On the outside rear edge draw a curved line starting about 1″ from the end of the tail (for the ⅛-scale animal) and meeting the bottom corner on the right-hand (romance) side (Illus. 3, bottom right). Cut out this segment with a scroll saw and glue it to the right-hand side of the carving block. Shape the tail as previously explained. The tail will curve around the rump, over the hind leg, and will be close to the side of the body. The finished carved tail may be seen in a number of the photographs, such as that of the Stander with Bells.

Each tail should be carved separately and glued in place after the horse is carved, sanded, and ready for painting. The tail tapers towards the end and the edges are rounded to resemble a natural horse's tail. Each tail is carved in a similar manner, but the thickness may be varied. For the ⅛-scale horse, a thinner tail may be achieved by using a ½″ thickness carving block, rather than the ¾″ thickness suggested in the tables of critical dimensions. A Number 1 2-mm gouge and a Number 15 3-mm "V" gouge are helpful in carving the shallow areas. The final hair texturing is done with a burning pen.

BODY

The body carving block for the ⅛th-scale horse is solid. The larger-sized carving blocks are hollow, as explained in Chapter VII. The hole in the body that will hold the pole is drilled at a right angle to the base that the horse will stand on. For the ⅛-scale horse it is ¼″ in diameter. This hole should be drilled before the actual carving is started. On those plans where a base line may not be obvious—for example, for the horses in the jumping position—a base reference line has been provided on the plan to ensure that the hole is properly located (see, for example, Illus. 32). The hole for the tail also should be made before the actual carving begins. Care must be taken in drilling the tail hole as the drill will have a tendency to "wander" when drilling end grain at an angle. After the holes are drilled, use a coping saw, scroll saw, or band saw to shape the outline of the body, depending on the size wood you need to cut.

HORSESHOES

For the ⅛-scale horse, cut the four horseshoes from 3/32″ stock (see Illus. 3) and glue one shoe to the bottom of each leg. End-grain gluing will be involved, so be certain to "butter" the bottom of each leg with glue before the actual gluing. Reduce the shaded areas in Illus. 3 to a shoe thickness of ³⁄₆₄″. For larger horses, see instructions in Chapter VIII.

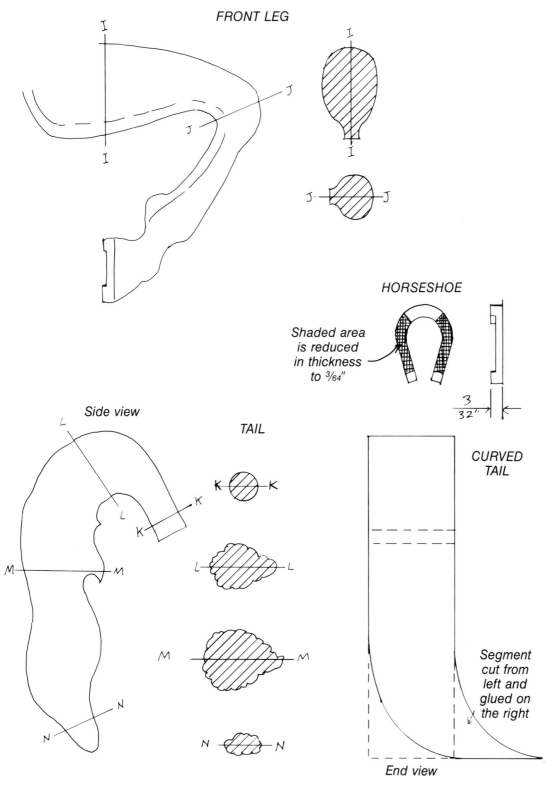

Illus. 3. Top: side view (left) and cross section (right) of bent front leg. Middle: carving horseshoe. Bottom (left): side view of tail and cross sections. Bottom right: block for tail carving.

CHAPTER III

Outside Row Horses

The animals on the outside row are larger and more ornate than the other animals on the carousel. These carvings were designed to catch the eyes of potential riders to increase their desire to want to get on the carousel, thus boosting ticket sales.

The outside row might contain menagerie figures, usually the larger ones (Lion, Tiger, Deer). Without exception all of the horses on the outside row were standers. A horse is designated a "stander" when it has at least three feet on the platform. These outside-row animals traveled with the rotation of the carousel, but they did not move up and down, as was characteristic of the inside-row animals.

The average time to make a ⅛th-scale carving of an outside-row animal is 26 hours. This includes the time needed to prepare the carving block, carve it, sand it, and paint it. Of course the experience and ability of each carver to carve and paint affects the amount of time required.

1. Patriotic Horse

Circa 1914

Using Illus. 4 as a plan, cut out the nine patterns and glue each pattern to wood of the proper thickness, as defined in Table 1. Refer to Illus. 2 for the complete pattern of the left front and hind legs. The length of each part should follow the direction of the grain. Table 2 provides the critical dimensions for the various sizes of horse.

The complete carving block consists of the nine parts listed in Table 1. For the ⅛-scale animal, drill a ¼″ hole perpendicularly through the body for the pole. Drill a ¼″ hole at a 60° angle from the perpendicular for the tail before gluing the legs in place (see Illus. 4). Size the end grain of each leg part and glue the legs in place. The head faces straight ahead with no sideways tilt.

From ³⁄₁₆″ stock, cut out the head and body of the decorative eagle and glue them to the romance side of the horse (see Illus. 4). This extra stock will permit the eagle to stand out from the body of the horse.

Use a burning pen to put the hair texture in the mane and tail. For the ⅛-scale animal, cut four horseshoes from ³⁄₃₂″ stock and glue one

Table 1   Parts List for the Patriotic Horse (⅛ Scale)

Part	Length	Width	Thickness
Body and head	6½″	5″	1½″
Right front leg	3⅛″	¾″	½″
Left front leg	1⅜″	⅜″	½″
Left front hoof	1″	½″	⁷⁄₁₆″
Right hind thigh	1″	1½″	¾″
Right hind leg	2¼″	⅝″	⁷⁄₁₆″
Left hind thigh	1⅜″	1⅜″	¾″
Left hind leg	2³⁄₁₆″	⅝″	⁷⁄₁₆″
Tail	2¹¹⁄₁₆″	1½″	¾″

to the bottom of each hoof. End-grain gluing will be involved, so be certain to "butter" the bottom of each leg with glue (see instructions on gluing in Chapter I). Reduce the middle sections of the horse-shoes to a shoe thickness of ³⁄₆₄″ (Illus. 3) for the ⅛-scale animal. Refer to Illus. 4 and 5 and to Table 2, the critical dimensions for a full-sized horse or a reduced-scale model, to complete the final shapes and details. After final sanding, glue the tail into the ¼″ hole and against the outside surface of the right hind leg.

After carving and sanding, paint the horse in accordance with the suggested color symbols in circles on the plans (see color chart in Chapter VI), or according to your own taste. For the ⅛-scale ani-mal, insert a 10½″ length of a ¼″-diameter brass pole (Illus. 79), brass tubing, or a gold-painted dowel through the hole in the body so that 5″ extends above the saddle. Glue the pole in place. Add the footrest (Illus. 80) to the pole ¹³⁄₁₆″ below the body. Make a base (see the section on bases in Chapter VI) and glue the pole of the

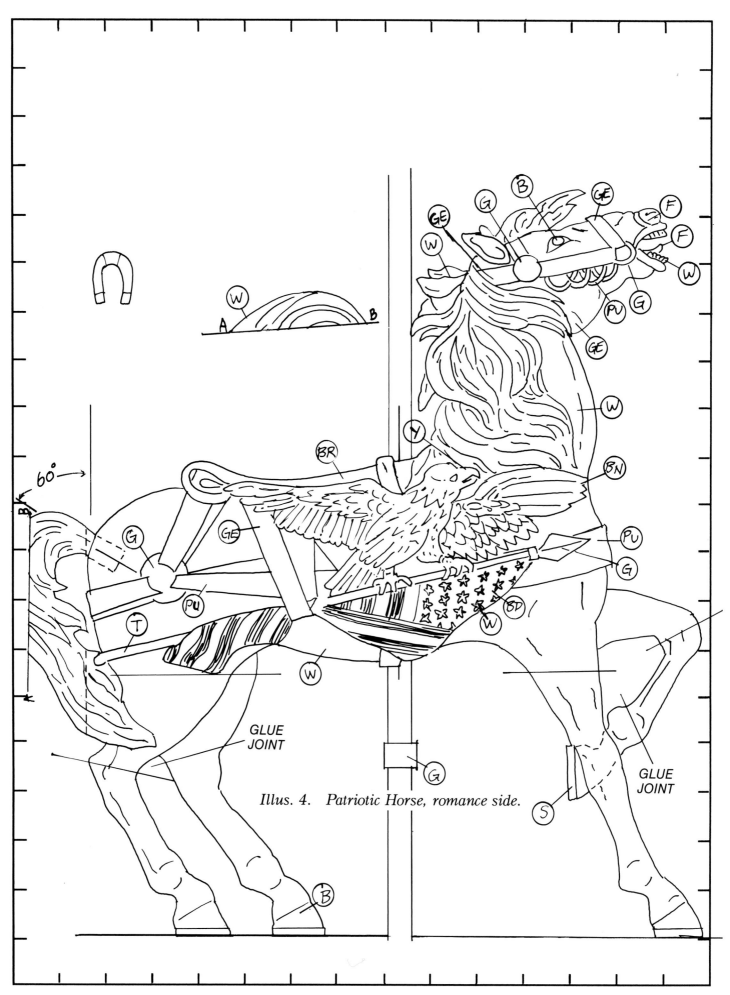

Illus. 4.   Patriotic Horse, romance side.

GLUE JOINT

GLUE JOINT

60°

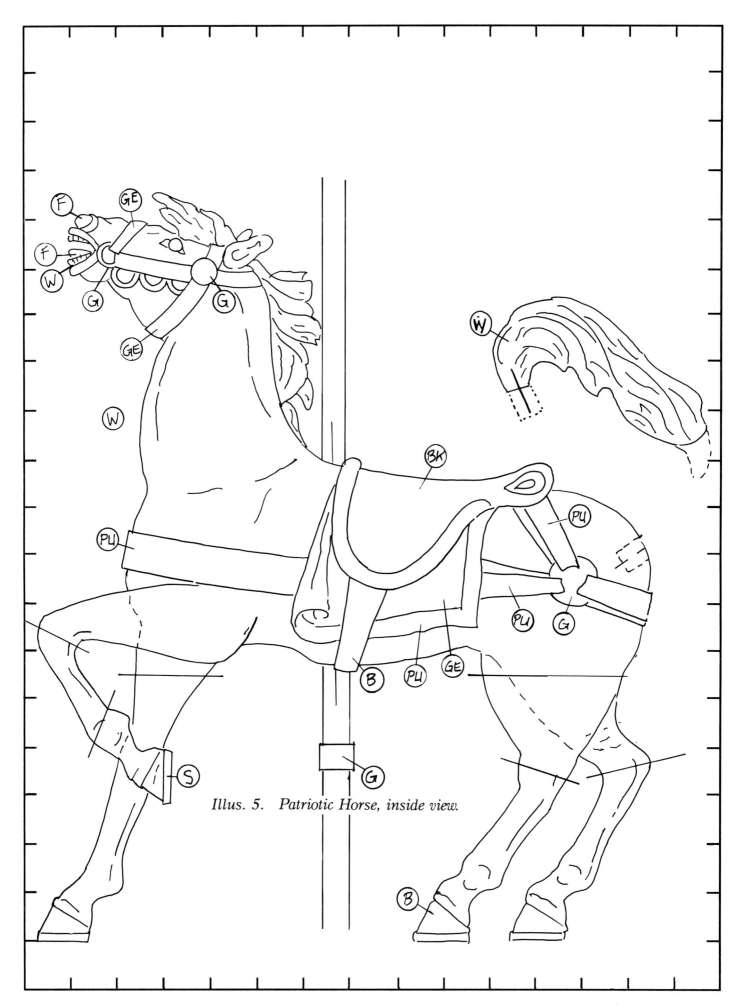

Illus. 5. Patriotic Horse, inside view.

completed horse to it. Instructions for large-scale animals are given in chapters VII and VIII.

For the ⅛-scale horse, the approximate carving time is 15½ hours; approximately 29 hours are required to carve, sand, and paint this Patriotic Horse.

Table 2 Critical Dimensions of the Patriotic Horse

	Scale				*Full*
	⅛	¼	½	¾	*Size*
From hoof to top of mane	7⅝″	15¼″	30½″	45¾″	61″
From rump to breast	5 9/16″	11⅛″	22¼″	33⅜″	44½″
From tail to front right knee	7½″	15″	30″	45″	60″
Width of head (including mane)	⅞″	1¾″	3½″	5¼″	7″
Width of nose	½″	1″	2″	3″	4″
Distance between tips of ears	13/16″	1⅝″	3¼″	4⅞″	6½″
Width of neck at head	1″	2″	4″	6″	8″
Width of neck at body	1⅜″	2¾″	5½″	8¼″	11″
Width of body at pole	1½″	3″	6″	9″	12″
Width of saddle at rear	1½″	3″	6″	9″	12″
Width of rump	1½″	3″	6″	9″	12″
Width of front leg at body	½″	1″	2″	3″	4″
Width of front leg at knee	⅜″	¾″	1½″	2¼″	3″
Width of hind leg at body	¾″	1½″	3″	4½″	6″
Width of hind leg at knee	⅜″	¾″	1½″	2¼″	3″
Width of tail	¾″	1½″	3″	4½″	6″
Length of hoof	9/16″	1⅛″	2¼″	3⅜″	4½″
Width of hoof	13/32″	13/16″	1⅝″	2 7/16″	3¼″

2. Dapple White with Flowers

Circa 1922

Using Illus. 6 as a plan, cut out the ten patterns and glue each pattern to wood of the correct thickness, given in Table 3. Refer to Illus. 7 for the complete patterns of the left front and hind legs. The length of each part should follow the direction of the wood grain.

The complete carving block consists of the ten parts listed in Table 3. For the ⅛-scale horse, drill a ¼″ hole perpendicularly through the

body for the pole and a ¼″ hole at a 60° angle from the perpendicular for the tail before gluing the head or legs in place (see Illus. 6). Size the end grain of each part (see instructions on gluing in Chapter I) and glue the head and legs to the body. The head tilts on a vertical axis 20° towards the romance side. Instructions for large-scale animals are given in chapters VII and VIII.

Cut four horseshoes from ³⁄₃₂″ stock (for the ⅛-scale horse) and glue one to the bottom of each hoof. End-grain gluing will be involved, so be certain to "butter" the bottom of each hoof (see gluing instructions in Chapter I). Reduce the middle areas of the horseshoes (see Illus. 3) to a shoe thickness of ³⁄₆₄″. Refer to Illus. 6 and 7 and Table 4 to complete the final shapes and details. Cut out the flowers from ¹⁄₁₆″ stock and glue them in place on the body. This will provide the added depth needed for the flowers. Use a burning pen to add texture to the mane, tail, and tassels. After final sanding, glue the tail into the hole in the body and glue it against the romance side of the right hind leg.

Table 4 provides the critical dimensions that you will need to carve a full-size or reduced-scale replica.

After carving and sanding the horse, paint it in accordance with the colors suggested in circles on plans (see color chart in Chapter VI), or select your own colors. The fine painted details are applied with a draftsman's ruling pen, as explained in Chapter VI. For the ⅛-scale horse, insert a 10½″ length of a ¼″-diameter brass pole (Illus. 79), brass tubing, or a gold-painted dowel through the hole in the body so that ½″ of the pole extends below the bottom of the hooves. Glue the pole in place. Add the footrest (Illus. 80) to the pole ¹³⁄₁₆″

below the body. Make a stand and glue the pole of the completed horse to it.

The approximate carving time for the ⅛-scale Dappled White with Flowers is 15½ hours; approximately 29 hours are needed to carve, sand, and paint the horse.

Table 3   Parts List for the Dapple White with Flowers (⅛ Scale)

Part	Length	Width	Thickness
Head	2¼″	1³⁄₁₆″	⅞″
Body and neck	6⅝″	4½″	1½″
Right front leg	3³⁄₁₆″	⅞″	½″
Left front leg	1¼″	½″	½″
Left front hoof	¾″	⁹⁄₁₆″	½″
Right hind thigh	1¾″	1¼″	¾″
Right hind leg	2⁵⁄₁₆″	⅝″	½″
Left hind thigh	⅞″	1⅜″	¾″
Left hind leg	2½″	⅝″	½″
Tail	2⅞″	1⅝″	¾″

Table 4   Critical Dimensions for Dapple White with Flowers

	Scale				Full Size
	⅛	¼	½	¾	
From hoof to tip of mane	7⅛″	14¼″	28½″	42¾″	57″
From rump to breast	5¹⁵⁄₁₆″	11⅞″	23¾″	35⅝″	47½″
From tail to front right knee	7⅞″	15¾″	31½″	47¼″	63″
Width of head	⅞″	1¾″	3½″	5¼″	7″
Width of nose	½″	1″	2″	3″	4″
Distance between tips of ears	⅝″	1¼″	2½″	3¾″	5″
Width of neck at head (with mane)	⅞″	1¾″	3½″	5¼″	7″
Width of neck at body	1¼″	2½″	5″	7½″	10″
Width of body at pole	1½″	3″	6″	9″	12″
Width of saddle across eagle nose	¾″	1½″	3″	4½″	6″
Width of saddle at eagle head	1⅛″	2¼″	4½″	6¾″	9″
Width of rump	1½″	3″	6″	9″	12″
Width of front leg at body	½″	1″	2″	3″	4″
Width of front leg at knee	⅜″	¾″	1½″	2¼″	3″
Width of hind leg at body	¾″	1½″	3″	4½″	6″
Width of hind leg at knee	⅜″	¾″	1½″	2¼″	3″
Width of tail	¾″	1½″	3″	4½″	6″
Length of hoof	⅝″	1¼″	2½″	3¾″	5″
Width of hoof	½″	1″	2″	3″	4″

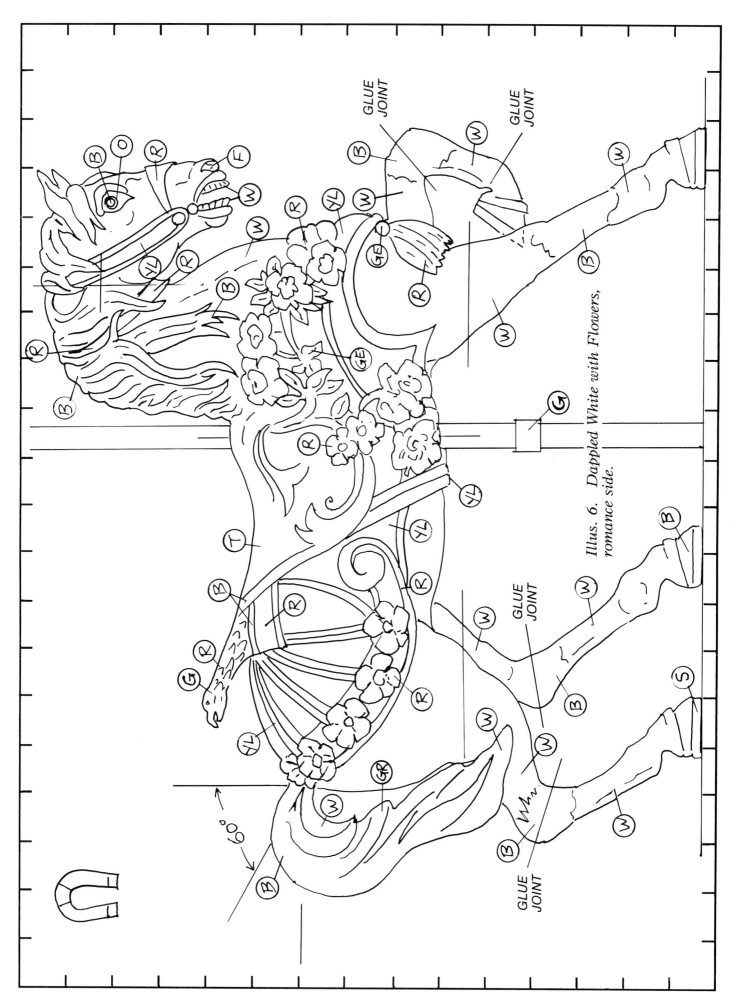

Illus. 6. Dappled White with Flowers, romance side.

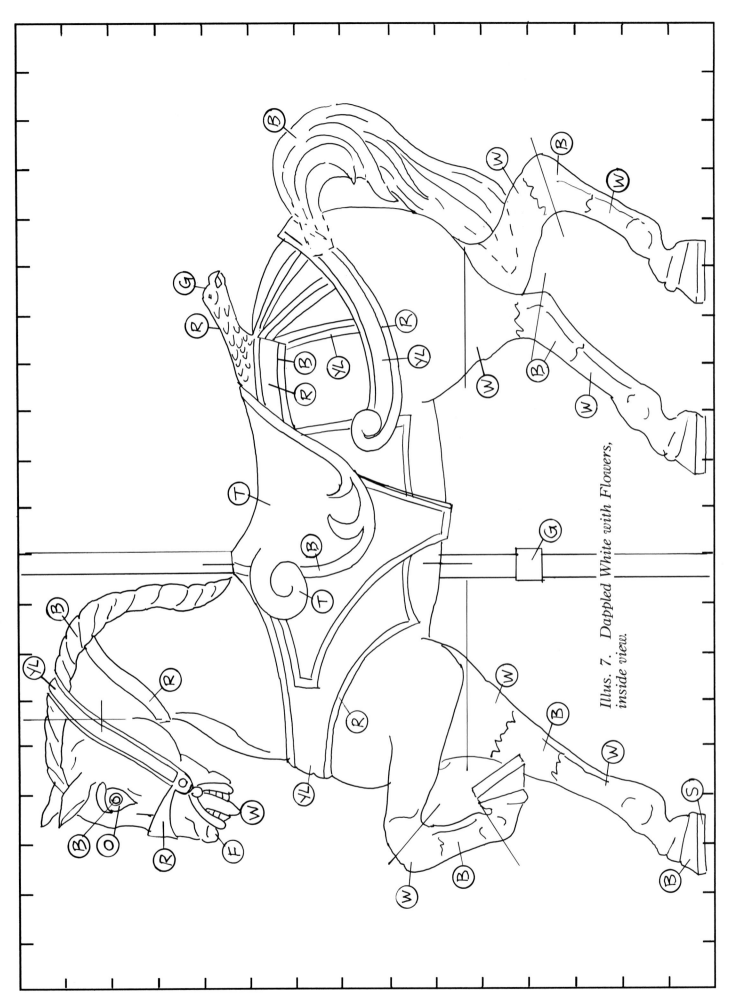

Illus. 7. Dappled White with Flowers, inside view.

3. Armored Horse

Circa 1917

Using Illus. 8 as a plan, cut out the seven patterns given and glue each pattern to wood of the correct thickness, as defined in Table 5. The length of each part should follow the direction of the wood grain.

The complete carving block consists of the seven parts listed in Table 5. For the ⅛-scale horse, drill a ¼″ hole perpendicularly through the body for the pole, using the base reference line on Illus. 8 as a guide, and drill a ¼″ hole at a 60° angle from the perpendicular for the tail (see Illus. 8). Drill these holes before the legs are glued in place. Size the end grain of all parts (see gluing instructions in Chapter I) and glue the four legs in place. The head faces straight ahead; there is no sideways tilt. Instructions for large-scale animals are given in chapters VII and VIII.

Table 5   Parts List for the Armored Horse (⅛ Scale)

Part	Length	Width	Thickness
Head and body	7⅜″	5⅝″	1⅝″
Right front leg	1¹⁵⁄₁₆″	¾″	½″
Left front leg	1⁵⁄₁₆″	⁷⁄₁₆″	½″
Left front hoof	¹¹⁄₁₆″	½″	½″
Right hind leg	2⅛″	⅝″	1⅛″
Left hind leg	2¼″	⅝″	1⅛″
Tail	1⅞″	1⁹⁄₁₆″	¾″

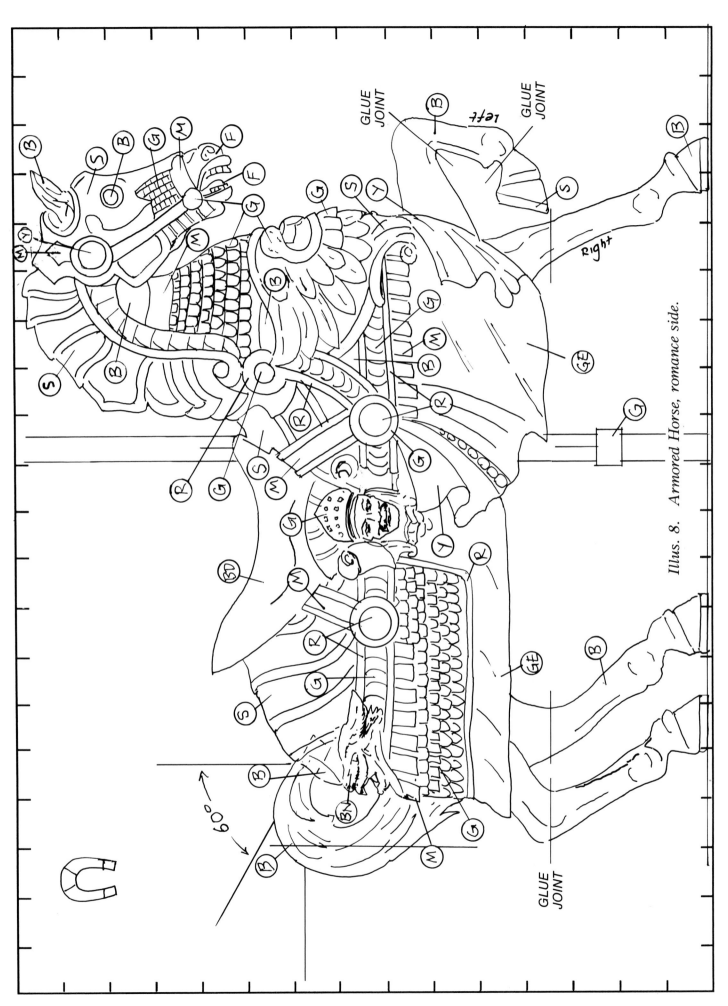

Illus. 8. Armored Horse, romance side.

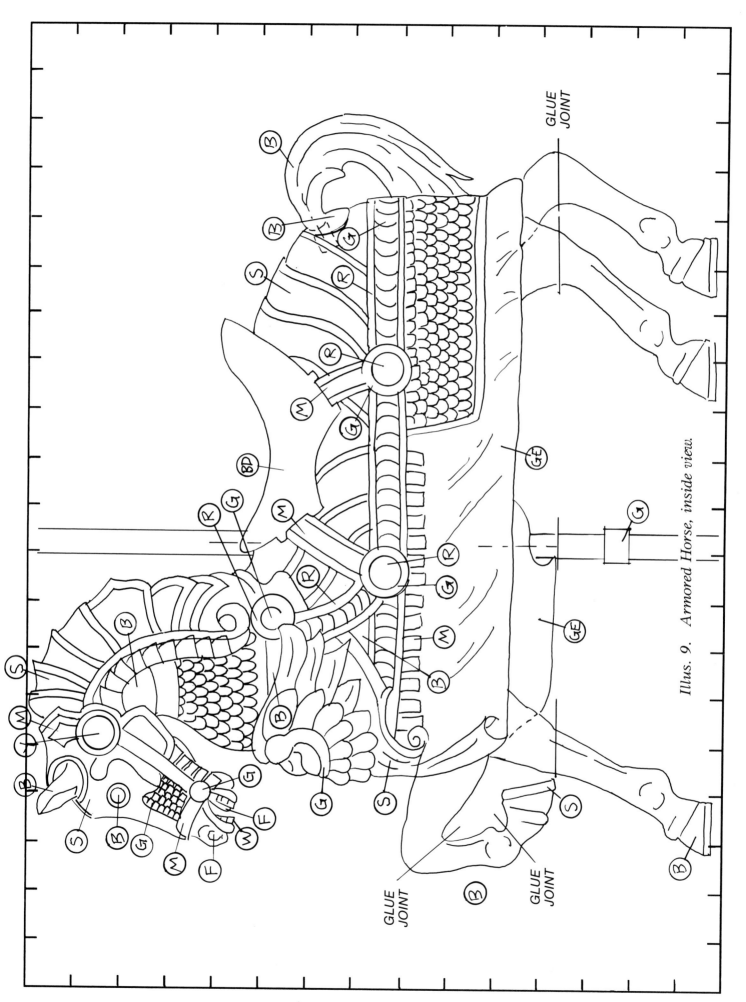

Illus. 9. Armored Horse, inside view.

GLUE JOINT

GLUE JOINT

GLUE JOINT

31

Cut four horseshoes from $\frac{3}{32}''$ stock for the $\frac{1}{8}$-scale horse, and glue one to the bottom of each leg. End-grain gluing is involved, so be certain to "butter" the bottom of each leg with glue. Reduce the middle areas of the horseshoes to a shoe thickness of $\frac{3}{64}''$ (Illus. 3). Refer to Illus. 8 and 9 and Table 6, the critical dimensions for a full-sized horse or a reduced-scale model, to complete the final shapes and details.

Table 6   Critical Dimensions for the Armored Horse

	Scale				Full Size
	$\frac{1}{8}$	$\frac{1}{4}$	$\frac{1}{2}$	$\frac{3}{4}$	
From hoof to tip of head armor	$7\frac{1}{4}''$	$14\frac{1}{2}''$	$29''$	$43\frac{1}{2}''$	$58''$
From rump to breast	$6''$	$12''$	$24''$	$36''$	$48''$
From tail to front right knee	$7\frac{3}{4}''$	$15\frac{1}{2}''$	$31''$	$46\frac{1}{2}''$	$62''$
Width of head	$1\frac{1}{8}''$	$2\frac{1}{4}''$	$4\frac{1}{2}''$	$6\frac{3}{4}''$	$9''$
Width of nose	$\frac{7}{16}''$	$\frac{7}{8}''$	$1\frac{3}{4}''$	$2\frac{5}{8}''$	$3\frac{1}{2}''$
Distance between tips of ears	$\frac{7}{8}''$	$1\frac{3}{4}''$	$3\frac{1}{2}''$	$5\frac{1}{4}''$	$7''$
Width of neck at head	$1\frac{1}{8}''$	$2\frac{1}{4}''$	$4\frac{1}{2}''$	$6\frac{3}{4}''$	$9''$
Width of neck at body	$2''$	$4''$	$8''$	$12''$	$16''$
Width of body at pole	$2\frac{1}{4}''$	$4\frac{1}{2}''$	$9''$	$13\frac{1}{2}''$	$18''$
Width of saddle at rear	$2\frac{1}{8}''$	$4\frac{1}{4}''$	$8\frac{1}{2}''$	$12\frac{3}{4}''$	$17''$
Width of rump	$2\frac{1}{4}''$	$4\frac{1}{2}''$	$9''$	$13\frac{1}{2}''$	$18''$
Width of front leg at body	$\frac{1}{2}''$	$1''$	$2''$	$3''$	$4''$
Width of front leg at knee	$\frac{3}{8}''$	$\frac{3}{4}''$	$1\frac{1}{2}''$	$2\frac{1}{4}''$	$3''$
Width of hind leg at body	$1\frac{1}{8}''$	$2\frac{1}{4}''$	$4\frac{1}{2}''$	$6\frac{3}{4}''$	$9''$
Width of hind leg at knee	$\frac{3}{8}''$	$\frac{3}{4}''$	$1\frac{1}{2}''$	$2\frac{1}{4}''$	$3''$
Length of hoof	$\frac{9}{16}''$	$1\frac{1}{8}''$	$2\frac{1}{4}''$	$3\frac{3}{8}''$	$4\frac{1}{2}''$
Width of hoof	$\frac{7}{16}''$	$\frac{7}{8}''$	$1\frac{3}{4}''$	$2\frac{5}{8}''$	$3\frac{1}{2}''$

Since the horse has a free-standing tail, an extra step to strengthen it is recommended. Drill a hole on the center line of the doweled end of the tail and insert a $1''$ long Number 20 brad. After sanding, glue the tail into the hole in the body. Use a burning pen to add texture to the tail. The individual pieces of mail in the armor can be made using a pointed knife and Number 11 1-, 2-, and 3-mm gouges. From $\frac{1}{4}''$ stock, cut out the face on the saddle and glue it to the horse's body to give extra depth for carving the relief.

After carving and sanding the horse, paint it in accordance with the suggested color symbols given in circles in the illustrations (see color chart in Chapter VI), or choose colors according to your own taste. For the $\frac{1}{8}$-scale horse, insert a $10\frac{1}{2}''$ length of a $\frac{1}{4}''$-diameter brass pole (Illus. 79), brass tubing, or a gold-painted dowel through the hole in the body so that $5''$ extends above the saddle. Glue the

*Dapple White with Flowers
(Project 2).*

A

*Stander with Bells
(Project 4).*

Indian Stander (Project 6).

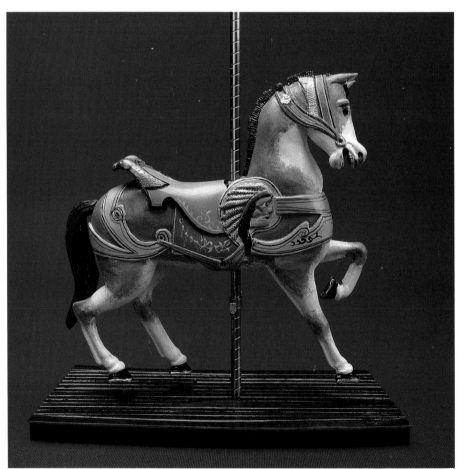

B

*Stander with Garlands
(Project 7).*

*Tassels and Disks
(Project 10).*

*Yellow-Fringe Prancer
(Project 16).*

*Western Prancer
(Project 18).*

D

Red Stripe Jumper
(Project 19).

Diamond Light (Project 20).

E

Flying Mane (Project 23).

*Flying Tassels
(Project 21).*

F

Armored Horse (Project 3).

Military Horse (Project 5).

G

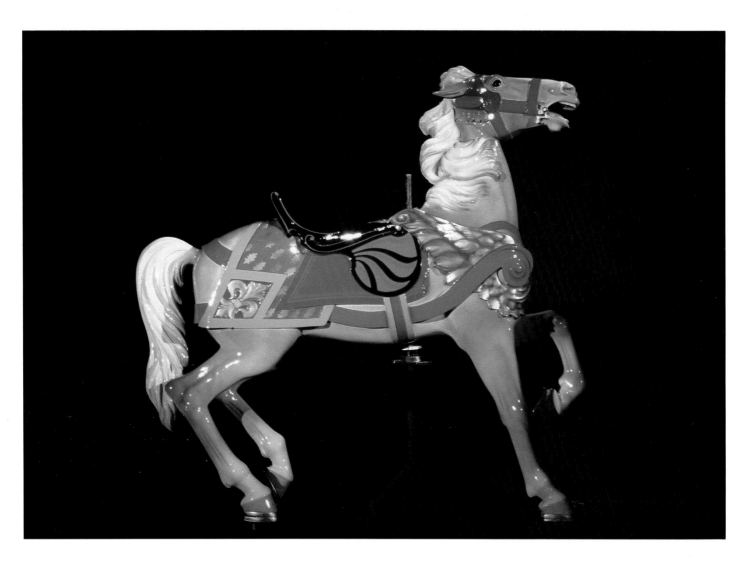

Orange Blanket Stander (Project 11).
Top: view of romance side.
Bottom: close-up of head.

H

pole in place. Add the footrest (Illus. 80) to the pole ¹³⁄₁₆″ below the body. Make a base (see section on bases in Chapter VI) and glue the pole of the completed horse to it.

The approximate carving time is 2½ hours, and approximately 29 hours are required to carve, sand, and paint the ⅛-scale Armored Horse.

4. Stander with Bells

Circa 1922

Using Illus. 10 as a plan, cut out the nine patterns and glue each pattern to wood of the correct thickness, as defined in Table 7. Refer to Illus. 11 for the complete patterns of the left front and hind legs. The length of each part should follow the direction of the wood grain.

The complete carving block consists of the nine parts listed in Table 7. For the ⅛-scale horse drill a ¼″ hole perpendicularly through the body for the pole, and drill a ¼″ hole at a 60° angle from the perpendicular for the tail (see Illus. 10) before gluing the head and legs in place. Size the end grain of each part and glue the head and legs in place (see gluing instructions in Chapter I). The head tilts on a vertical axis towards the romance side at approximately a 20° angle. Instructions for large-scale animals are given in chapters VII and VIII.

Use a Number 11 15-mm gouge to shape the bottoms of the bell hangings. Use a Number 11 2-mm gouge to cut the top spaces between the bell hangings. Use a Number 1 2-mm straight gouge

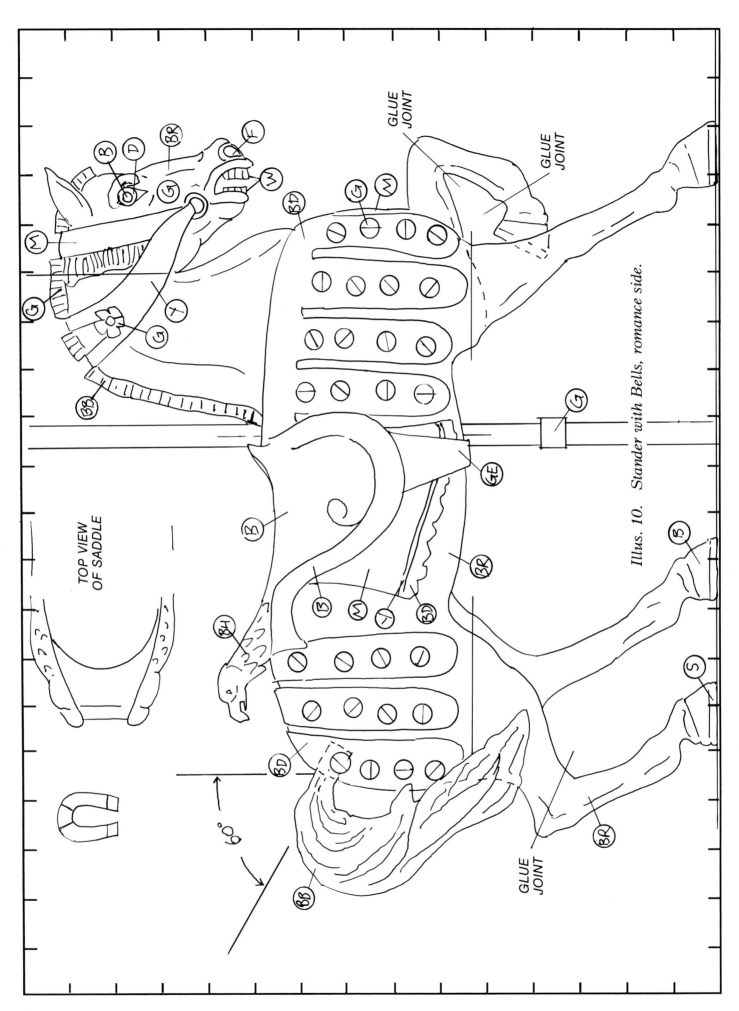

TOP VIEW
OF SADDLE

GLUE
JOINT

GLUE
JOINT

GLUE
JOINT

Illus. 10. Stander with Bells, romance side.

34

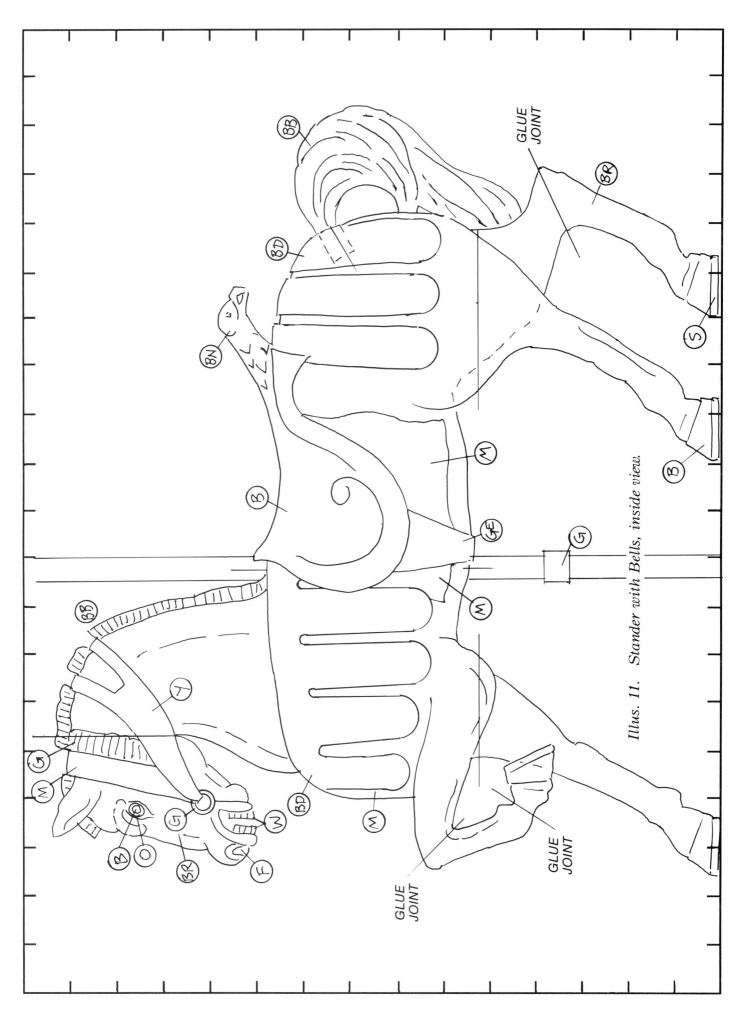

Illus. 11. *Stander with Bells, inside view.*

Table 7   Parts List for the Stander with Bells (⅛ Scale)

Part	Length	Width	Thickness
Head	2³⁄₈″	1⁵⁄₁₆″	⅞″
Body and neck	6⅝″	4½″	1½″
Right front leg	3¼″	1″	½″
Left front leg	1³⁄₈″	⁷⁄₁₆″	½″
Left front hoof	¾″	⅝″	½″
Right hind thigh	2″	1¹⁄₁₆″	¾″
Right hind leg	2³⁄₈″	⅝″	½″
Left hind leg	3³⁄₈″	1¼″	½″
Tail	2³⁄₈″	1⅝″	¾″

Table 8   Critical Dimensions for the Stander with Bells

	Scale				Full Size
	⅛	¼	½	¾	
From hoof to tip of ear	7⅛″	14¼″	28½″	42¾″	57″
From rump to breast	5¹⁵⁄₁₆″	11⅞″	23¾″	35⅝″	47½″
From tail to front right knee	7¹³⁄₁₆″	15⅝″	31¼″	46⅜″	62½″
Width of head	⅞″	1¾″	3½″	5¼″	7″
Width of nose	½″	1″	2″	3″	4″
Distance between tips of ears	⁹⁄₁₆″	1⅛″	2¼″	3⅜″	4½″
Width of neck at head	¹³⁄₁₆″	1⅝″	3¼″	4⅞″	6½″
Width of neck at body	1⅜″	2¾″	5½″	8¼″	11″
Width of body at pole	1½″	3″	6″	9″	12″
Width of saddle across eagle's nose	¾″	1½″	3″	4½″	6″
Width of saddle at eagle head	1⅛″	2¼″	4½″	6¾″	9″
Width of rump	1½″	3″	6″	9″	12″
Width of front leg at body	½″	1″	2″	3″	4″
Width of front leg at knee	⅜″	¾″	1½″	2¼″	3″
Width of hind leg at body	¾″	1½″	3″	4½″	6″
Width of hind leg at knee	⅜″	¾″	1½″	2¼″	3″
Width of tail	¾″	1½″	3″	4½″	6″
Length of hoof	⅝″	1¼″	2½″	3¾″	5″
Width of hoof	½″	1″	2″	3″	4″

to clean out the spaces between the hangings. Use a burning pen to put the design on the saddle and the hair texture on the roached mane.

The bells are made separately and glued in place after the horse is sanded and ready for painting. The bells can best be made by the following procedure (sizes for ⅛ scale): On a length of a ³⁄₁₆″ dowel mark a line around the entire circumference ³⁄₃₂″ in from the end of the dowel. Score this line with a knife. Using a knife, start to round the end of the dowel. The knife cut made around the circumference makes it easier to start this rounding process, since the knife blade will "feel" the indentation and this will help to keep the bell to the 3/32" length. Use sandpaper to smooth the dome that has been created at the end of the dowel. Using a 24-teeth-per-inch blade on the scroll saw, cut a slot into the dome of the bell, approximately 1/16" deep. Separate the completed bell from the dowel, 3/32" from the top of the dome. Glue the twenty-eight bells in place on the romance side, as shown in Illus. 10.

Cut four horseshoes from 3/32" stock for the 1/8-scale horse and glue one to the bottom of each hoof. End-grain gluing is involved, so be certain to "butter" the bottom of each leg with glue. Reduce the middle horseshoe areas (see Illus. 3) to a thickness of 3/64". Refer to Illus. 10 and 11 and Table 8 to complete the final shapes and details. After final sanding, glue the tail into the hole in the body and glue it against the outside surface of the right hind leg. Use a burning pen to develop the texture details on the tail, roached mane, eagle saddle, and harness fringe.

Table 8 provides the critical dimensions that you will need when carving a full-size Stander with Bells or a reduced-scale model.

After carving and sanding, paint the horse in accordance with the suggested color symbols given in circles in the illustrations (see color chart in Chapter VI) or use colors to your own taste. For the 1/8-scale horse, insert a 10½" length of a ¼"-diameter brass pole (Illus. 79), brass tubing, or gold-painted dowel through the body of the horse so that 5⅜" extends above the saddle. Glue it in place. Add the footrest (Illus. 80) to the pole 13/16" below the body. Make a base (see Chapter VI) and glue the pole of the completed horse to it.

The approximate carving time is 14 hours for the 1/8-scale horse; approximately 25 hours are required to carve, sand, and paint the 1/8-scale Stander with Bells.

5. Military Horse
Circa 1917

Using Illus. 12 as a plan, cut out the eight patterns and glue each pattern to wood of the correct thickness, as defined in Table 9. Refer to Illus. 13 for the complete patterns of the left front and hind legs. The length of each part should follow the direction of the wood grain. Instructions for large-scale animals are given in chapters VII and VIII.

Table 9   Parts List for the Military Horse (⅛ Scale)

Part	Length	Width	Thickness
Head and body	6⁵⁄₁₆″	4⅞″	1½″
Right front leg	3¹⁄₁₆″	¹¹⁄₁₆″	½″
Left front leg	1¼″	½″	½″
Left front hoof	¾″	⁹⁄₁₆″	½″
Right hind thigh	1⅝″	1¹⁄₁₆″	¾″
Right hind leg	2⁵⁄₁₆″	⅝″	½″
Left hind leg	2¼″	1¼″	¾″
Tail	2½″	1¼″	¾″

The complete carving block consists of the eight parts listed in Table 9. For the ⅛-scale horse, drill a ¼″ hole perpendicularly through the body for the pole and a ¼″ hole at a 60° angle from the perpendicular for the tail (see Illus. 12) before gluing the legs in place. Size the end grain of each leg part and glue the legs in place (see gluing instructions in Chapter I). There is no sideways tilt to the head; it faces straight ahead.

For the ⅛-scale horse, cut four horseshoes from ³⁄₃₂″ stock and glue one to the bottom of each leg. End-grain gluing will be involved so be certain to "butter" the bottom of each leg with glue. Reduce the middle areas of the horseshoes to a shoe thickness of ³⁄₆₄″ (Illus. 3). Refer to Illus. 12 and 13 and Table 10 to complete the final shapes and details. Table 10 provides the critical dimensions you will need when carving a full-size horse or a reduced-scale model.

After final sanding, glue the tail into the hole in the body, so that it

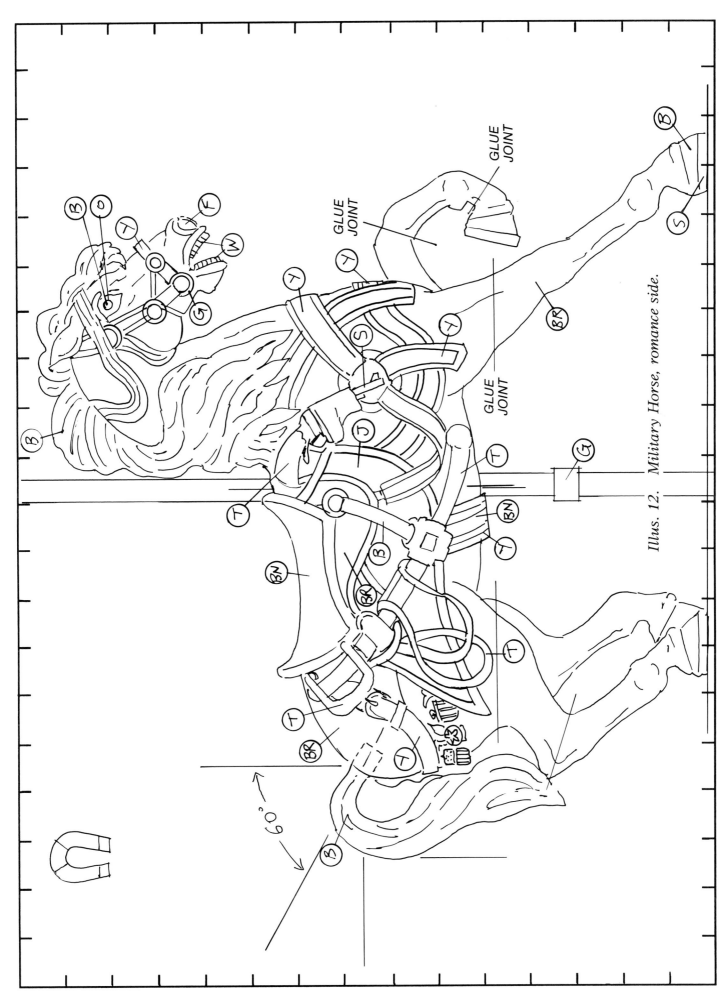

Illus. 12. Military Horse, romance side.

GLUE JOINT

GLUE JOINT

GLUE JOINT

60°

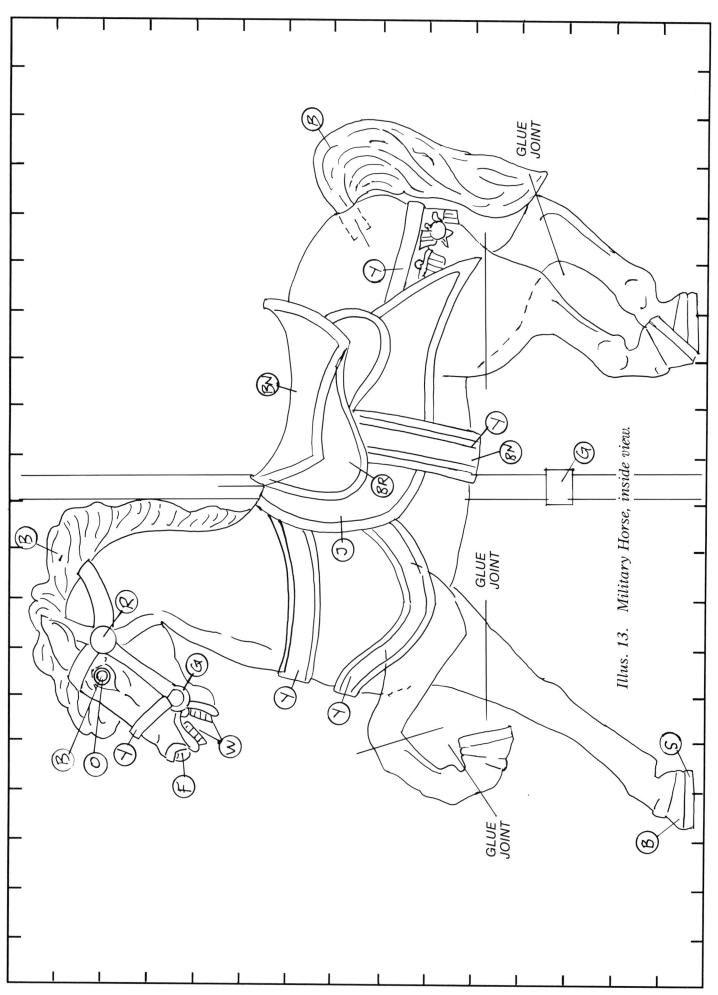

Illus. 13. *Military Horse, inside view.*

GLUE JOINT

is just touching the top of the right hind leg. Use a burning pen to add texture to the mane and tail.

After carving and sanding, paint the horse in accordance with the colors suggested in circles in the illustrations (see color chart in Chapter VI) or in colors of your choice. Insert a 10½″ length of a ¼″ diameter brass pole (Illus. 79), brass tubing or gold-painted dowel through the hole in the body of the ⅛-scale horse so that 5³⁄₁₆″ extends above the saddle. Glue the pole in place. Add the footrest (Illus. 80) to the pole ¹³⁄₁₆″ below the body. Make a base (see Chapter VI) and glue the pole of the completed horse to it.

Table 10   Critical Dimensions for the Military Horse

	Scale				Full Size
	⅛	¼	½	¾	
From hoof to top of mane	7⅛″	14¼″	28½″	42¾″	57″
From rump to breast	5⅛″	10¼″	20½″	30¾″	41″
From tail to front right ankle	7¹⁄₁₆″	14⅛″	28¼″	42⅜″	56½″
Width of head	⅞″	1¾″	3½″	5¼″	7″
Width of nose	½″	1″	2″	3″	4″
Distance between tips of ears	⁹⁄₁₆″	1⅛″	2¼″	3⅜″	4½″
Width of neck at head	¹³⁄₁₆″	1⅝″	3¼″	4⅞″	6½″
Width of neck at body	1⅜″	2¾″	5½″	8¼″	11″
Width of body at pole	1½″	3″	6″	9″	12″
Width of saddle at rear	1″	2″	4″	6″	8″
Width of rump	1½″	3″	6″	9″	12″
Width of front leg at body	½″	1″	2″	3″	4″
Width of front leg at knee	⅜″	¾″	1½″	2¼″	3″
Width of hind leg at body	¾″	1½″	3″	4½″	6″
Width of hind leg at knee	⅜″	¾″	1½″	2¼″	3″
Length of hoof	⅝″	1¼″	2½″	3¾″	5″
Width of hoof	½″	1″	2″	3″	4″

6. Indian Stander

Circa 1922

Using Illus. 14 as a plan, cut out the ten patterns and glue each pattern to wood of the correct thickness, as defined in Table 11. Refer to Illus. 15 for the complete pattern for the left hind leg. The length of each pattern should follow the direction of the wood grain. Table 12 provides the critical dimensions you need when carving a full-size horse or a reduced-scale model. Instructions for large-scale animals are given in chapters VII and VIII.

The complete carving block consists of the ten parts listed in Table 11. For the ⅛ scale horse, drill a ¼″ hole perpendicularly through the body for the pole and a ¼″ hole horizontally for the tail before gluing the head and legs to the body. Size the end grain of each part and glue the legs in place. You may want to carve the head before gluing it to the body; if not, glue the head in place at this time also. The head tilts on a horizontal axis towards the romance side at approximately a 15° angle.

Cut four horseshoes from ³⁄₃₂″ stock and glue one to the bottom of each leg. End-grain gluing is involved so be certain to "butter" these areas with glue. Reduce the middle areas of the horseshoes (Illus. 3) to a thickness of ³⁄₆₄″. Refer to Illus. 14 and 15 and to Table 12 to complete the final shapes and details. Using a burning pen develop the hair texture for the tail, roached mane, Indian-head hair, and for the feather details on the Indian's headdress, for details on the eagle saddle, and for the fringe on the harness. After a final sanding, glue the tail into the body and against the inside of the right hind leg.

After carving and sanding, paint the horse in accordance with the suggested color symbols in circles on the illustrations (see color chart in Chapter VI); or choose other colors that are pleasing to you. The many fine painted lines are best applied using a draftsman's ruling pen, as explained in Chapter VI. For the ⅛-horse, insert a 10½″ length of a ¼″-diameter brass pole (Illus. 79), brass tubing, or gold-painted dowel through the hole in the body of the horse so that 5⅜″ extends above the saddle. Glue it in place. Add the footrest (Illus. 80) to the pole ¹³⁄₁₆″ below the underside of the body. Make a base (see Chapter VI) and glue the pole of the completed carving to it. The approximate carving time is 14.6 hours; almost 28 hours are required to carve, sand, and paint the ⅛-scale Indian Stander.

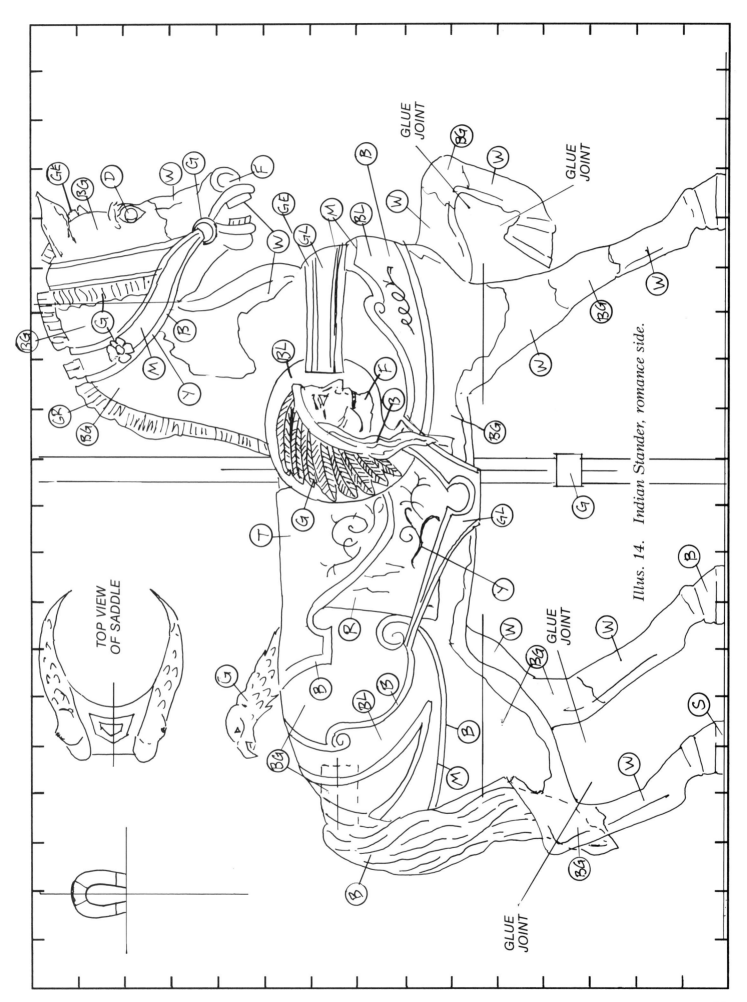

TOP VIEW
OF SADDLE

GLUE
JOINT

GLUE
JOINT

GLUE
JOINT

GLUE
JOINT

Illus. 14. Indian Stander, romance side.

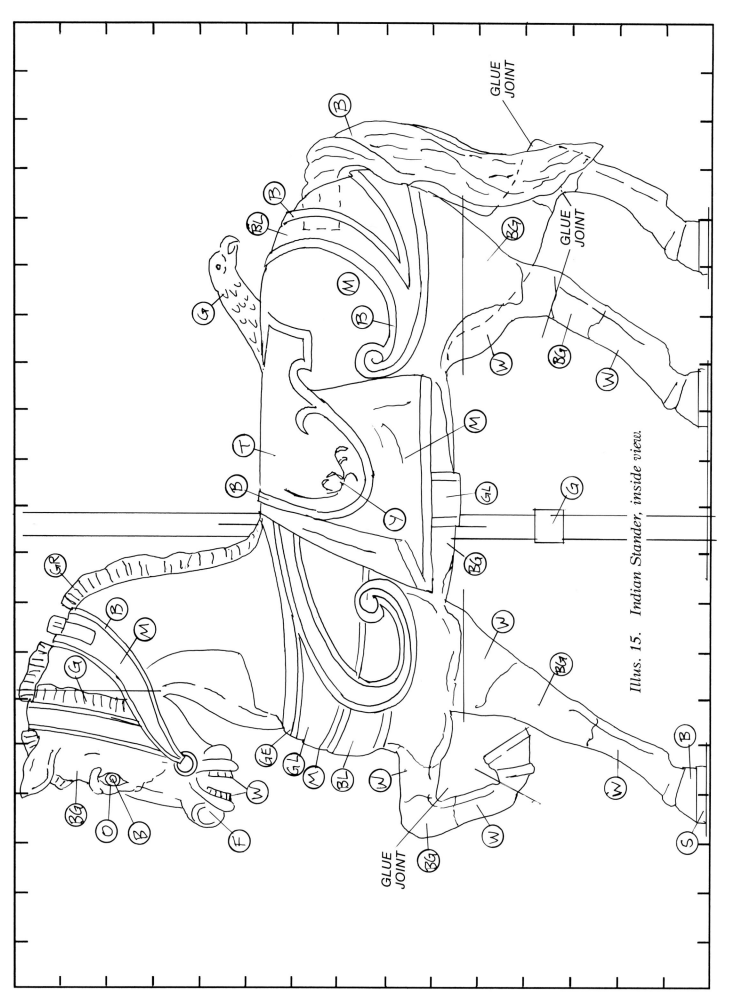

Illus. 15. Indian Stander, inside view.

Table 11   Parts List for the Indian Stander (⅛ Scale)

Part	Length	Width	Thickness
Head	2⁹/₁₆″	1½″	⅞″
Body	6¹³/₁₆″	4¾″	1½″
Right front leg	3³/₁₆″	1″	½″
Left front leg	1⁵/₁₆″	⅜″	½″
Left front hoof	⅝″	½″	⁷/₁₆″
Right hind thigh	1⅞″	1⅛″	¾″
Right hind leg	2¼″	⅝″	⁷/₁₆″
Left hind thigh	1⅜″	1⁵/₁₆″	¾″
Left hind leg	2¹/₁₆″	⅝″	⁷/₁₆″
Tail	3¹/₁₆″	1⅜″	¾″

Table 12   Critical Dimensions for the Indian Stander

	Scale				Full Size
	⅛	¼	½	¾	
From hoof to tip of ear	7⁵/₁₆″	14⅝″	29¼″	43⅞″	58½″
From rump to breast	5⅞″	11¾″	23½″	35¼″	47″
From tail to front right knee	7⅜″	14¾″	29½″	44¼″	59″
Width of head	⅞″	1¾″	3½″	5¼″	7″
Width of nose	½″	1″	2″	3″	4″
Distance between tips of ears	⁹/₁₆″	1⅛″	2¼″	3⅜″	4½″
Width of neck at head	¹³/₁₆″	1⅝″	3¼″	4⅞″	6½″
Width of neck at body	1¼″	2½″	5″	7½″	10″
Width of body at pole	1⅜″	2¾″	5½″	8¼″	11″
Width of saddle across eagle nose	¾″	1½″	3″	4½″	6″
Width of saddle at eagle head	1⅛″	2¼″	4½″	6¾″	9″
Width of rump	1½″	3″	6″	9″	12″
Width of front leg at body	½″	1″	2″	3″	4″
Width of front leg at knee	⁷/₁₆″	⅞″	1¾″	2⅝″	3½″
Width of hind leg at body	¾″	1½″	3″	4½″	6″
Width of hind leg at knee	⁷/₁₆″	⅞″	1¾″	2⅝″	3½″
Length of hoof	⁹/₁₆″	1⅛″	2¼″	3⅜″	4½″
Width of hoof	⁷/₁₆″	⅞″	1¾″	2⅝″	3½″
Width of tail	¾″	1½″	3″	4½″	6″

7. Stander with Garlands

Circa 1922

Using Illus. 16 as a plan, cut out the ten patterns and glue each
pattern to wood of the correct thickness, given in Table 13. Refer to
Illus. 17 for the complete patterns of the left front and hind legs.
The length of each part should follow the direction of the wood

grain. Instructions for large-scale horses are given in chapters VII and VIII.

The complete carving block consists of the ten parts given in Table 13. For the ⅛-scale horse, drill a ¼″ hole perpendicularly through the body for the pole and drill a ¼″ hole at a 60° angle from the perpendicular for the tail (see Illus. 16) before gluing the legs in place. If you do not prefer to carve the head separately, it too can be glued to the body at this time. Size the end grain of each part and glue the legs and head to the body. The head tilts on a vertical axis towards the romance side at approximately a 15° angle.

Cut the four horseshoes from ³⁄₃₂″ stock for the ⅛-scale horse and glue one to the bottom of each hoof. End-grain gluing is involved so be certain to "butter" the bottom of each leg with glue. Reduce the middle areas of the horseshoes (Illus. 3) to a thickness of ³⁄₆₄″. Refer to Illus. 16 and 17 and to Table 14 to complete the final shapes and details. Using a burning pen put the hair or feather texture on the mane, tail, and eagle saddle and to make the decorations on the saddle blanket. After the final sanding, glue the tail into the hole in the body and to the outside surface of the right hind leg.

Table 14 provides the critical dimensions for carving a full-size horse or a reduced-scale model.

When the carving and sanding are completed, paint the horse in the colors suggested in circles on the illustrations (see color chart in Chapter VI) or according to your own desires. For the ⅛-scale horse, insert a 10½″ length of a ¼″-diameter brass pole (Illus. 79), brass tubing or gold-painted dowel through the hole in the body so that 5⅜″ extends above the saddle. Glue the pole in place. Add the footrest (Illus. 80) to the pole ¹³⁄₁₆″ below the underbelly of the horse. Make a base (see Chapter VI) and glue the pole of the completed horse to it.

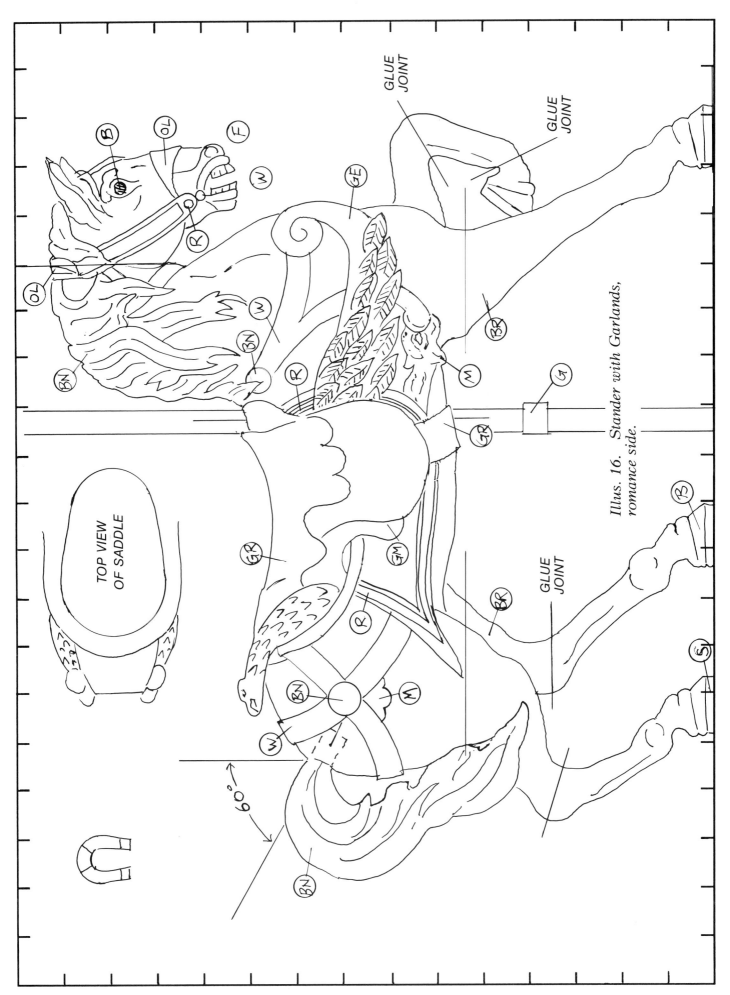

Illus. 16. *Stander with Garlands, romance side.*

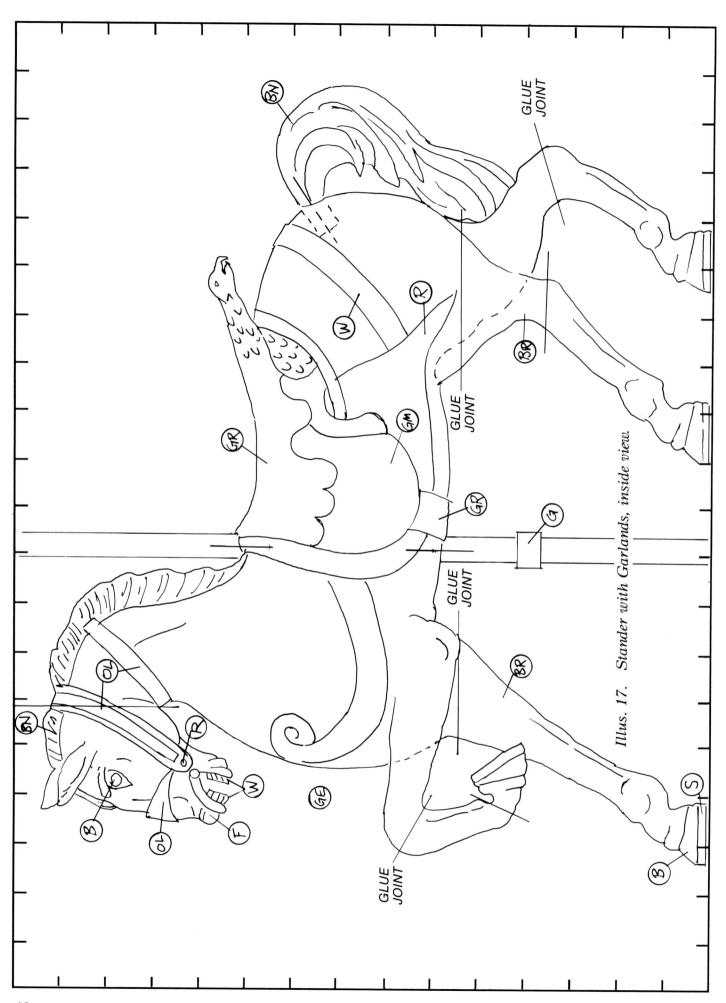

Illus. 17. *Stander with Garlands, inside view.*

The approximate carving time is 15 hours; about 26 hours are required to carve, sand, and paint the ⅛-scale Stander with Garlands.

Table 13   Parts List for the Stander with Garlands (⅛ Scale)

Part	Length	Width	Thickness
Head	2⅛″	1⁵⁄₁₆″	⅞″
Body and neck	6¾″	4⁷⁄₁₆″	1½″
Right front leg	3⁵⁄₁₆″	1″	½″
Left front leg	1⁵⁄₁₆″	⁷⁄₁₆″	½″
Left front hoof	¾″	⁹⁄₁₆″	½″
Right hind thigh	2″	1¹⁄₁₆″	¾″
Right hind leg	2¼″	⁹⁄₁₆″	½″
Left hind thigh	1⁵⁄₁₆″	1¼″	¾″
Left hind leg	2⁷⁄₁₆″	⅝″	½″
Tail	2⅞″	1⅝″	¾″

Table 14   Critical Dimensions for the Stander with Garlands

	Scale				Full Size
	⅛	¼	½	¾	
From hoof to tip of ear	7⅛″	14¼″	28½″	42¾″	57″
From rump to breast	5⅞″	11¾″	23½″	35¼″	47″
From tail to front right knee	7⅞″	15¾″	31½″	47¼″	63″
Width of head	⅞″	1¾″	3½″	5¼″	7″
Width of nose	½″	1″	2″	3″	4″
Distance between tips of ears	⁷⁄₁₆″	⅞″	1¾″	2⅝″	3½″
Width of neck at head (with mane)	1¹⁄₁₆″	2⅛″	4¼″	6⅜″	8½″
Width of neck at body	1⅜″	2¾″	5½″	8¼″	11″
Width of body at pole	1½″	3″	6″	9″	12″
Width of saddle across eagle nose	¾″	1½″	3″	4½″	6″
Width of saddle at eagle head	1⅛″	2¼″	4½″	6¾″	9″
Width of rump	1½″	3″	6″	9″	12″
Width of front leg at body	½″	1″	2″	3″	4″
Width of front leg at knee	⅜″	¾″	1½″	2¼″	3″
Width of hind leg at body	¾″	1½″	3″	4½″	6″
Width of hind leg at knee	⅜″	¾″	1½″	2¼″	3″
Width of tail	¾″	1½″	3″	4½″	6″
Length of hoof	⁹⁄₁₆″	1⅛″	2¼″	3⅜″	4½″
Width of hoof	¹⁵⁄₃₂″	¹⁵⁄₁₆″	1⅞″	2¹³⁄₁₆″	3¾″

8. Cerni's Figure

Circa 1905

Use Illus. 18 as a plan to cut out the nine patterns, and glue each pattern to wood of the correct thickness, given in Table 15. Refer to Illus. 19 for the complete patterns of the left front and hind legs. The length of each part should follow the direction of the wood grain. Instructions for large-scale animals are given in chapters VII and VIII.

The complete carving block consists of the nine parts given in Table 15. For the ⅛-scale horse, drill a ¼″ hole perpendicularly through the body for the pole and a ¼″ hole at a 55° angle from the perpendicular (see Illus. 18) for the tail. Use the base reference line given in Illus. 18 as a guideline. Drill the holes before the legs are glued in place. Size the end grain of each part and glue the head and legs in place. The head tilts on a vertical axis towards the romance side at a 20° angle.

For the ⅛-scale horse, cut the four horseshoes from ³⁄₃₂″ stock and glue one to the bottom of each leg. End grain gluing is involved, so be certain to "butter" the bottom of each leg with glue. Reduce the middle horseshoe areas (Illus. 3) to a thickness of ³⁄₆₄″. Refer to Illus. 18 and 19 to complete the final shapes and details and to Table 16, which provides the critical dimensions needed to carve a full-sized horse or to make a reduced-scale model.

After the final sanding, glue the tail into the hole in the body and against the outside surface of the right hind leg. Use a burning pen to reproduce the texture in the roached mane and tail, the feathers, and the eagle saddle. Cut out the figure on the horse's side from ⅛″ stock and glue it to the side of the body to provide greater relief.

After carving and sanding, paint the horse in accordance with the

Table 15   Parts List for Cerni's Figure (⅛ Scale)

Part	Length	Width	Thickness
Head	2¹⁄₁₆″	1³⁄₈″	⅞″
Body and neck	6¹⁵⁄₁₆″	4¹¹⁄₁₆″	1½″
Right front leg	3⅝″	¹⁵⁄₁₆″	½″
Left front leg	1⁷⁄₁₆″	⁷⁄₁₆″	½″
Left front hoof	¹¹⁄₁₆″	⁷⁄₁₆″	½″
Right hind thigh	2¹⁄₁₆″	⅞″	¾″
Right hind leg	2⁵⁄₁₆″	¾″	½″
Left hind leg	3½″	2″	¾″
Tail	2¹³⁄₁₆″	1⅝″	¾″

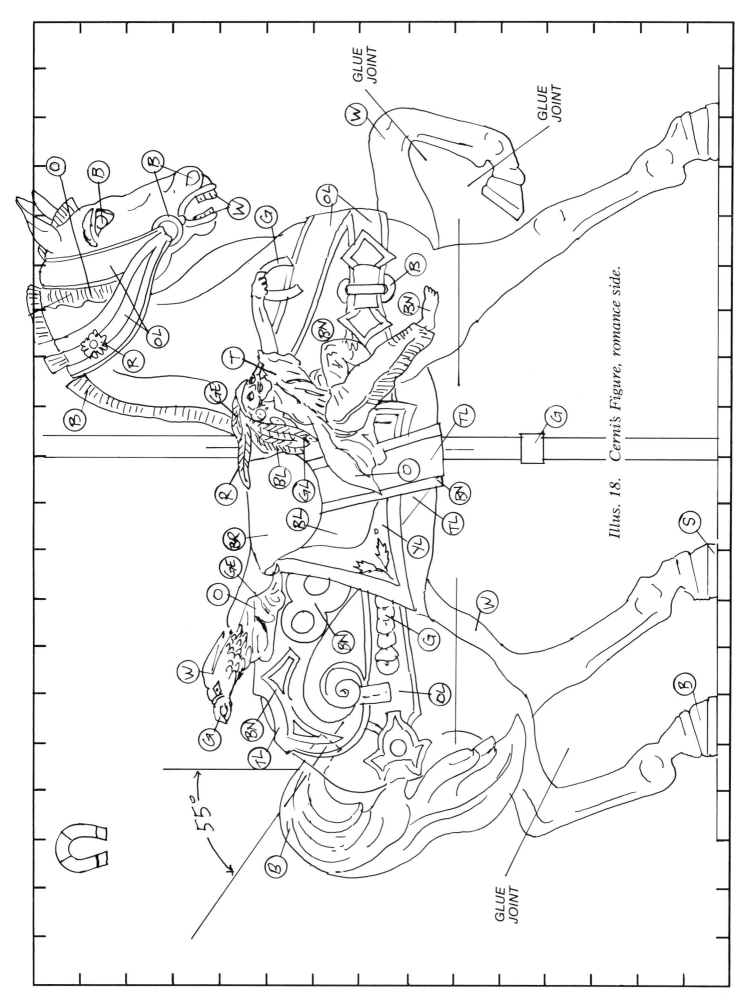

GLUE
JOINT

GLUE
JOINT

GLUE
JOINT

55°

Illus. 18. Cerni's Figure, romance side.

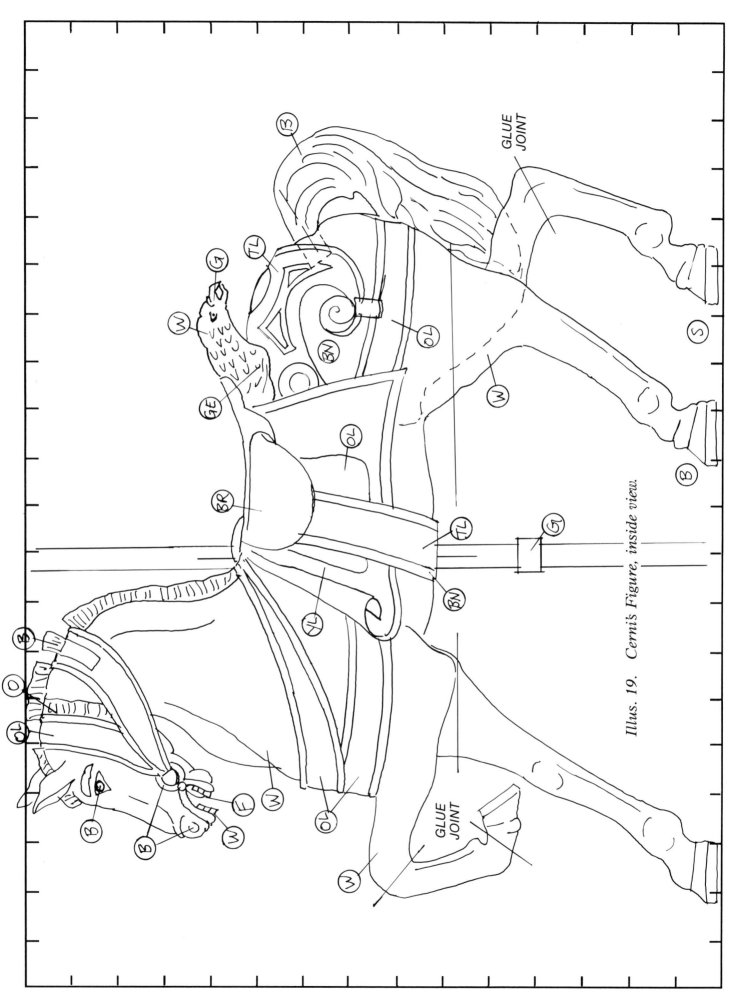

Illus. 19. Cerni's Figure, inside view.

GLUE JOINT

GLUE JOINT

colors suggested in circles in the illustrations (see color chart in
Chapter VI); or choose other colors that are pleasing to you. Insert
a 10½″ length of a ¼″-diameter brass pole (Illus. 79), brass tubing,
or gold-painted dowel through the body for the ⅛-scale horse so that
4⅞″ extends above the saddle. Glue the pole in place. Add the footrest (Illus. 80) to the pole ¹³⁄₁₆″ below the body. Make a base (see
Chapter VI) and glue the pole of the completed carving to it.

Table 16   Critical Dimensions for Cerni's Figure

	Scale				Full Size
	⅛	¼	½	¾	
From hoof to tip of ear	7½″	15″	30″	45″	60″
From rump to breast	6″	12″	24″	36″	48″
From tail to front right knee	7⅞″	15¾″	31½″	47¼″	63″
Width of head	⅞″	1¾″	3½″	5¼″	7″
Width of nose	½″	1″	2″	3″	4″
Distance between tips of ears	⁷⁄₁₆″	⅞″	1¾″	2⅝″	3½″
Width of neck at head	¹³⁄₁₆″	1⅝″	3¼″	4⅞″	6½″
Width of neck at body	1⅜″	2¾″	5½″	8¼″	11″
Width of body at pole	1½″	3″	6″	9″	12″
Width of saddle at eagle's beak	¾″	1½″	3″	4½″	6″
Width of saddle at eagle's head	1⅛″	2¼″	4½″	6¾″	9″
Width of rump	1½″	3″	6″	9″	12″
Width of front leg at body	½″	1″	2″	3″	4″
Width of front leg at knee	⅜″	¾″	1½″	2¼″	3″
Width of hind leg at body	¾″	1½″	3″	4½″	6″
Width of hind leg at knee	⅜″	¾″	1½″	2¼″	3″
Width of tail	¾″	1½″	3″	4½″	6″
Length of hoof	⁹⁄₁₆″	1⅛″	2¼″	3⅜″	4½″
Width of hoof	¹⁵⁄₃₂″	¹⁵⁄₁₆″	1⅞″	2¹³⁄₁₆″	3¾″

9. Roached Stander

Circa 1926

Using Illus. 20 as a plan, cut out the ten patterns and glue each
pattern to wood of the correct thickness, given in Table 17. You will
need to refer to Illus. 21 for the complete patterns for the left front
and hind legs. The length of each part should follow the direction of
the wood grain. Instructions for large-scale animals are given in
chapters VII and VIII.

The complete carving block consists of the ten parts listed in Table
17. For the ⅛-scale horse, drill a ¼″-hole perpendicularly through
the body for the pole and a ¼″ hole at a 60° angle from the perpendicular for the tail before gluing the head and legs in place. Size the

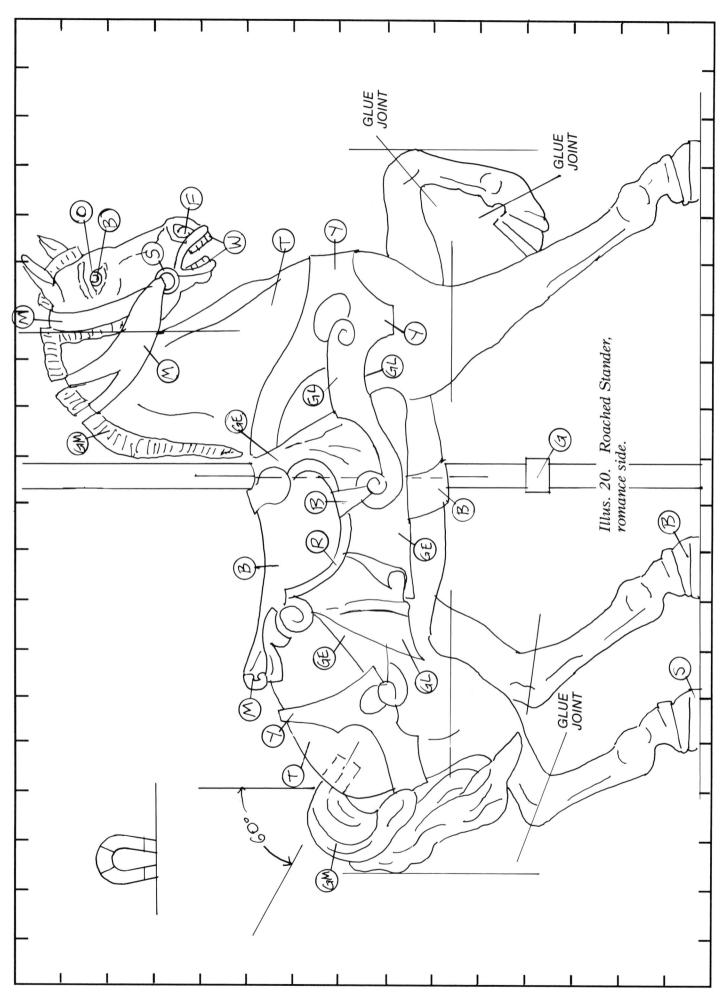

Illus. 20. Roached Stander, romance side.

GLUE JOINT

GLUE JOINT

GLUE JOINT

60°

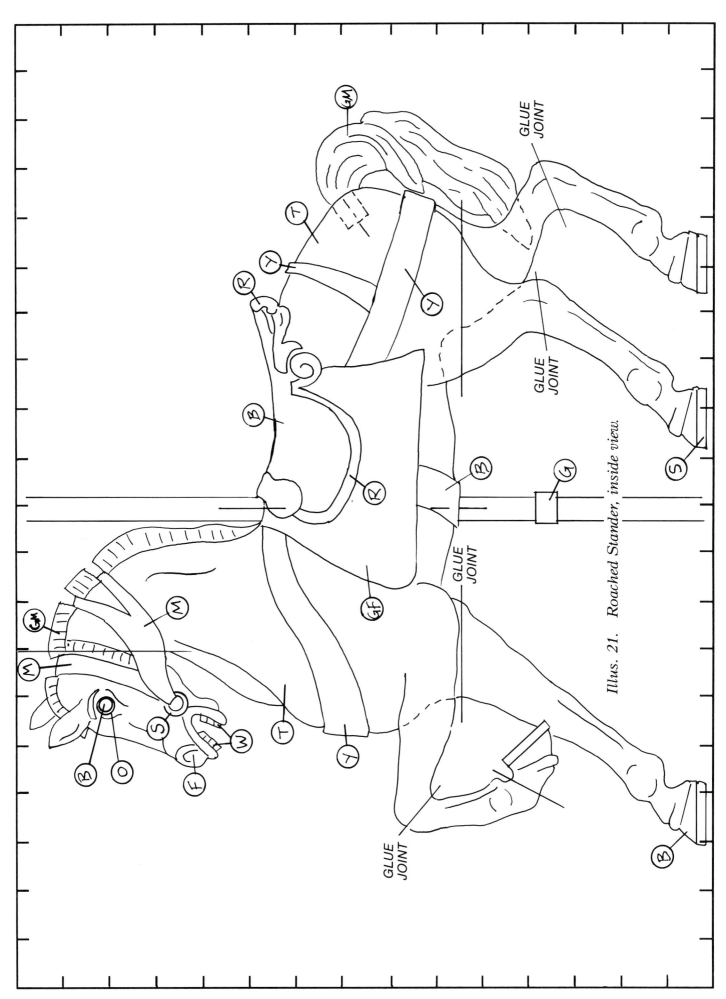

Illus. 21. Roached Stander, inside view.

Table 17 Parts List for the Roached Stander (1/8 Scale)

Part	*Length*	*Width*	*Thickness*
Head	2″	1 9/16″	7/8″
Body and neck	6 1/2″	4 9/16″	1 1/2″
Right front leg	3 1/2″	13/16″	1/2″
Left front leg	1 1/2″	7/16″	1/2″
Left front hoof	3/4″	1/2″	1/2″
Right hind thigh	1 1/2″	1 3/16″	3/4″
Right hind leg	2 3/16″	9/16″	1/2″
Left hind thigh	1 1/2″	1 5/16″	3/4″
Left hind leg	2 3/8″	5/8″	1/2″
Tail	2 7/16″	1 3/8″	3/4″

Table 18 Critical Dimensions for the Roached Stander

	Scale				*Full*
	1/8	1/4	1/2	3/4	*Size*
From hoof to tip of ear	7 1/4″	14 1/2″	29″	43 1/2″	58″
From rump to breast	5 5/8″	11 1/4″	22 1/2″	33 3/4″	45″
From tail to front left knee	7 3/8″	14 3/4″	29 1/2″	44 1/4″	59″
Width of head	7/8″	1 3/4″	3 1/2″	5 1/4″	7″
Width of nose	1/2″	1″	2″	3″	4″
Distance between tips of ears	7/16″	7/8″	1 3/4″	2 5/8″	3 1/2″
Width of neck at head	13/16″	1 5/8″	3 1/4″	4 7/8″	6 1/2″
Width of neck at body	1 3/8″	2 3/4″	5 1/2″	8 1/4″	11″
Width of body at pole	1 1/2″	3″	6″	9″	12″
Width of saddle at rear	1″	2″	4″	6″	8″
Width of rump	1 1/2″	3″	6″	9″	12″
Width of front leg at body	1/2″	1″	2″	3″	4″
Width of front leg at knee	3/8″	3/4″	1 1/2″	2 1/4″	3″
Width of hind leg at body	3/4″	1 1/2″	3″	4 1/2″	6″
Width of hind leg at knee	3/8″	3/4″	1 1/2″	2 1/4″	3″
Width of tail	3/4″	1 1/2″	3″	4 1/2″	6″
Length of hoof	5/8″	1 1/4″	2 1/2″	3 3/4″	5″
Width of hoof	1/2″	1″	2″	3″	4″

end grain of the head and each leg part and glue them in place. The head tilts on a vertical axis towards the romance side at approximately a 10° angle.

For the 1/8-scale horse, cut four horseshoes from 3/32″ stock and glue one to the bottom of each leg. End-grain gluing is involved, so be certain to "butter" the bottom of each leg with glue. Reduce the middle areas of the horseshoes (Illus. 3) to a thickness of 3/64″. Refer to Illus. 20 and 21 to complete the final shapes and details, and to Table 18, which provides the critical dimensions for carving a full-size horse or a reduced-scale model. After a final sanding, glue the tail into the hole in the body and against the outside surface of the right hind leg. Use a burning pen to add texture to the mane, tail, and fringe.

After carving and sanding the horse, paint it in accordance with the suggested color scheme given in circles in the illustrations (see color chart in Chapter VI) or other colors that are pleasing to you. For the ⅛-scale horse, insert a 10½″ length of a ¼″-diameter brass pole (Illus. 79), brass tubing, or gold-painted dowel through the hole in the body so that 5³⁄₁₆″ extends above the saddle. Glue the pole in place. Add the footrest (Illus. 80) to the pole ¹³⁄₁₆″ below the body. Make a base (see Chapter VI) and glue the pole of the completed horse to it.

10. Tassels and Disks

Circa 1922

Using Illus. 22 as a plan, cut out the nine patterns and glue each pattern to wood of the correct thickness, as given in Table 19. Refer to Illus. 23 for the complete patterns of both the left front and hind legs. The length of each part should follow the direction of the wood grain. Instructions for large-scale animals are given in chapters VII and VIII.

The complete carving block consists of nine parts, given in Table 19. For the ⅛-scale horse, drill a ¼″ hole perpendicularly through the body for the pole and a ¼″ hole at a 60° angle for the tail (see Illus. 22). Drill these holes before gluing the legs in place. Size the end grain of each part and glue the head and legs in place. The head tilts 15° towards the romance side on the vertical axis.

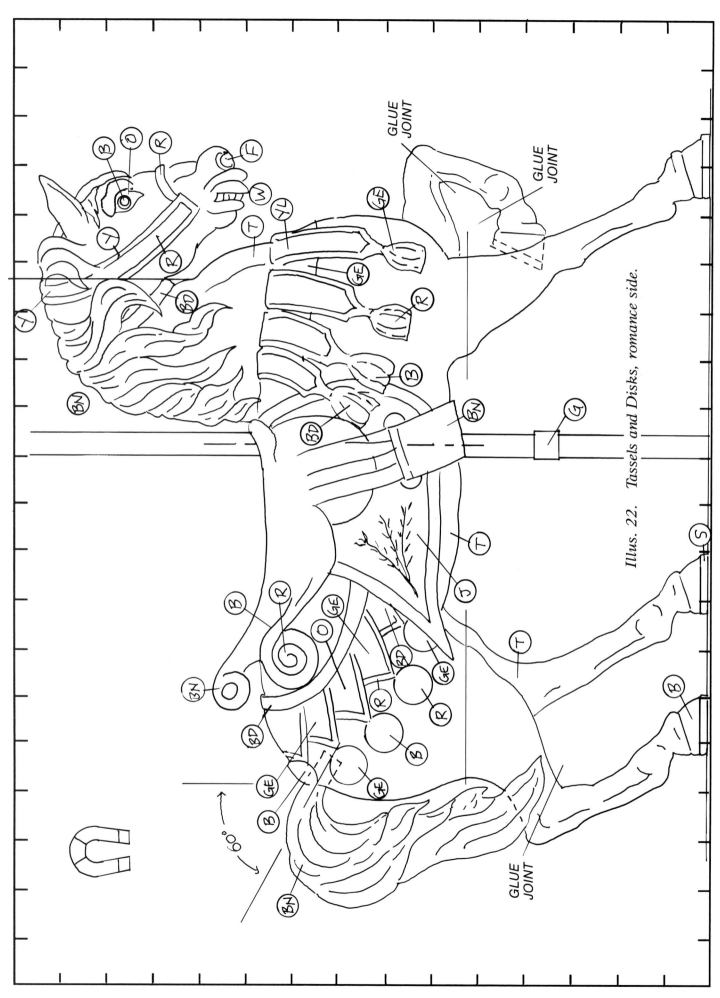

Illus. 22.   *Tassels and Disks, romance side.*

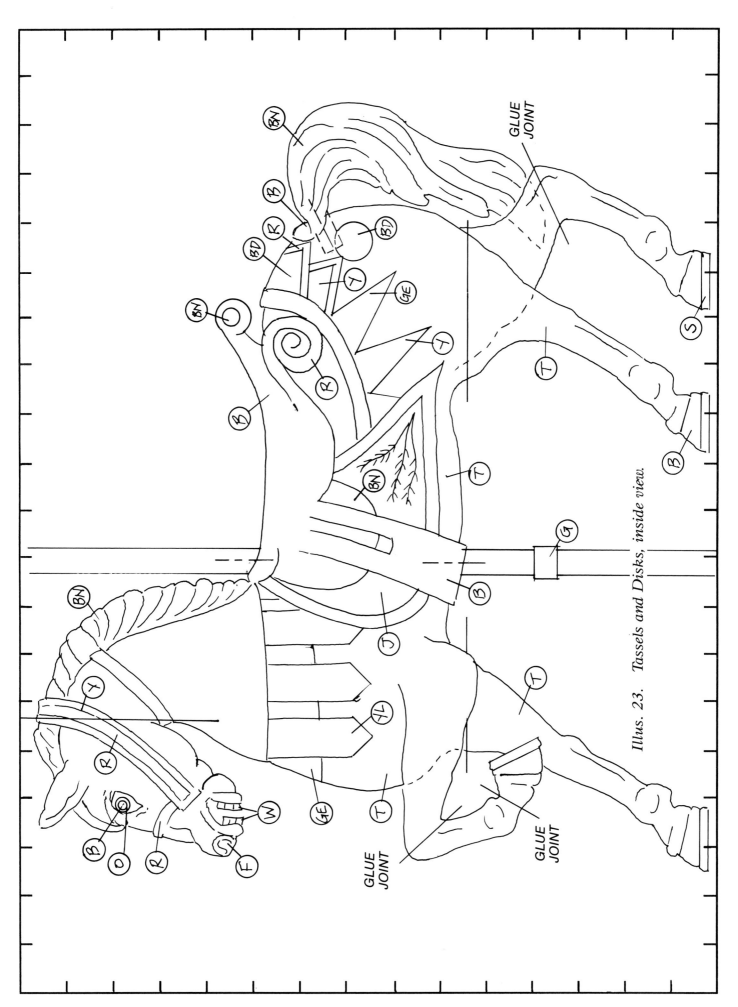

Illus. 23. *Tassels and Disks, inside view.*

Table 19   Parts List for Tassels and Disks (⅛ Scale)

Part	Length	Width	Thickness
Head	2⁷⁄₁₆″	1½″	⅞″
Body and neck	6⅝″	4½″	1½″
Right front leg	3⁵⁄₁₆″	¹⁵⁄₁₆″	½″
Left front leg	1⁵⁄₁₆″	⁷⁄₁₆″	½″
Left front hoof	¹¹⁄₁₆″	⁹⁄₁₆″	½″
Right hind thigh	1¾″	1¹⁄₁₄″	¾″
Right hind leg	2⁵⁄₁₆″	¹¹⁄₁₆″	½″
Left hind leg	3⁵⁄₁₆″	1¼″	¾″
Tail	2⅞″	1¹¹⁄₁₆″	¾″

Table 20   Critical Dimensions for Tassels and Disks

	Scale				Full Size
	⅛	¼	½	¾	
From hoof to top of mane	7⅛″	14¼″	28½″	42¾″	57″
From rump to breast	6″	12″	24″	36″	48″
From tail to front right knee	7¹³⁄₁₆″	15⅝″	31¼″	46⅞″	62½″
Width of head (with mane)	⅞″	1¾″	3½″	5¼″	7″
Width of nose	½″	1″	2″	3″	4″
Distance between tips of ears	⁹⁄₁₆″	1⅛″	2¼″	3⅜″	4½″
Width of neck at head (with mane)	⅞″	1¾″	3½″	5¼″	7″
Width of neck at body	1⅜″	2¾″	5½″	8¼″	11″
Width of body at pole	1½″	3″	6″	9″	12″
Width of saddle at rear	1″	2″	4″	6″	8″
Width of rump	1½″	3″	6″	9″	12″
Width of front leg at body	½″	1″	2″	3″	4″
Width of front leg at knee	⅜″	¾″	1½″	2¼″	3″
Width of hind leg at body	¾″	1½″	3″	4½″	6″
Width of hind leg at knee	⅜″	¾″	1½″	2¼″	3″
Width of tail	¾″	1½″	3″	4½″	6″
Length of hoof	⅝″	1¼″	2½″	3¾″	5″
Width of hoof	½″	1″	2″	3″	4″

Cut four horseshoes from ³⁄₃₂″ stock and glue one to the bottom of each hoof. End-grain gluing is involved so be certain to size the bottom of each leg before gluing the horseshoes in place. Reduce the middle areas of the horseshoes (Illus. 3) to a thickness of ³⁄₆₄″. Cut the four tassels from ⅛″ stock and glue in place on the romance side, to give the tassels depth. Refer to Illus. 22 and 23 to complete the final shapes and details, and to Table 20, which provides the critical dimensions that you will need to carve a full-sized horse or a reduced-scale model. After final sanding, carve the tail (Illus. 3) and glue it into the hole in the body and against the upper side of the right hind leg. Use a burning pen to put the hair texture in the mane and tail and the thread texture to the tassels. Place a ⁹⁄₁₆″ length of a ¹⁄₁₆″ wide dowel in the mouth for the bit.

After carving and sanding, paint the horse in accordance with the suggested color scheme given in circles on the illustrations (see color chart in Chapter VI) or select other colors that are pleasing to you. The fine painted details are applied with a draftsman's ruling pen, as explained in Chapter VI. For the ⅛-scale horse, insert a 10½″ length of a ¼″-diameter brass pole (Illus. 79), brass tubing, or gold-painted dowel through the hole in the body so that ½″ extends below the level of the feet. Glue the pole in place. Add the footrest (Illus. 80) to the pole ¹³⁄₁₆″ underneath the body. Make a base (see Chapter VI) and glue the pole to it. The approximate carving time is 15 hours; approximately 27 hours are required to carve, sand, and paint the ⅛-scale stander.

11. Orange Blanket Stander

Circa 1926

Using Illus. 24 as a plan, cut out the ten patterns and glue each pattern to wood of the correct thickness, given in Table 21. Refer to Illus. 25 for a complete pattern of the left front and hind legs. The length of each part should follow the direction of the wood grain. Instructions for large-scale animals are given in chapters VII and VIII.

The complete carving block consists of the ten parts given in Table 21. For the ⅛-scale horse, drill a ¼″ hole perpendicularly through the body for the pole and drill a ¼″ hole at a 60° angle from the perpendicular for the tail (see Illus. 24) before gluing the head and legs

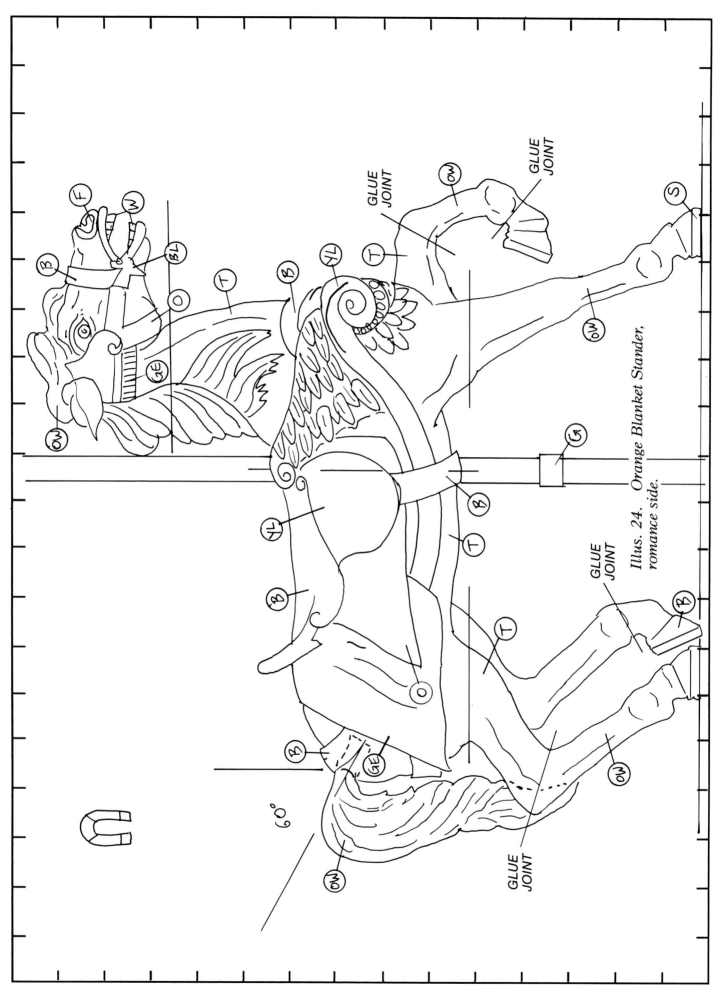

Illus. 24. Orange Blanket Stander, romance side.

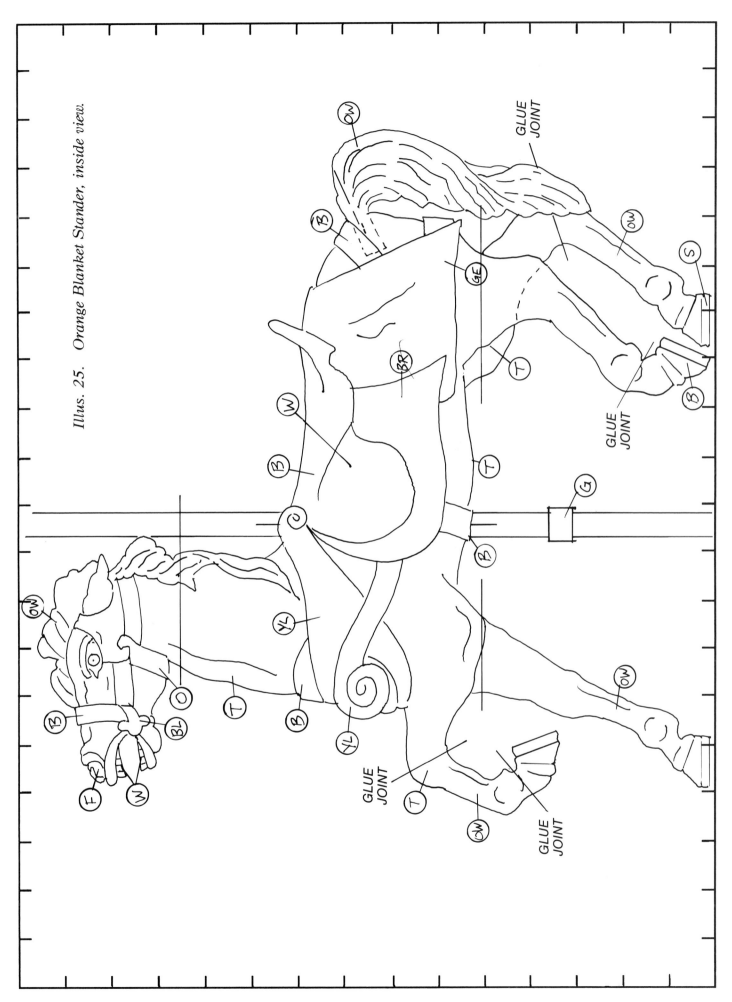

Illus. 25. Orange Blanket Stander, inside view.

63

Table 21   Parts List of Orange Blanket Stander (⅛ Scale)

Part	Length	Width	Thickness
Head	2⁹/₁₆″	1½″	¾″
Body and neck	5¹¹/₁₆″	3³/₁₆″	1½″
Right front leg	2⅞″	¾″	½″
Left front leg	1⁵/₁₆″	½″	½″
Left front hoof	⅝″	½″	⅜″
Right hind thigh	1¾″	¾″	¾″
Right hind leg	2⅜″	½″	½″
Left hind leg	2⅛″	1⅛″	¾″
Left hind hoof	⅞″	⁷/₁₆″	⅜″
Tail	2¹³/₁₆″	1⅜″	¾″

Table 22   Critical Dimensions for Orange Blanket Stander

	Scale				Full Size
	⅛	¼	½	¾	
From hoof to top of mane	7⅛″	14¼″	28½″	42¾″	57″
From rump to breast	5³/₁₆″	10⅜″	20¾″	31⅛″	41½″
From tail to front left knee	7″	14″	28″	42″	56″
Width of head	¾″	1½″	3″	4½″	6″
Width of nose	⁷/₁₆″	⅞″	1¾″	2⅝″	3½″
Distance between tips of ears	⁹/₁₆″	1⅛″	2¼″	3⅜″	4½″
Width of neck at head (with mane)	⅞″	1¾″	3½″	5½″	7″
Width of neck at body	1⅜″	2¾″	5½″	8¼″	11″
Width of body at pole	1½″	3″	6″	9″	12″
Width of saddle at rear	1″	2″	4″	6″	8″
Width of rump	1½″	3″	6″	9″	12″
Width of front leg at body	½″	1″	2″	3″	4″
Width of front leg at knee	⅜″	¾″	1½″	2¼″	3″
Width of hind leg at body	¾″	1½″	3″	4½″	6″
Width of hind leg at knee	⅜″	¾″	1½″	2¼″	3″
Length of hoof	½″	1″	2″	3″	4″
Width of hoof	⅜″	¾″	1½″	2¼″	3″
Width of tail	¾″	1½″	3″	4½″	6″

in place. Size the end grain of each leg part and glue the legs and head to the body. The head tilts on a horizontal axis 15° towards the romance side.

For the ⅛-scale horse, cut four horseshoes from ³/₃₂″ stock and glue one to the bottom of each hoof. End-grain gluing is involved, so be certain to "butter" the bottom of each hoof with glue. Reduce the middle horseshoe area (Illus. 3) to a thickness of ³/₆₄″. Refer to Illus. 24 and 25 to complete the final shapes and details, and to Table 22, which provides the critical dimensions that you will need to carve a full-size horse or a reduced-scale replica. After a final sanding, glue the tail into the hole in the body and against the inside of the right hind leg. Use a burning pen to put the hair texture in the mane and tail and add the feather details on the breast band.

After carving and sanding, paint the horse in the colors suggested by the color codes in circles on the illustrations (see color chart in Chapter VI); or use other colors that are pleasing to you. For the ⅛-size animal, insert a 10½″ length of a ¼″-diameter brass pole (Illus. 79), brass tubing, or gold-painted dowel through the hole in the body so that ½″ extends below the hooves. Glue the pole in place. Add the footrest (Illus. 80) to the pole ¹³⁄₁₆″ below the body. Make a base (see Chapter VI) and glue the pole of the completed carving to it. The approximate carving time is 13 hours; approximately 23 hours are required to carve, sand, and paint the ⅛-scale stander.

12. Lead Horse

Circa 1926

Using Illus. 26 as a plan, cut out the ten patterns and glue each pattern to wood of the correct thickness, given in Table 23. Refer to Illus. 27 for the complete patterns for the left front and hind legs. The length of each part should follow the direction of the wood grain. Instructions for large-scale animals are given in chapters VII and VIII.

The complete carving block consists of the ten parts given in Table 23. For the ⅛-scale horse, drill a ¼″ hole perpendicularly through the body for the pole and a ¼″ hole at a 60° angle to the perpendicular for the tail, before gluing the legs in place (see Illus. 26). Size all end-grain surfaces of each part and glue the head and legs in position. The head tilts on a horizontal axis towards the romance side at approximately a 15° angle.

For the ⅛-scale horse, cut four horseshoes of ³⁄₃₂″ stock and glue one to the bottom of each leg. End-grain gluing is involved so be certain to "butter" the bottom of each leg with glue. Reduce the middle areas of each horseshoe to a thickness of ³⁄₆₄″ (Illus. 3). Refer to Illus. 26 and 27 to complete the final shaping and details, and to Table 24, which provides the critical dimensions that you will need when carving a full-sized horse or a reduced-scale model.

After final sanding, glue the tail into the hole in the body and against the inside surface of the right hind leg. Use a burning pen to add texture to the mane and tail.

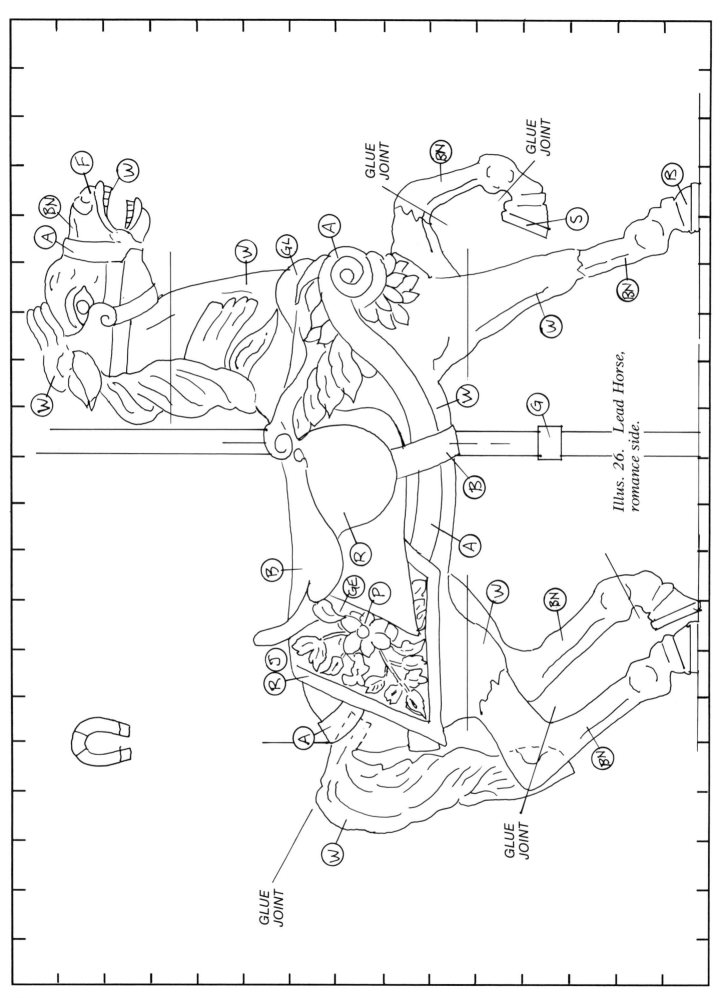

Illus. 26. Lead Horse, romance side.

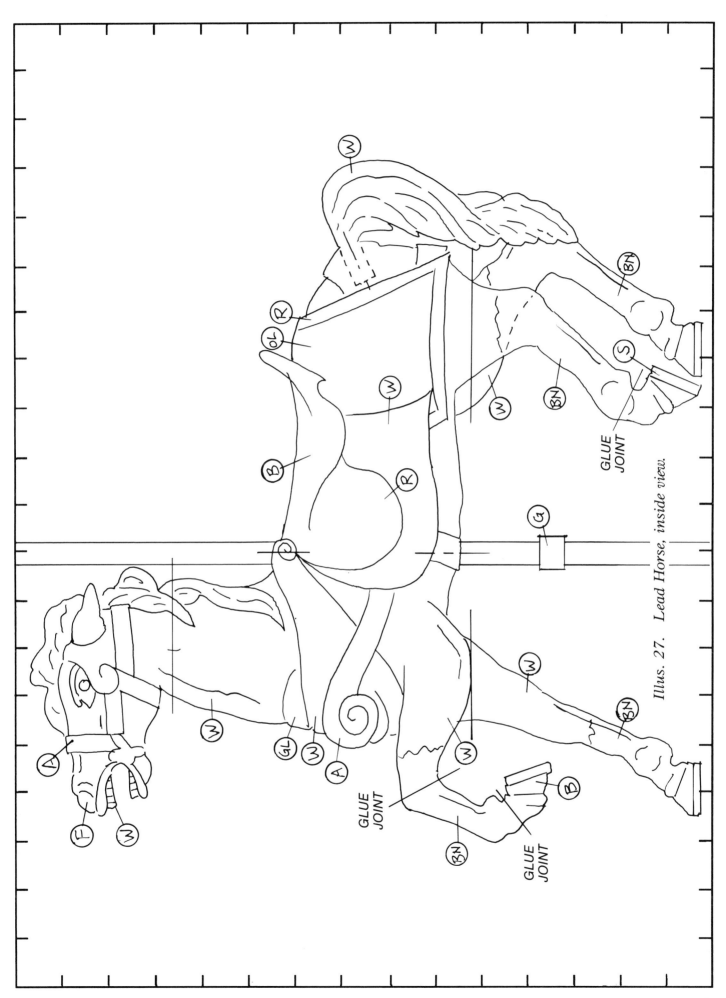

Illus. 27. Lead Horse, inside view.

After carving and sanding, paint the horse in accordance with the suggested color symbols given in the illustrations in circles (see color chart in Chapter VI) or according to your own taste. For the ⅛-scale horse, insert a 10½″ length of ¼″-diameter brass pole (Illus. 79), brass tubing, or gold-painted dowel through the hole in the body of the horse so that 5⅜″ extends above the saddle. Glue the pole in place. Add the footrest (Illus. 80) to the pole ¹³⁄₁₆″ below the body. Make a base (see Chapter VI) and glue the pole of the completed carving to it.

Table 23 Parts List for the Lead Horse (⅛ Scale)

Part	Length	Width	Thickness
Head	2⁹⁄₁₆″	1½″	⅞″
Body and neck	5¹¹⁄₁₆″	3³⁄₁₆″	1½″
Right front leg	3¹⁄₁₆″	¾″	½″
Left front leg	1⅜″	½″	½″
Left front hoof	⅝″	⁷⁄₁₆″	⅜″
Right hind thigh	2″	¾″	¾″
Right hind leg	2⅜″	½″	½″
Left hind thigh	1⅞″	¾″	¾″
Left hind hoof	⅞″	½″	⅜″
Tail	2¹³⁄₁₆″	1⁵⁄₁₆″	¾″

Table 24 Critical Dimensions for the Lead Horse

	Scale				Full Size
	⅛	¼	½	¾	
From hoof to top of mane	7³⁄₁₆″	14⅜″	28¾″	43⅛″	57½″
From rump to breast	5¼″	10½″	21″	31½″	42″
From tail to front left knee	7″	14″	28″	42″	56″
Width of head	⅞″	1¾″	3½″	5¼″	7″
Width of nose	½″	1″	2″	3″	4″
Distance between tips of ears	⁹⁄₁₆″	1⅛″	2¼″	3⅜″	4½″
Width of neck at head (with mane)	⅞″	1¾″	3½″	5¼″	7″
Width of neck at body	1⅜″	2¾″	5½″	8½″	11″
Width of body at pole	1½″	3″	6″	9″	12″
Width of saddle at rear	1″	2″	4″	6″	8″
Width of rump	1½″	3″	6″	9″	12″
Width of front leg at body	½″	1″	2″	3″	4″
Width of front leg at knee	⅜″	¾″	1½″	2¼″	3″
Width of hind leg at body	¾″	1½″	3″	4½″	6″
Width of hind leg at knee	⅜″	¾″	1½″	2¼″	3″
Width of tail	¾″	1½″	3″	4½″	6″
Length of hoof	½″	1″	2″	3″	4″
Width of hoof	⅜″	¾″	1½″	2¼″	3″

CHAPTER IV
Prancers and Jumpers

he inside row horses of Chapter IV and the menagerie animals of Chapter V are smaller and less ornate than the outside row animals. On an actual carousel, they are often preferred by very young riders or by the parents of such riders, because of their smaller size.

All of the plans in Chapter IV are of prancers or jumpers. A prancer is a horse with the two hind feet resting on the platform and the two front feet in the air. A jumper is an animal with bent legs and all four feet in the air; these are usually the horses that move up and down while the carousel rotates.

The average time needed to make one of the ⅛-scale carvings is 23 hours.

13. Red Blanket Prancer

Using Illus. 28 as a plan, cut out the ten patterns and glue each pattern to wood of the correct thickness, given in Table 25. Refer to Illus. 29 for the complete patterns for the left front and hind legs. The length of each part should follow the direction of the wood grain. Instructions for large-scale animals are given in chapters VII and VIII.

The complete carving block consists of the ten parts given in Table 25. For the ⅛-scale horse, drill a ¼″ hole perpendicular through the body to hold the pole. The base reference line given in Illus. 28 should be used to be certain that the hole is properly placed. Drill a ⅛″ hole approximately ½″ deep at a 35° angle to the horizontal for the tail. The holes should be drilled before the legs are glued in place. The head and neck assembly involves a compound angle (see Illus. 1). The head tilts 20° toward the romance side on the vertical axis. Butter all end-grain surfaces with glue and glue the head and legs to the body.

For the ⅛-scale horse, cut four horseshoes from ³⁄₃₂″ stock and glue one to the bottom of each hoof. End-grain gluing is involved so be certain to "butter" the bottom of each leg with glue. Reduce the middle area of the horseshoes (Illus. 3) to a thickness of ³⁄₆₄″. Refer to Illus. 28 and 29 to complete the final shapes and details, and to Table 26, which provides the critical dimensions needed to carve a full-sized or reduced-scale model. Use a burning pen to develop the

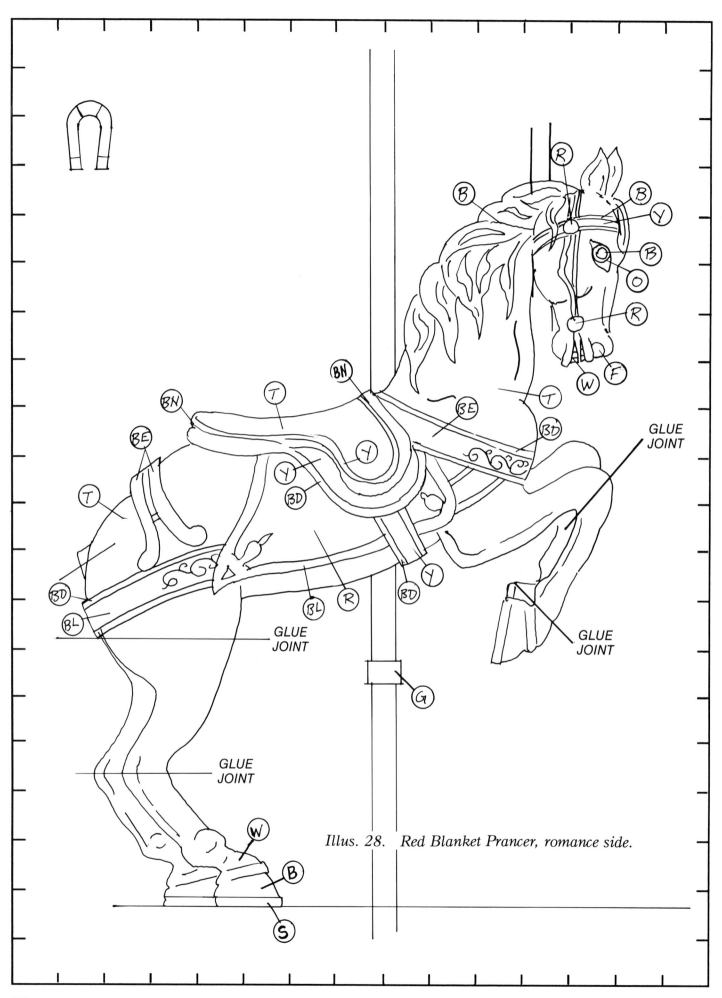

Illus. 28.   *Red Blanket Prancer, romance side.*

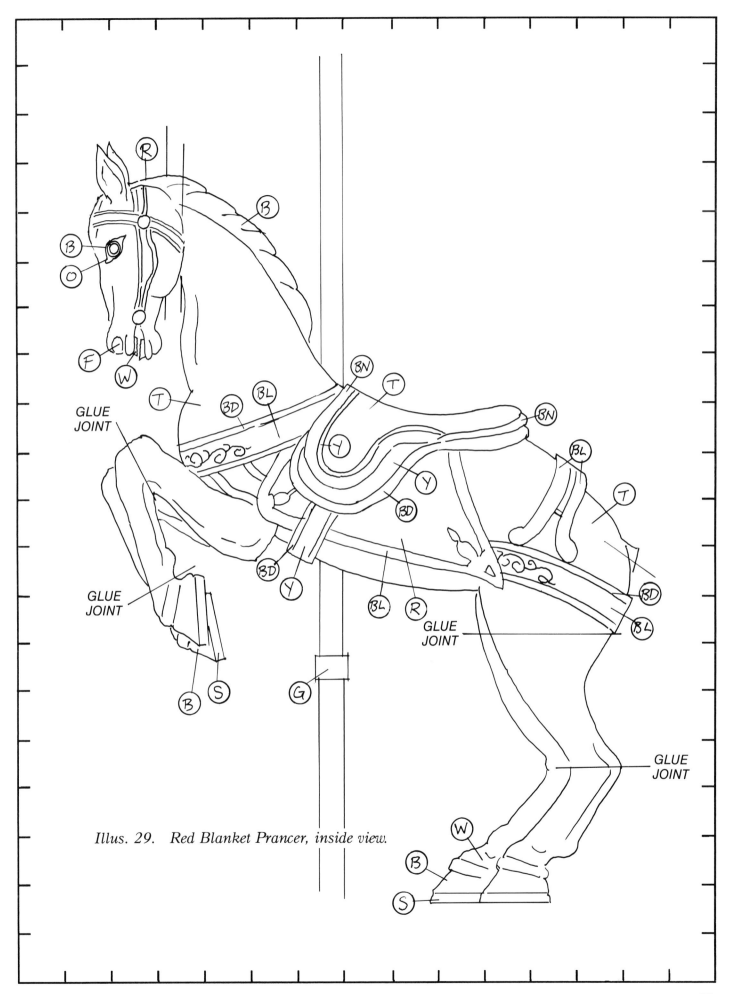

Illus. 29.   Red Blanket Prancer, inside view.

GLUE JOINT

GLUE JOINT

GLUE JOINT

GLUE JOINT

texture of the mane. The tail is made from 30 strands of 3″ long heavy black sewing thread for the ⅛-scale model.

After carving and sanding the horse, paint it in accordance with the suggested color scheme given in circles on the illustrations (see color chart in Chapter VI), or choose other pleasing colors. For the ⅛-scale horse, insert a 10½″ length of a ¼″-diameter brass pole (Illus. 79), brass tubing, or gold-painted dowel through the hole in the body so that 4¾″ extends above the saddle. Glue the pole in place. Add the footrest (Illus. 80) to the pole, ¹³⁄₁₆″ below the body. Make a base (see Chapter VI) and glue the pole of the completed horse to it.

Table 25   Parts List for Red Blanket Prancer (⅛ Scale)

Part	Length	Width	Thickness
Head	2⁵⁄₁₆″	1″	⅞″
Body and neck	5¹¹⁄₁₆″	4⅝″	1⅜″
Right front leg	1⅝″	⅜″	½″
Right front hoof	¹¹⁄₁₆″	¾″	½″
Left front leg	1½″	⁷⁄₁₆″	½″
Left front hoof	¹¹⁄₁₆″	¾″	½″
Right hind thigh	1¹⁵⁄₁₆″	1⅜″	¹¹⁄₁₆″
Right hind leg	2″	¾″	½″
Left hind thigh	1¾″	1¼″	¹¹⁄₁₆″
Left hind leg	1⅞″	¾″	½″

Table 26   Critical Dimensions of the Red Blanket Prancer

	Scale				Full Size
	⅛	¼	½	¾	
From hoof to tip of ear	7¾″	15½″	31″	46½″	62″
From rump to breast	4⅞″	9¾″	19½″	29¼″	39″
From rump to front right knee	5¾″	11½″	23″	34½″	46″
Width of head	⅞″	1¾″	3½″	5¼″	7″
Width of nose	½″	1″	2″	3″	4″
Distance between tips of ears	⅝″	1¼″	2½″	3¾″	5″
Width of neck at head	1⅛″	2¼″	4½″	6¾″	9″
Width of neck at body	1¼″	2½″	5″	7½″	10″
Width of body at pole	1⅜″	2¾″	5½″	8¼″	11″
Width of saddle at widest point	1⁷⁄₁₆″	2⅞″	5¾″	8⅝″	11½″
Width of rump	1⅜″	2¾″	5½″	8¼″	11″
Width of front leg at body	½″	1″	2″	3″	4″
Width of front leg at knee	⅜″	¾″	1½″	2¼″	3″
Width of hind leg at body	¹¹⁄₁₆″	1⅜″	2¾″	4⅛″	5½″
Width of hind leg at knee	⅜″	¾″	1½″	2¼″	3″
Length of hoof	¹¹⁄₁₆″	1⅜″	2¾″	4⅛″	5½″
Width of hoof	¾″	1½″	3″	4½″	6″

14. Indian Prancer

Using Illus. 30 and 31 as plans, cut out the 10 patterns and glue each pattern on wood of the correct thickness, given in Table 27. The length of each part should follow the direction of the wood grain. Instructions for large-scale animals are given in chapters VII and VIII.

The complete carving block is made up of the ten parts listed in Table 27. Use the base reference line on Illus. 30 and drill a ¼″ hole (for ⅛-scale horse) perpendicularly through the body for the pole. Drill a ⅛″ hole at a 35° angle to the horizontal for the tail. Drill the holes before the legs are glued in place.

The head and neck meet at a compound angle (see Illus. 1), with the head at a 20° tilt towards the romance side on the vertical axis. Size all end-grain surfaces and glue the head and legs in place.

For the ⅛-scale horse, cut four horseshoes from ³⁄₃₂″ stock and glue one to the bottom of each leg. End-grain gluing is involved, so be certain to size the bottom of each leg with glue. Reduce the middle area of the horseshoes (Illus. 3) to a thickness of ³⁄₆₄″. Refer to Illus. 30 and 31 to complete the final shapes and details, and to Table 28, which provides the critical dimensions that are required to carve a full-sized or a reduced-scale model. Use a burning pen to provide texture to the mane, fringe, and Indian feathers. The tail for the ⅛-scale horse is made from 30 lengths of 3″ heavy black sewing thread.

After carving and sanding the horse, paint it in accordance with the suggested colors given in circles in the illustrations (see color chart in Chapter VI), or choose other colors that best meet your needs.

Table 27   Parts List for Indian Prancer (⅛ Scale)

Part	Length	Width	Thickness
Head	2¼″	1⅛″	⅞″
Body and neck	5¹¹⁄₁₆″	4″	1⅜″
Right front leg	1⁹⁄₁₆″	⅜″	½″
Right front hoof	¹³⁄₁₆″	⁹⁄₁₆″	½″
Left front leg	⁹⁄₁₆″	⅜″	½″
Left front hoof	¹³⁄₁₆″	⁹⁄₁₆″	½″
Right hind thigh	1¾″	1⅜″	¹¹⁄₁₆″
Right hind leg	2″	¹¹⁄₁₆″	½″
Left hind thigh	1¾″	1⅜″	¹¹⁄₁₆″
Left hind leg	2″	¹¹⁄₁₆″	½″

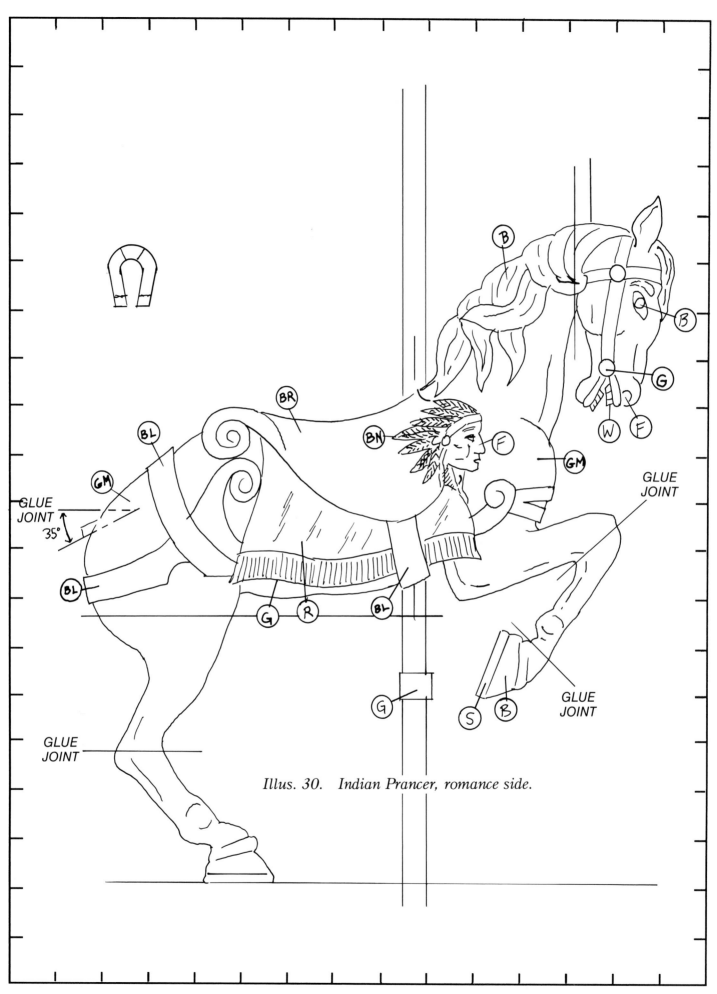

Illus. 30. Indian Prancer, romance side.

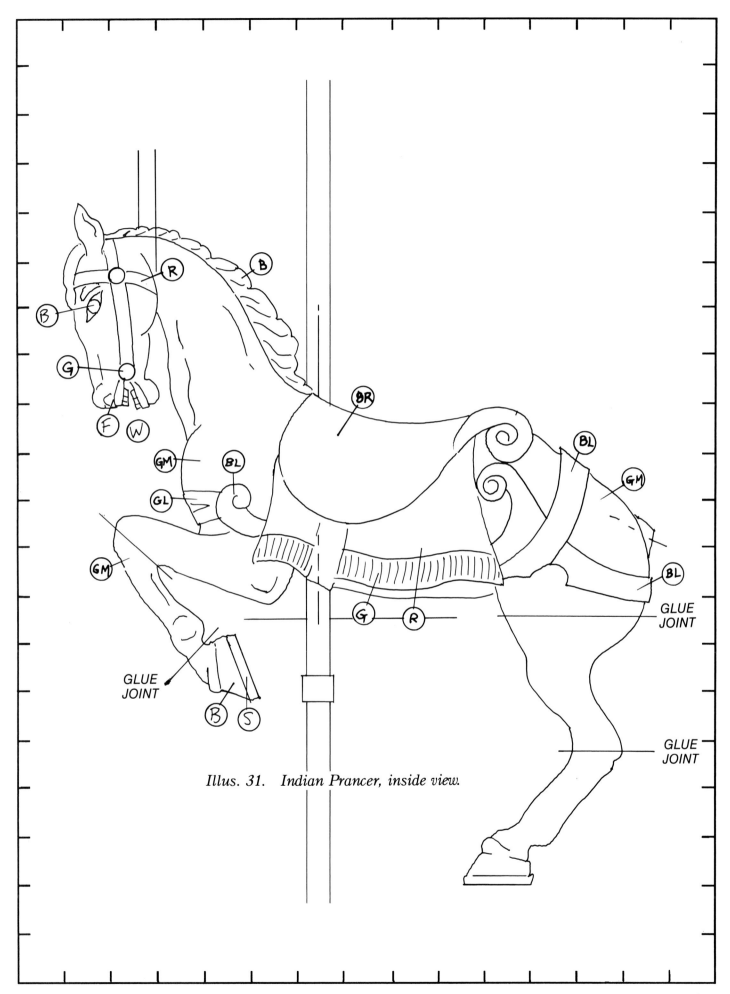

Illus. 31. Indian Prancer, inside view.

75

For the ⅛-scale horse, insert a 10½″ length of a ¼″-diameter brass pole (Illus. 79), brass tubing, or a gold-painted dowel through the hole in the body so that 5″ extends above the saddle. Glue the pole in place. Add the footrest (Illus. 80) to the pole 13⁄16″ below the body, make a base (see Chapter VI), and glue the pole of the completed horse to it.

Table 28 Critical Dimensions for the Indian Prancer

	Scale				*Full Size*
	⅛	*¼*	*½*	*¾*	
From hoof to tip of ear	7″	14″	28″	42″	56″
From rump to breast	5″	10″	20″	30″	40″
From rump to front right knee	5¾″	11½″	23″	34½″	46″
Width of head	⅞″	1¾″	3½″	5¼″	7″
Width of nose	½″	1″	2″	3″	4″
Distance between tips of ears	½″	1″	2″	3″	4″
Width of neck at head	1⅛″	2¼″	4½″	6¾″	9″
Width of neck at body	1¼″	2½″	5″	7½″	10″
Width of body at pole	1⅜″	2¾″	5½″	8¼″	11″
Width of saddle at rear	1⅜″	2¾″	5½″	8¼″	11″
Width of rump	1⅜″	2¾″	5½″	8¼″	11″
Width of front leg at body	½″	1″	2″	3″	4″
Width of front leg at knee	⅜″	¾″	1½″	2¼″	3″
Width of hind leg at body	11⁄16″	1⅜″	2¾″	4⅛″	5½″
Width of hind leg at knee	⅜″	¾″	1½″	2¼″	3″
Length of hoof	¾″	1½″	3″	4½″	6″
Width of hoof	½″	1″	2″	3″	4″

15. Buccaneer

Using Illus. 32 as a plan, cut out the eleven patterns and glue each pattern to wood of the correct thickness, given in Table 29. Refer to Illus. 33 for the complete pattern of the left front and hind legs. The length of each part should follow the directions of the wood grain. Instructions for large-scale animals are given in chapters VII and VIII.

The complete carving block is made up of the 11 parts listed in Table 29. Using the base reference line given in Illus. 32 as a guide, drill a ¼″ hole (for the ⅛-scale horse) perpendicularly through the body for the pole. Drill another ¼″ hole at a 62° angle to the perpendicular for the tail. The two holes should be drilled before the legs are glued in place. Size the end grain of each part and glue the head and legs in place. The head tilts on a vertical axis toward the romance side at approximately a 10° angle.

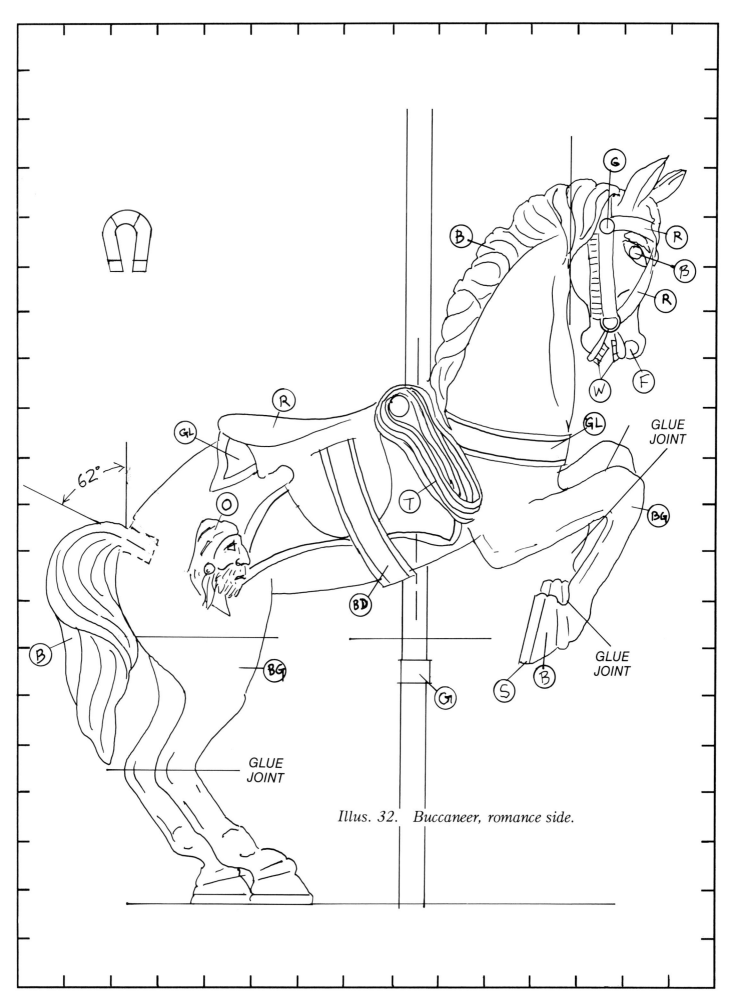

Illus. 32.   Buccaneer, romance side.

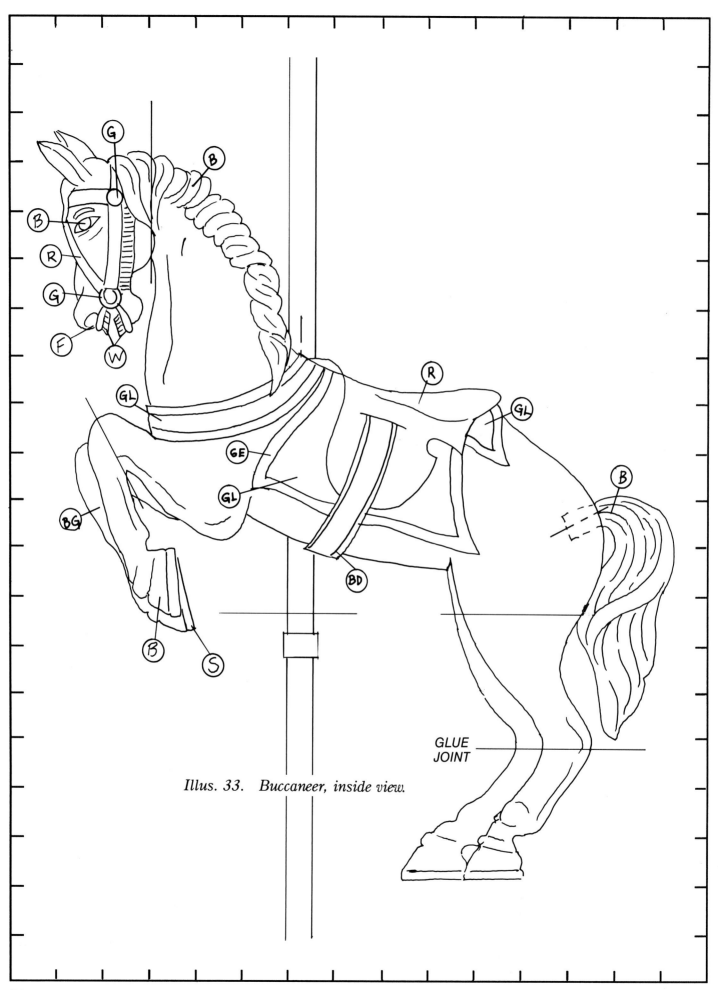

Illus. 33.   Buccaneer, inside view.

For the ⅛-scale horse, cut four horseshoes from ³⁄₃₂″ stock and glue one to the bottom of each hoof. End-grain gluing is involved, so be certain to "butter" the bottom of each leg with glue. Reduce the middle area of the horseshoes (Illus. 3) to a thickness of ³⁄₆₄″. Refer to Illus. 32 and 33 to complete the final shapes and details, and to Table 30, which provides the critical dimensions needed to carve a full-sized prancer or a reduced-scale model.

After the final sanding, glue the tail into the hole in the rump. It is supported only at the rump, so to strengthen the tail, insert a ¾″

Table 29 Parts List for the Buccaneer (⅛ Scale)

Part	Length	Width	Thickness
Head	2³⁄₁₆″	1¼″	⅞″
Body and neck	5⁹⁄₁₆″	4¹¹⁄₁₆″	1⅜″
Right front leg	1⅜″	⅜″	½″
Right front hoof	¾″	⅝″	½″
Left front leg	2¼″	½″	½″
Left front hoof	¾″	⅝″	½″
Right hind thigh	1⅞″	1⅜″	¹¹⁄₁₆″
Right hind leg	2″	¹¹⁄₁₆″	½″
Left hind thigh	1¾″	1¼″	¹¹⁄₁₆″
Left hind leg	1¹³⁄₁₆″	¾″	½″
Tail	2½″	1¼″	¾″

Table 30 Critical Dimensions for the Buccaneer

	Scale				Full Size
	⅛	¼	½	¾	
From hoof to tip of ear	7¹¹⁄₁₆″	15⅜″	30¾″	46⅛″	61½″
From rump to breast	4¹³⁄₁₆″	9⅝″	19¼″	28⅞″	38½″
From tail to front right knee	5⅝″	11¼″	22½″	33¾″	45″
Width of head	⅞″	1¾″	3½″	5¼″	7″
Width of nose	½″	1″	2″	3″	4″
Distance between tips of ears	½″	1″	2″	3″	4″
Width of neck at head	⅞″	1¾″	3½″	5¼″	7″
Width of neck at body	1¼″	2½″	5″	7½″	10″
Width of body at pole	1⅜″	2¾″	5½″	8¼″	11″
Width of saddle at widest point	1″	2″	4″	6″	8″
Width of rump	1⅜″	2¾″	5½″	8¼″	11″
Width of front leg at body	½″	1″	2″	3″	4″
Width of front leg at knee	⅜″	¾″	1½″	2¼″	3″
Width of hind leg at body	¹¹⁄₁₆″	1⅜″	2¾″	4⅛″	5½″
Width of hind leg at knee	⅜″	¾″	1½″	2¼″	3″
Width of tail	¾″	1½″	3″	4½″	6″
Length of hoof	¾″	1½″	3″	4½″	6″
Width of hoof	½″	1″	2″	3″	4″

long Number 20 brad along the center line of the dowel area. This is best done before the tail is carved. Use a burning pen to add texture to the mane, fringe, rope, and to the buccaneer's beard.

After carving and sanding the horse, paint it in accordance with the suggested color symbols in circles on the illustrations (see color chart in Chapter VI); or choose other colors that are pleasing to you. For the ⅛-scale horse, insert a 10½" length of a ¼"-diameter brass pole, brass tubing, or gold-painted dowel through the hole in the body (Illus. 79) with 4¹¹⁄₁₆" extending above the saddle. Glue the pole in place. Add the footrest (Illus. 80) to the pole ¹³⁄₁₆" below the body. Make a base (see Chapter VI) and glue the pole of the completed prancer to it.

16. Yellow-Fringe Prancer

Circa 1895–1900

Using Illus. 34 as a plan, cut out the nine patterns and glue each pattern to wood of the correct thickness as defined in Table 31. Refer to Illus. 35 for the complete pattern of the left front and hind legs. The length of each part should follow the direction of the wood grain. Instructions for large-scale animals are given in chapters VII and VIII.

The complete carving block consists of the nine parts listed in Table 31. For the ⅛-scale horse, drill a ¼" hole perpendicularly through the body for the pole. Drill a ¼" hole at a 52° angle from the

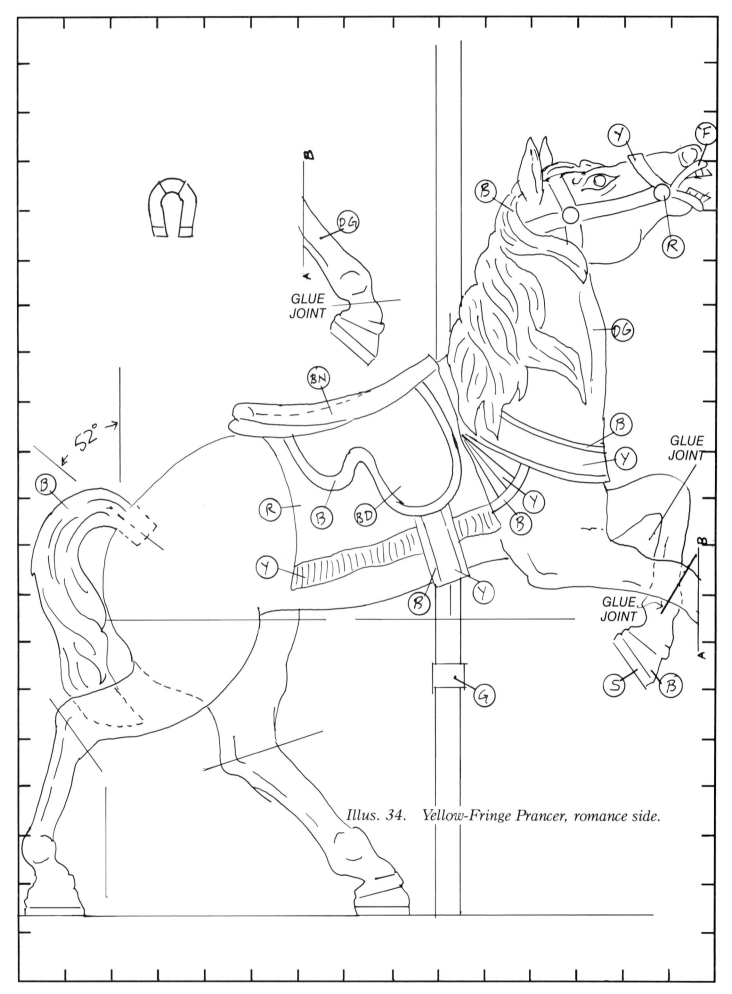

Illus. 34.   *Yellow-Fringe Prancer, romance side.*

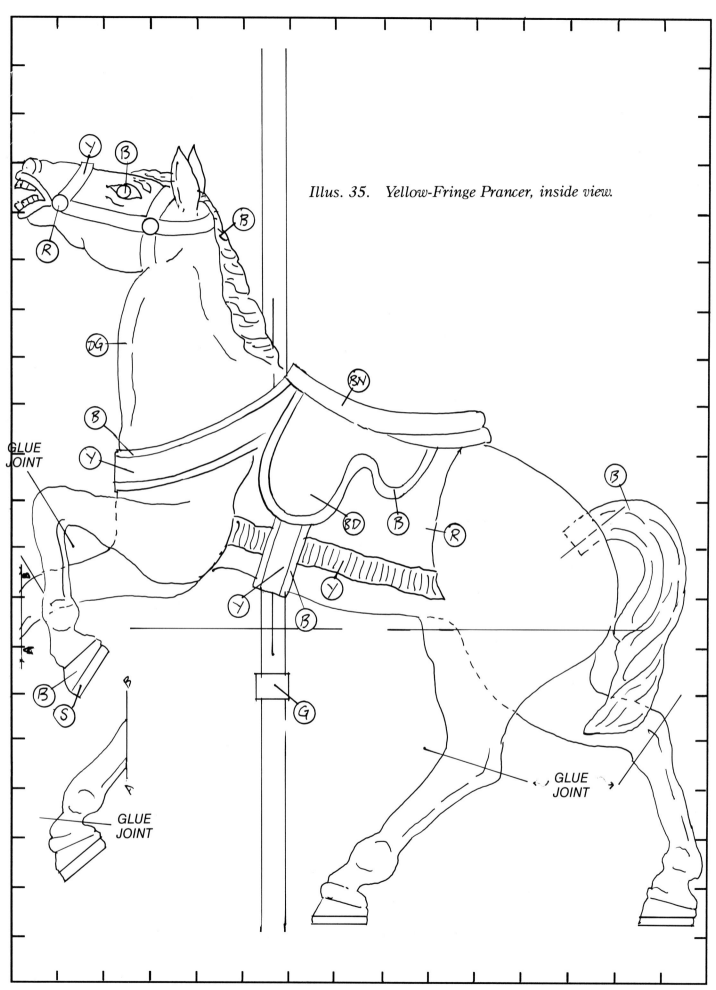

Illus. 35. *Yellow-Fringe Prancer, inside view.*

GLUE
JOINT

GLUE
JOINT

GLUE
JOINT

Table 31   Parts List for the Yellow-Fringe Prancer (⅛ Scale)

Part	Length	Width	Thickness
Head and body	6⅜″	4⅞″	1½″
Right front leg	1⁷⁄₁₆″	½″	½″
Right front hoof	⁹⁄₁₆″	⁹⁄₁₆″	½″
Left front leg	2⅛″	⅝″	½″
Right hind thigh	2¼″	1⅜″	¾″
Right hind leg	1⅞″	¹³⁄₁₆″	½″
Left hind thigh	2″	1¾″	¾″
Left hind leg	2⁷⁄₁₆″	⅝″	½″
Tail	2⁷⁄₁₆″	1⁷⁄₁₆″	¾″

Table 32   Critical Dimensions for the Yellow-Fringe Prancer

	Scale				Full Size
	⅛	¼	½	¾	
From hoof to tip of ear	7¹⁵⁄₁₆″	15⅞″	31¾″	47⅝″	63½″
From rump to breast	5⅜″	10¾″	21½″	32¼″	43″
From tail to front right knee	7⅛″	14¼″	28½″	42¾″	57″
Width of head	⅞″	1¾″	3½″	5¼″	7″
Width of nose	½″	1″	2″	3″	4″
Distance between tips of ears	⅝″	1¼″	2½″	3¾″	5″
Width of neck at head	¹³⁄₁₆″	1⅝″	3¼″	4⅞″	6½″
Width of neck at body	1⅜″	2¾″	5½″	8¼″	11″
Width of body at pole	1½″	3″	6″	9″	12″
Width of saddle at widest point	1⅜″	2¾″	5½″	8¼″	11″
Width of rump	1½″	3″	6″	9″	12″
Width of front leg at body	½″	1″	2″	3″	4″
Width of front leg at knee	⅜″	¾″	1½″	2¼″	3″
Width of hind leg at body	¾″	1½″	3″	4½″	6″
Width of hind leg at knee	⅜″	¾″	1½″	2¼″	3″
Width of tail	¾″	1½″	3″	4½″	6″
Length of hoof	⅝″	1¼″	2½″	3¾″	5″
Width of hoof	½″	1″	2″	3″	4″

perpendicular for the tail. Drill both holes before gluing the legs in place. Size the end grain of each part and glue the legs to the body. The head is facing straight ahead; there is no sideways tilt.

For the ⅛-scale horse, cut out four horseshoes from ³⁄₃₂″ stock and glue one to the bottom of each leg. End-grain gluing is involved, so be certain to "butter" the bottom of each leg with glue. Reduce the middle areas of each horseshoe (Illus. 3) to a thickness of ³⁄₆₄″. Refer to Illus. 34 and 35 to complete the final shapes and details, and to Table 32, which provides the critical dimensions needed to carve the full-sized horse or a reduced-scale model. Use a burning pen to develop the texture in the flowing mane, tail, and in the fringe on the saddle blanket. After final sanding, glue the tail to the body and against the inside of the right hind leg and paint the horse in accordance with the suggested color symbols given in Illus. 34 and 35 (see color chart in Chapter VI), or with colors of your own choice. Insert a 10½″ length of a ¼″-diameter brass pole, brass tubing, or a gold-painted dowel (Illus. 79) through the hole in the body of the horse so that ½″ extends below the hind feet for the ⅛-scale horse. Glue the pole in place. Add the footrest (Illus. 80) to the pole ¹³⁄₁₆″ below the body. Make a base (see Chapter VI) and glue the pole of the completed carving to it. For the ⅛-scale horse, the approximate carving time is 12 hours; approximately 23 hours are needed to carve, sand, and paint the ⅛-scale Yellow-Fringe Prancer.

17. Prancer with Brown Saddle

Circa 1900

Using Illus. 36 as a plan, cut out the seven patterns and glue each pattern to wood of the correct thickness, as given in Table 33. Refer to Illus. 37 for the complete pattern of the right front and hind legs. The length of each part should follow the direction of the wood grain.

The complete carving block consists of the seven parts given in Table 33. Using the base reference line, drill a ¼″ hole perpendicularly through the body for the pole. Drill a ⅛″ hole at a 60° angle to the perpendicular for the tail. Both of these holes should be drilled before the legs are glued in place. There is no sideways tilt to the head. Size all end grain and glue the legs in place.

For the ⅛-scale horse, cut four horseshoes from ³⁄₃₂″ stock and glue one to the bottom of each leg. End-grain gluing is involved, so be certain to "butter" the bottom of each leg with glue. Reduce the middle areas of the horseshoes (Illus. 3) to a thickness of ³⁄₆₄″. Refer to Illus. 36 and 37 to complete the final shapes and details, and to Table 34, which provides the critical dimensions that you will need to carve a full-sized horse or a reduced-scale model. Use a burning pen to add texture to the mane. The tail for the ⅛-scale horse is made up of 30 lengths of heavy-duty white sewing thread, each 3″ long. After the final sanding, glue the fabric tail into the hole in the rump and paint the horse as suggested by the color symbols in circles on illustrations (see color chart in Chapter VI), or in other colors that please you. For the ⅛-scale horse, insert a 10½″ length of a ¼″-diameter brass pole (Illus. 79), brass tubing, or gold-painted

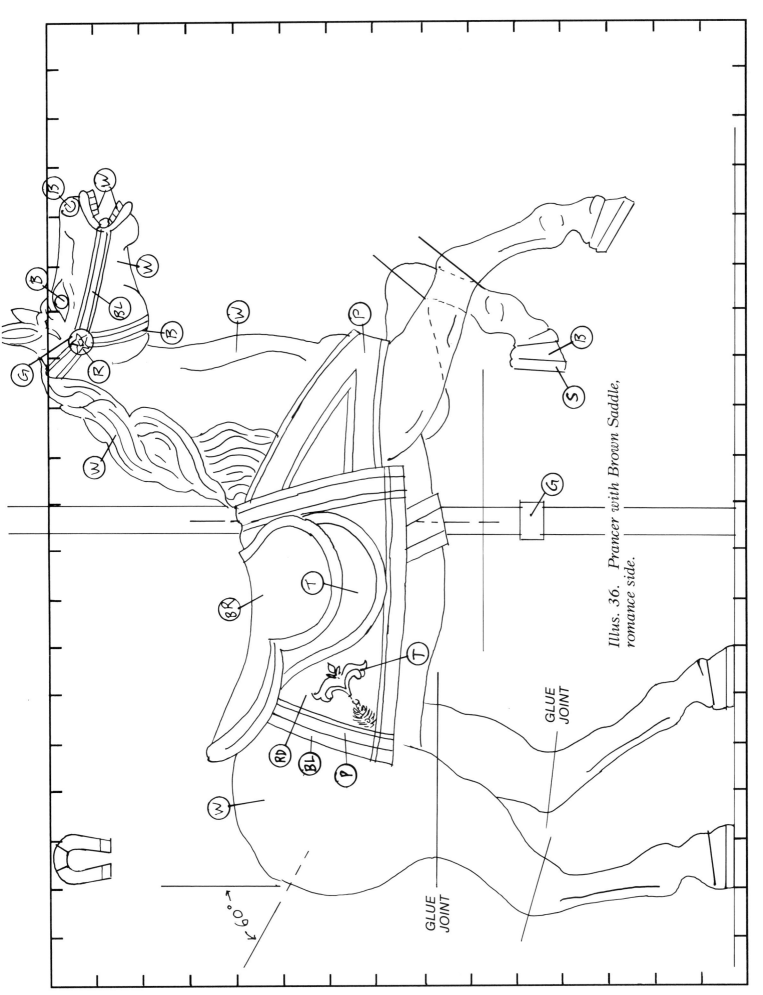

Illus. 36. Prancer with Brown Saddle, romance side.

GLUE JOINT

GLUE JOINT

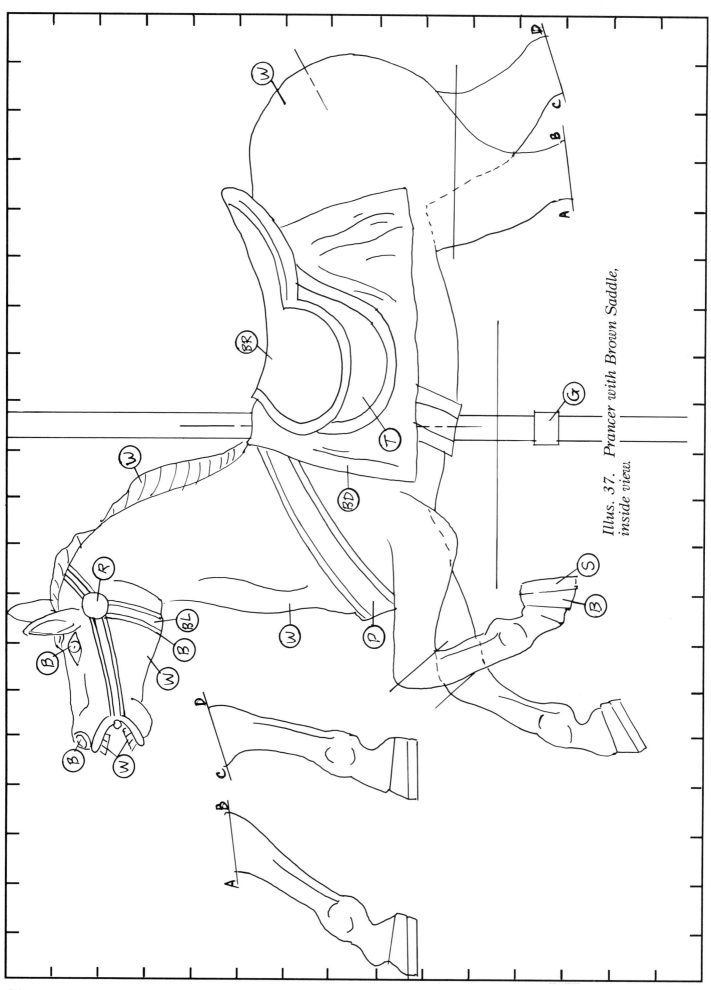

Illus. 37. *Prancer with Brown Saddle, inside view.*

dowel through the hole in the body so that 4¹¹⁄₁₆" of pole extends above the saddle. Glue the pole in place. Add the footrest (Illus. 80) to the pole ¹³⁄₁₆" below the body. Make a base (see Chapter VI) and glue the pole of the completed horse to it.

Table 33   Parts List for the Prancer with Brown Saddle (⅛ Scale)

Part	Length	Width	Thickness
Head and body	7³⁄₁₆"	4⅞"	1⅜"
Right front leg	2¹⁄₁₆"	⅝"	½"
Left front leg	2⅛"	⅝"	½"
Right hind thigh	1¹¹⁄₁₆"	¹⁵⁄₁₆"	¹¹⁄₁₆"
Right hind leg	2¼"	¹¹⁄₁₆"	½"
Left hind thigh	1½"	1⅜"	¹¹⁄₁₆"
Left hind leg	2½"	⅝"	½"

Table 34   Critical Dimensions for the Prancer with Brown Saddle

	Scale				Full Size
	⅛	¼	½	¾	
From hoof to tip of ear	7¹⁵⁄₁₆"	15⅞"	31¾"	47⅝"	63½"
From rump to breast	5¹³⁄₁₆"	11⅝"	23¼"	34⅞"	46½"
From tail to front right knee	7¼"	14½"	29"	43½"	58"
Width of head	⅞"	1¾"	3½"	5¼"	7"
Width of nose	½"	1"	2"	3"	4"
Distance between tips of ears	⅝"	1¼"	2½"	3¾"	5"
Width of neck at head	¹³⁄₁₆"	1⅝"	3¼"	4⅞"	6½"
Width of neck at body	1⅜"	2¾"	5½"	8¼"	11"
Width of body at pole	1⅜"	2¾"	5½"	8¼"	11"
Width of saddle at widest point	1⅛"	2¼"	4½"	6¾"	9"
Width of rump	1⅜"	2¾"	5½"	8¼"	11"
Width of front leg at body	½"	1"	2"	3"	4"
Width of front leg at knee	⅜"	¾"	1½"	2¼"	3"
Width of hind leg at body	¹¹⁄₁₆"	1⅜"	2¾"	4⅛"	5½"
Width of hind leg at knee	⅜"	¾"	1½"	2¼"	3"
Length of hoof	⅝"	1¼"	2½"	3¾"	5"
Width of hoof	½"	1"	2"	3"	4"

18. Western Prancer

Circa 1904

Using Illus. 38 as a plan, cut out the twelve patterns and glue each pattern to wood of the correct thickness, given in Table 35. Refer to Illus. 39 for the complete pattern of the left front and hind legs. The length of each part should follow the direction of the wood grain.

Instructions for large-scale animals are given in chapters VII and VIII.

The complete carving block consists of the twelve parts given in Table 35. For the ⅛-scale horse, drill a ¼″ hole perpendicularly through the body for the pole. Use the suggested reference line from Illus. 38 to assure accuracy. Drill a ¼″ hole at a 60° angle from the perpendicular for the tail before gluing the head or legs in place. Size the end grain of each part and glue the head and legs to the body. The head tilts on a vertical axis towards the romance side at approximately a 10° angle.

For the ⅛-scale horse, cut four horseshoes from ³⁄₃₂″ stock and glue one at the bottom of each hoof. End-grain gluing is involved, so be certain to "butter" the bottom of each leg with glue. Reduce the middle areas of each horseshoe (Illus. 3) to a thickness of ³⁄₆₄″. Refer to Illus. 38 and 39 to complete the final shapes and details, and to Table 36, which provides the critical dimensions needed to carve the full-sized prancer or a smaller-scale model. Use a burning pen to develop the hair texture in the flowing mane and tail, as well as the decorations on the saddle and saddle blanket. After a final sanding, glue the tail in the hole in the body and against the inside of the right hind leg.

Use a burning pen on mane, tail, fringe, and geometric design on saddle. For the ⅛-scale horse, the bit is a ½″ length of a ³⁄₃₂″-diameter dowel, which is added after painting. After carving and sanding the horse, paint it in the colors suggested by the color symbols in circles on the illustrations (see color chart in Chapter VI), or choose colors according to your own desires. Insert a 10½″ length of a ¼″-diameter brass pole (Illus. 79), brass tubing, or gold-painted dowel through the hole in the body of the horse so that 4¼″ extends above the saddle. Glue the pole in place. Add the footrest (Illus. 80) to the pole 13⁄16″ below the underbelly. Make a base (see Chapter VI) and glue the pole of the completed horse to it.

The approximate carving time is 14 hours; approximately 27 total hours are needed to carve, sand, and paint the ⅛-scale prancer.

Table 35 Parts List for the Western Prancer (⅛ Scale)

Part	*Length*	*Width*	*Thickness*
Head	2¼″	1″	½″
Body	6¼″	4¾″	1½″
Right front leg	1 7⁄16″	7⁄16″	½″
Right front hoof	⅝″	9⁄16″	½″
Left front leg	1 9⁄16″	⅜″	½″
Left front hoof	9⁄16″	9⁄16″	½″
Right hind thigh	2⅛″	1½″	¾″
Right hind leg	1⅞″	⅝″	½″
Right hind hoof	⅜″	⅝″	½″
Left hind thigh	1 15⁄16″	1 15⁄16″	¾″
Left hind leg	2 7⁄16″	11⁄16″	½″
Tail	2¾″	1⅜″	¾″

Table 36 Critical Dimensions for the Western Prancer

	Scale				*Full*
	⅛	¼	½	¾	*Size*
From hoof to tip of ear	8 3⁄16″	16⅜″	32¾″	49⅛″	65½″
From rump to breast	5⅜″	10¾″	21½″	32¼″	43″
From right hind hoof to front right ankle	8 1⁄16″	16⅛″	32¼″	48⅜″	64½″
Width of head	⅞″	1¾″	3½″	5¼″	7″
Width of nose	½″	1″	2″	3″	4″
Distance between tips of ears	½″	1″	2″	3″	4″
Width of neck at head	1⅛″	2¼″	4½″	6¾″	9″
Width of neck at body	1¼″	2½″	5″	7½″	10″
Width of body at pole	1⅜″	2¾″	5½″	8¼″	11″
Width of saddle at widest point	1 7⁄16″	2⅞″	5¾″	8⅝″	11½″
Width of rump	1½″	3″	6″	9″	12″
Width of front leg at body	½″	1″	2″	3″	4″
Width of front leg at knee	⅜″	¾″	1½″	2¼″	3″
Width of hind leg at body	¾″	1½″	3″	4½″	6″
Width of hind leg at knee	⅜″	¾″	1½″	2¼″	3″
Length of hoof	⅝″	1¼″	2½″	3¾″	5″
Width of hoof	½″	1″	2″	3″	4″

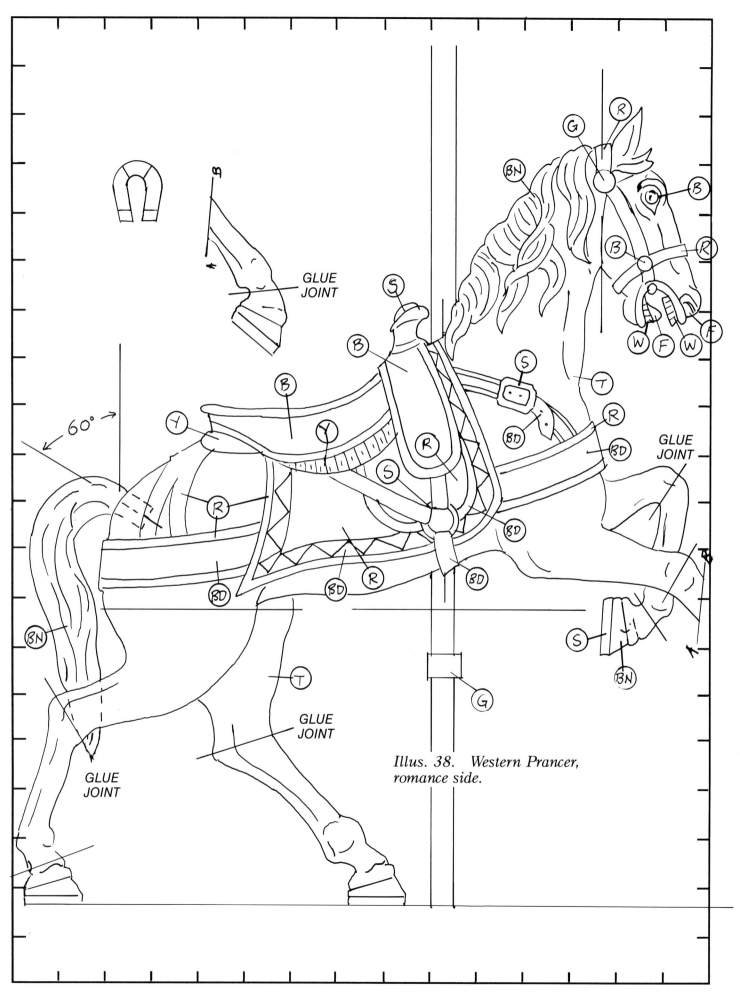

GLUE JOINT

60°

GLUE JOINT

GLUE JOINT

GLUE JOINT

Illus. 38. Western Prancer, romance side.

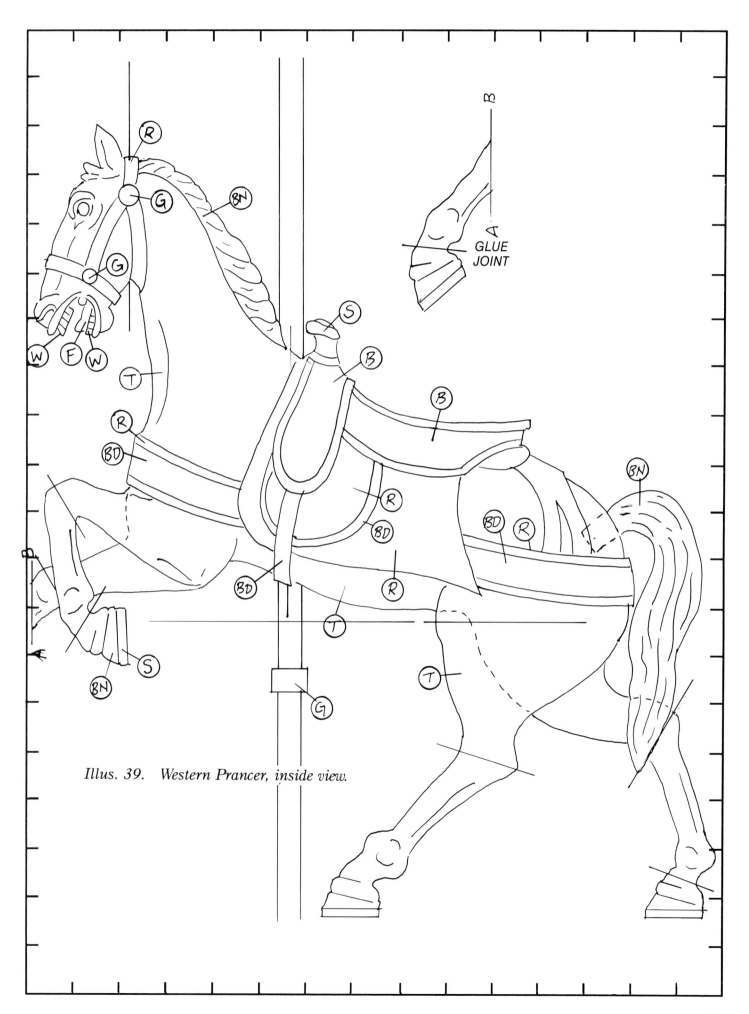

GLUE JOINT

Illus. 39.   Western Prancer, inside view.

19. Red Stripe Jumper

Circa 1926

Use Illus. 40 as a plan and cut out the thirteen patterns; glue each pattern to wood of the correct thickness as defined in Table 37. Refer to Illus. 41 for the complete pattern of the left front and hind legs. The length of each part should follow the direction of the wood grain. Instructions for large-scale animals are given in chapters VII and VIII. The complete carving block consists of the thirteen parts given in Table 37. For the ⅛-scale horse, drill a ¼″ hole perpendicularly through the body for the pole. Use the horizontal reference line provided on Illus. 40. Drill a ¼″ hole at a 60° angle from the perpendicular for the tail. Drill both holes before the head or legs are glued in place. Size the end grain of each part and glue the head and legs to the body. The head tilts on a vertical axis towards the romance side at approximately a 15° angle.

For the ⅛-scale horse, cut four horseshoes from ³⁄₃₂″ stock and glue one to the bottom of each hoof. End-grain gluing is involved, so be certain to "butter" the bottom of each leg with glue. Reduce the middle area of each horseshoe (Illus. 3) to a thickness of ³⁄₆₄″. Refer to Illus. 40 and 41 to complete the final shapes and details, and to Table 38, which provides the critical dimensions you will need when carving a full-sized Jumper or a reduced-scale model. After a final sanding, glue the tail into the hole in the body and against the inside of the right hind leg. Use a burning pen to develop the hair texture on the mane and tail.

Paint the horse in accordance with the suggested color symbols in circles on the illustrations (see color chart in Chapter VI), or according to your own taste. For the ⅛-scale horse, insert a 10½″

length of a ¼"-diameter brass pole (Illus. 79), brass tubing, or gold-painted dowel through the hole in the body of the horse so that 4⅜" extends above the saddle. Glue the pole in place. Add the footrest (Illus. 80) to the pole ¹³⁄₁₆" below the body. Make a base (see Chapter VI) and glue the pole of the completed horse to it. The approximate carving time is 13 hours; approximately 25 hours are required to carve, sand, and paint the ⅛-scale Jumper.

Table 37   Parts List for the Red Stripe Jumper (⅛ Scale)

Part	Length	Width	Thickness
Head	2¾"	1³⁄₁₆"	¾"
Body and neck	5¹³⁄₁₆"	4¾"	1⅜"
Right front leg	1⅜"	⁷⁄₁₆"	½"
Right front hoof	⅝"	⁷⁄₁₆"	⁷⁄₁₆"
Left front leg	1⅜"	⁷⁄₁₆"	½"
Left front hoof	¾"	⁷⁄₁₆"	⁷⁄₁₆"
Right hind thigh	2½"	⅝"	¹¹⁄₁₆"
Right hind leg	1¹¹⁄₁₆"	⁹⁄₁₆"	⁷⁄₁₆"
Right hind hoof	¾"	⁷⁄₁₆"	⁷⁄₁₆"
Left hind thigh	¹³⁄₁₆"	¾"	¹¹⁄₁₆"
Left hind leg	1⅜"	½"	⁷⁄₁₆"
Left hind hoof	¹¹⁄₁₆"	⁷⁄₁₆"	⁷⁄₁₆"
Tail	2¼"	1³⁄₁₆"	¾"

Table 38   Critical Dimensions for the Red Stripe Jumper

	Scale				Full Size
	⅛	¼	½	¾	
From left front hoof to top of mane	6⅛"	12¼"	24½"	36¾"	49"
From rump to breast	5¹⁄₁₆"	10⅛"	20¼"	30⅜"	40½"
From tail to front right knee	6¾"	13½"	27"	40½"	54"
Width of head	¾"	1½"	3"	4½"	6"
Width of nose	⁷⁄₁₆"	⅞"	1¾"	2⅝"	3½"
Distance between tips of ears	⁷⁄₁₆"	⅞"	1¾"	2⅝"	3½"
Width of neck at head	¹¹⁄₁₆"	1⅜"	2¾"	4⅛"	5½"
Width of neck at body	1⅛"	2¼"	4½"	6¾"	9"
Width of body at pole	1⅜"	2¾"	5½"	8¼"	11"
Width of saddle at rear	1⁵⁄₁₆"	2⅝"	5¼"	7⅞"	10½"
Width of rump	1⅜"	2¾"	5½"	8¼"	11"
Width of front leg at body	½"	1"	2"	3"	4"
Width of front leg at knee	⁷⁄₁₆"	⅞"	1¾"	2⅝"	3½"
Width of hind leg at body	¹¹⁄₁₆"	1⅜"	2¾"	4⅛"	5½"
Width of hind leg at knee	⁷⁄₁₆"	⅞"	1¾"	2⅝"	3½"
Length of hoof	½"	1"	2"	3"	4"
Width of hoof	⁷⁄₁₆"	⅞"	1¾"	2⅝"	3½"
Width of tail	¾"	1½"	3"	4½"	6"

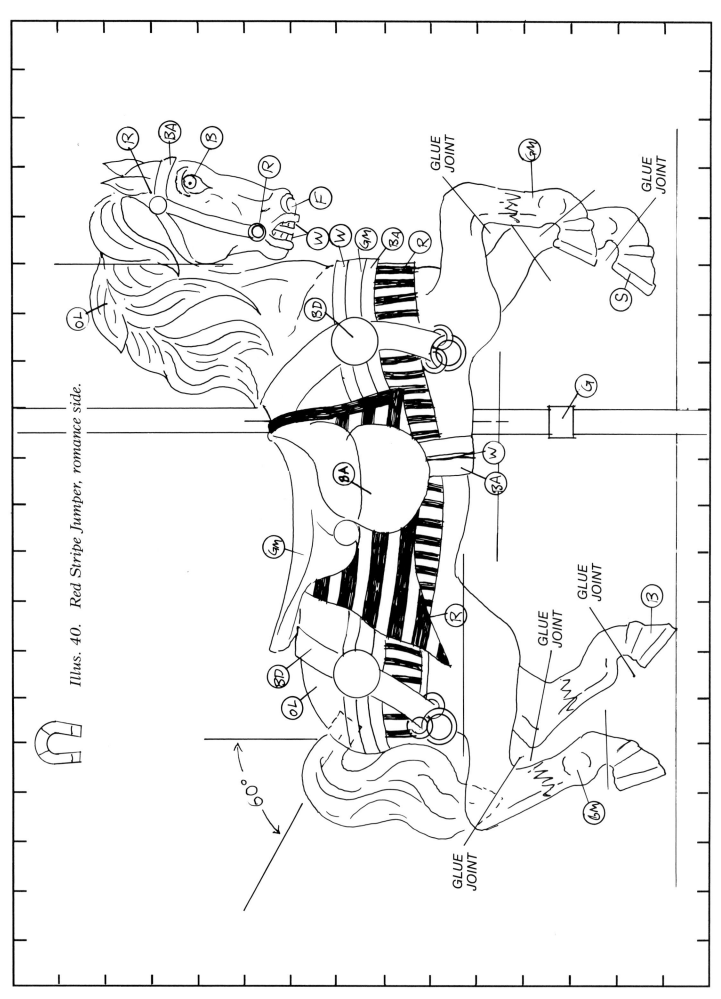

Illus. 40. Red Stripe Jumper, romance side.

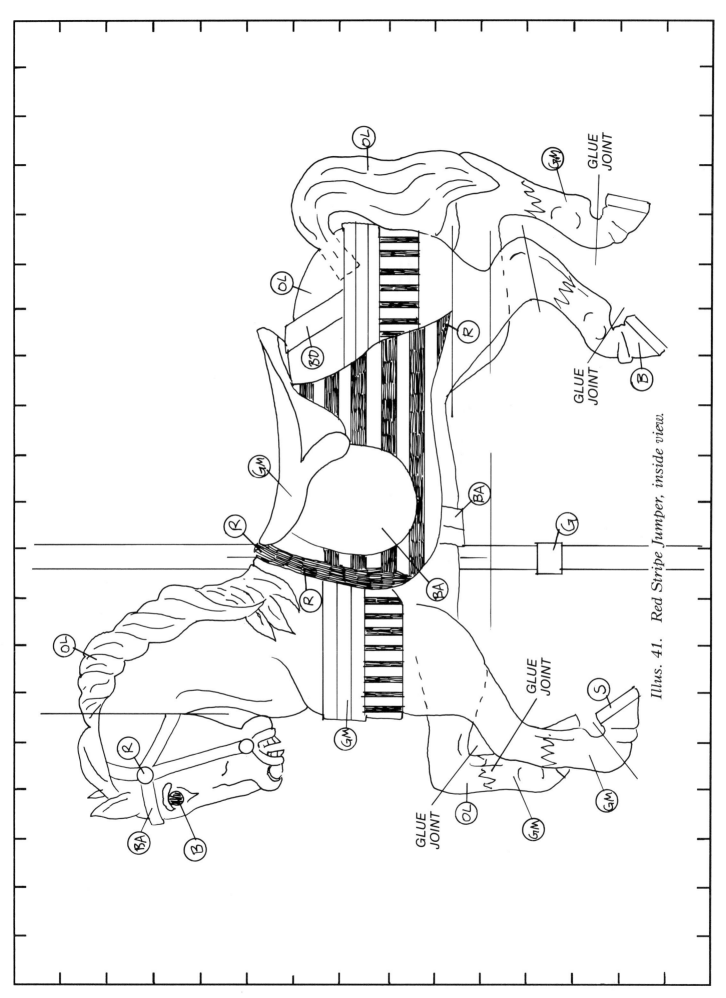

Illus. 41. Red Stripe Jumper, inside view.

20. Diamond Light

Circa 1922

Using Illus. 42 as a plan, cut out the thirteen patterns and glue each pattern to wood of the correct thickness, given in Table 39. Refer to Illus. 43 for the complete pattern for the left front and hind legs. The length of each part should follow the direction of the wood grain. Instructions for large-scale animals are given in chapters VII and VIII. The complete carving block is made up of the thirteen parts listed in Table 39. For the ⅛-scale horse, drill a ¼″ hole perpendicularly through the body for the pole and a ¼″ hole at a 30° angle for the tail (see Illus. 42). Drill these holes before the legs are glued in place. Note that the head is at a compound angle. Be certain to add ³⁄₁₆″ to the front of the neck block and follow the procedure for compound angles outlined in Chapter II (Illus. 1). Size all end-grain surfaces and glue legs and head in place. The head tilts on the vertical axis 25° towards the romance side.

For the ⅛-scale horse, cut four horseshoes from ³⁄₃₂″ stock and glue one to each hoof. Size the bottom of each leg before the horseshoe is glued in place since end-grain gluing is involved. Reduce the center sections of each horseshoe (Illus. 3) to a thickness of ³⁄₆₄″. Refer to Illus. 42 and 43 to complete the final shapes and details, and to Table 40, which provides the critical dimensions that will be needed to carve a full-sized horse or a reduced-scale model.

The tail is only attached at the rump (it does not rest against a leg), so an extra step to strengthen it is recommended. Drill a hole on the center line of the dowel end of the tail and insert a 1″ long Number 20 brad. After final sanding, glue the tail in place in the hole in the body. Use a burning pen to add the hair texture to the mane and tail.

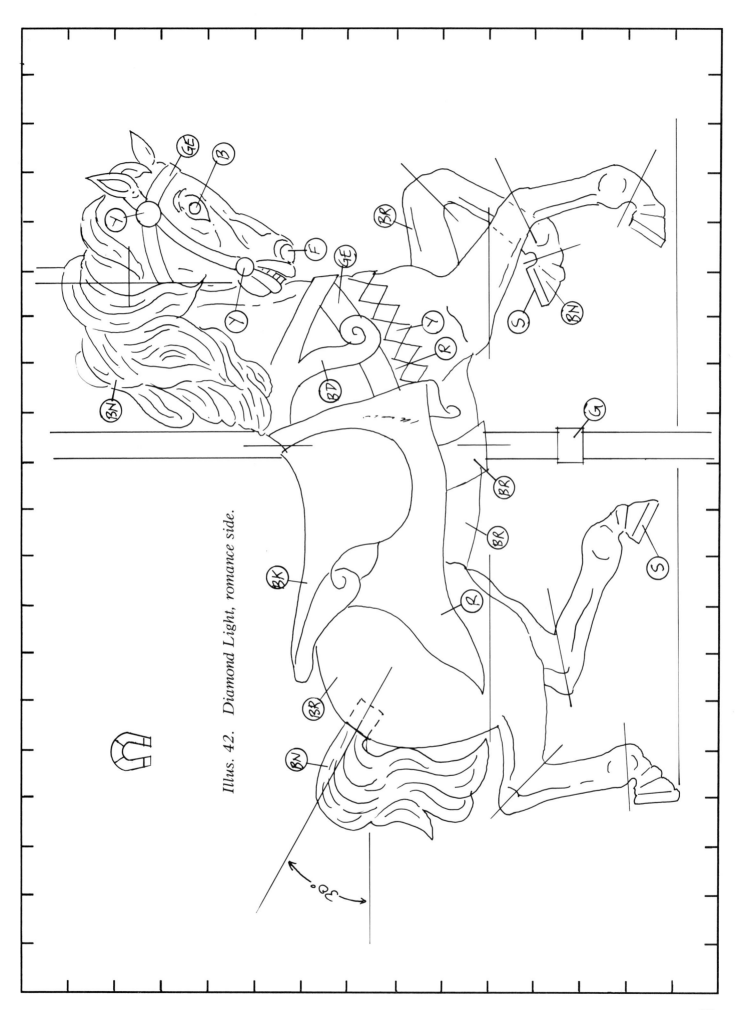

Illus. 42. *Diamond Light, romance side.*

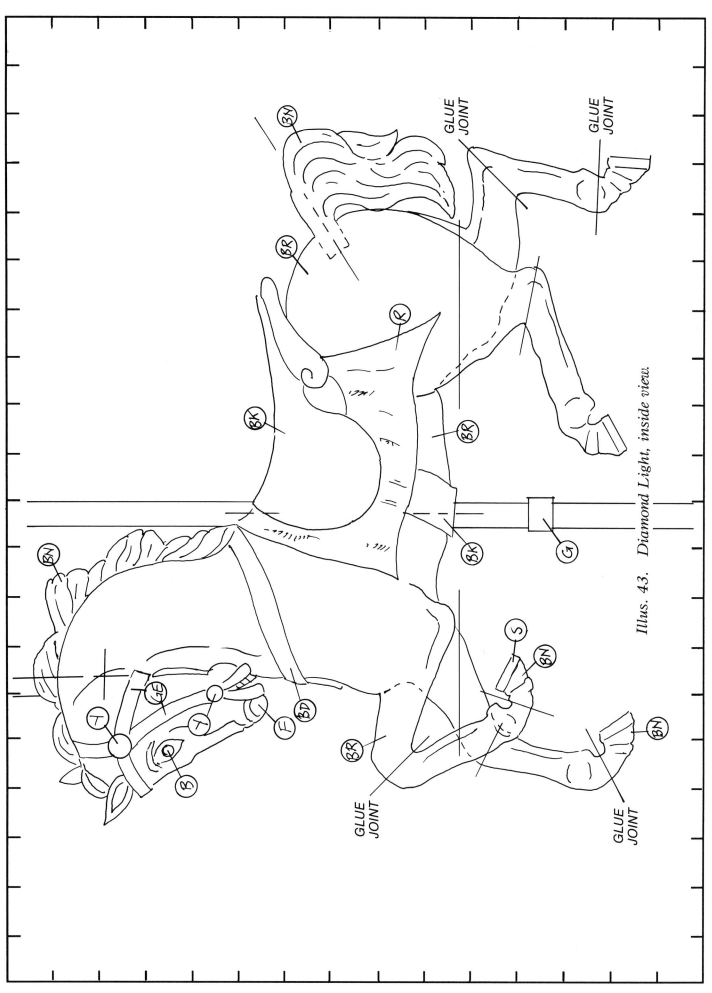

Illus. 43. Diamond Light, inside view.

After carving, final sanding, and burning, paint the horse the colors suggested in circles in the illustrations (see color chart in Chapter VI) or in other colors that are pleasing to you. For the ⅛-scale horse, insert a 10½″ length of ¼″-diameter brass pole (Illus. 79), brass tubing, or gold-painted dowel through the hole in the body of

Table 39   Parts List for the Diamond Light (⅛ Scale)

Part	Length	Width	Thickness
Head	2⅜″	1¾″	¾″
Body and neck	5⅞″	4⁹⁄₁₆″	1⅜″
Right front thigh	1½″	½″	¼″
Right front leg	1⅜″	⁷⁄₁₆″	½″
Right front hoof	¹¹⁄₁₆″	⅜″	⅜″
Left front leg	1¾″	⁷⁄₁₆″	½″
Left front hoof	⁹⁄₁₆″	⁵⁄₁₆″	⅜″
Right hind thigh	2³⁄₁₆″	¹¹⁄₁₆″	¹¹⁄₁₆″
Right hind leg	1½″	⁷⁄₁₆″	½″
Right hind hoof	¾″	⅜″	⅜″
Left hind thigh	1″	1⅜″	¹¹⁄₁₆″
Left hind leg	2⅛″	⁹⁄₁₆″	½″
Tail	2⅝″	1⁷⁄₁₆″	¾″

Table 40   Critical Dimensions for Diamond Light

	Scale				Full Size
	⅛	¼	½	¾	
From right front hoof to top of mane	6⁹⁄₁₆″	13⅛″	26¼″	39⅜″	52½″
From rump to breast	4⅞″	9¾″	19½″	29¼″	39″
From tail to front right knee	6⅞″	13¾″	27½″	41¼″	55″
Width of head	¾″	1½″	3″	4½″	6″
Width of nose	⁷⁄₁₆″	⅞″	1¾″	2⅝″	3½″
Distance between tips of ears	¾″	1½″	3″	4½″	6″
Width of neck at head (with mane)	1″	2″	4″	6″	8″
Width of neck at body	1¼″	2½″	5″	7½″	10″
Width of body at pole	1⅜″	2¾″	5½″	8¼″	11″
Width of saddle at rear	1⅜″	2¾″	5½″	8¼″	11″
Width of rump	1⅜″	2¾″	5½″	8¼″	11″
Width of front leg at body	½″	1″	2″	3″	4″
Width of front leg at knee	⅜″	¾″	1½″	2¼″	3″
Width of hind leg at body	⁷⁄₁₆″	⅞″	1¾″	2⅝″	3½″
Width of hind leg at knee	⅜″	¾″	1½″	2¼″	3″
Width of tail	¾″	1½″	3″	4½″	6″
Length of hoof	⁷⁄₁₆″	⅞″	1¾″	2⅝″	3½″
Width of hoof	⅜″	¾″	1½″	2¼″	3″

the horse so that 4⅜″ extends above the saddle. Glue the pole in place. Add the footrest (Illus. 80) to the pole ¹³⁄₁₆″ below the body. Make a base (see Chapter VI) and glue the pole of the completed horse to it. The approximate carving time is 10 hours; approximately 19 hours are needed to carve, sand, and paint the ⅛-scale Diamond Light.

21. Flying Tassels
Circa 1922

Using Illus. 44 as a plan, cut out the nine patterns and glue each pattern to wood of the correct thickness, given in Table 41. Refer to Illus. 45 for the complete pattern of the left front leg. The length of each part should follow the direction of the wood grain. Instructions for large-scale animals are given in chapters VII and VIII. The complete carving block consists of the nine parts given in Table 41. For the ⅛-scale horse, drill a ¼″ hole perpendicularly through the body for the pole and a ¼″ hole horizontally for the tail before gluing the legs in position. The horizontal reference line on Illus. 44 will serve as a ready reference for drilling the holes. There is no sideways tilt to the head; it faces straight ahead. The romance side of the mane extends beyond the breastbone.

For the ⅛-scale horse, cut four horseshoes from ³⁄₃₂″ stock and glue one to the bottom of each hoof. End-grain gluing is involved so be certain to "butter" the bottom of each leg with glue. Reduce the middle area of each horseshoe (Illus. 3) to a thickness of ³⁄₆₄″. Refer to Illus. 44 and 45 to complete the final shapes and details, and to Table 42, which provides the critical dimensions necessary to carve a full-sized horse or a reduced-scale model. After final sanding, glue

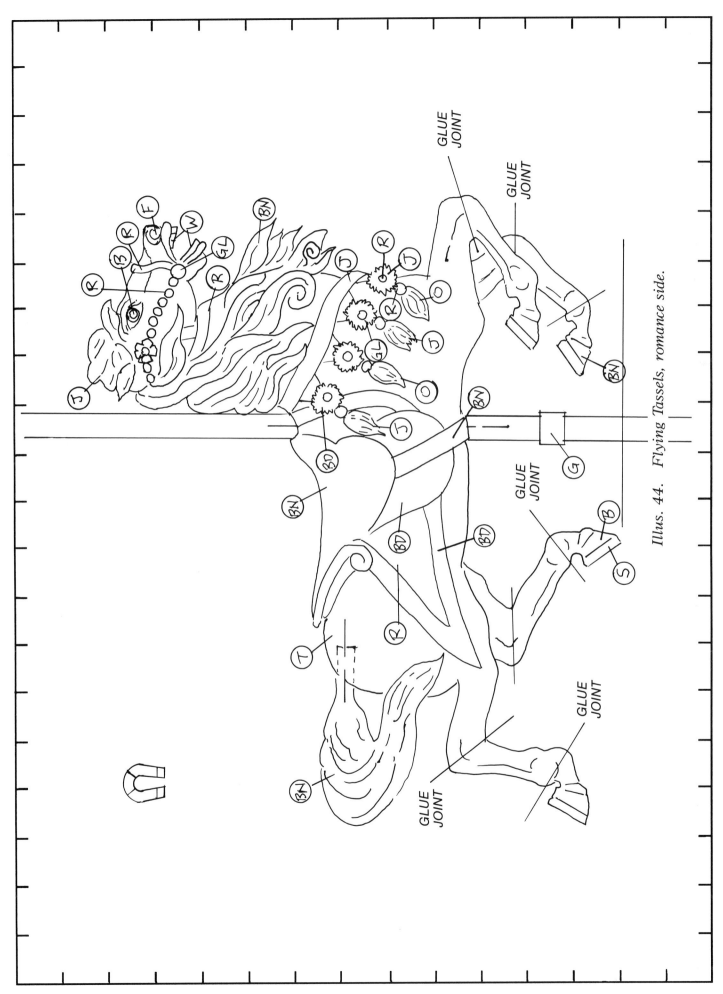

Illus. 44. Flying Tassels, romance side.

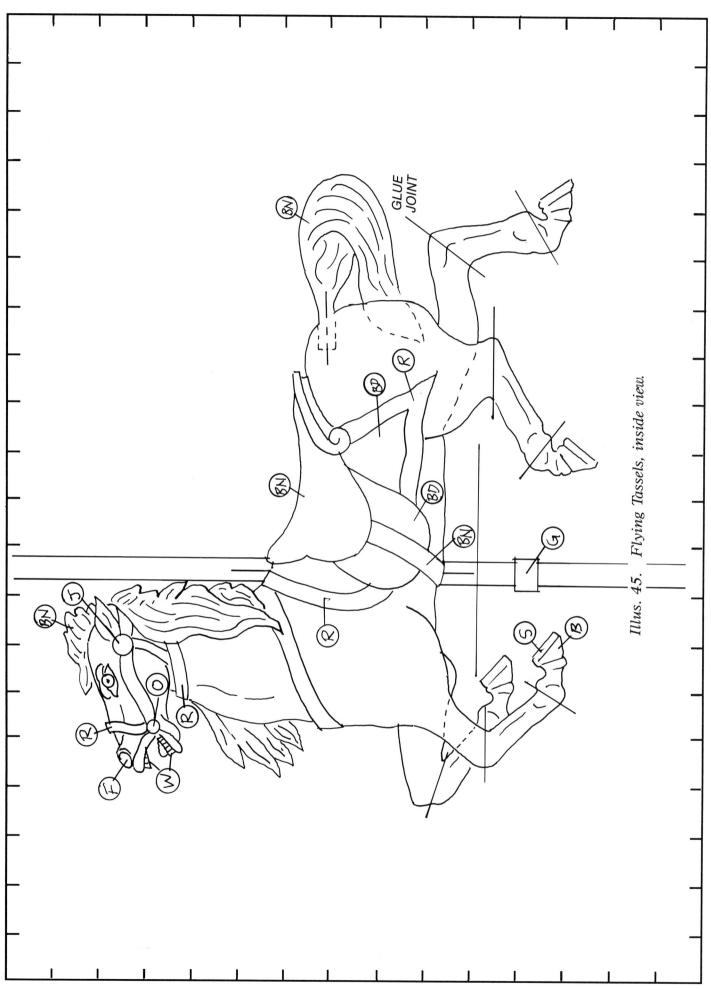

GLUE JOINT

Illus. 45. Flying Tassels, inside view.

the tail into the hole in the body and against the romance side of the flank. Use a burning pen to develop the hair texture on the mane and tail and the thread texture on the tassels.

After carving and sanding the horse, paint it as suggested by the color symbols in circles in the illustrations (see color chart in Chapter VI) or in other colors that are pleasing to you. For the ⅛-scale horse, insert a 10½″ length of a ¼″-diameter brass pole (Illus. 79), brass tubing, or gold-painted dowel through the hole in the body so

Table 41   Parts List for Flying Tassels (⅛ Scale)

Part	Length	Width	Thickness
Head and body	5⅛″	5⁹⁄₁₆″	1⅜″
Right front leg	1¾″	½″	½″
Left front leg	1¹⁄₁₆″	⅜″	½″
Left front hoof	¹¹⁄₁₆″	⁵⁄₁₆″	⁷⁄₁₆″
Right hind leg	1¼″	½″	⅜″
Right hind hoof	¾″	⁷⁄₁₆″	⁷⁄₁₆″
Left hind leg	1⅜″	⅜″	⅜″
Left hind hoof	¹¹⁄₁₆″	⁷⁄₁₆″	⁷⁄₁₆″
Tail	1⅞″	1⁵⁄₁₆″	1″

Table 42   Critical Dimensions for Flying Tassels

	Scale				Full Size
	⅛	¼	½	¾	
From hind left hoof to top of mane*	5¹¹⁄₁₆″	11⅜″	22¾″	34⅛″	45½″
From rump to breast	4⁵⁄₁₆″	8⅝″	17¼″	25⅞″	34½″
From tail to front right knee	6½″	13″	26″	39″	52″
Width of head	¾″	1½″	3″	4½″	6″
Width of nose	⁷⁄₁₆″	⅞″	1¾″	2⅝″	3½″
Distance between tips of ears	⅝″	1¼″	2½″	3¾″	5″
Width of neck at head (with mane)	1″	2″	4″	6″	8″
Width of neck at body (with mane)	1⅜″	2¾″	5½″	8¼″	11″
Width of body at pole	1⅜″	2¾″	5½″	8¼″	11″
Width of saddle at rear	1⅜″	2¾″	5½″	8¼″	11″
Width of rump	1¼″	2½″	5″	7½″	10″
Width of front leg at body	½″	1″	2″	3″	4″
Width of front leg at knee	⁷⁄₁₆″	⅞″	1¾″	2⅝″	3½″
Width of hind leg at body	⅝″	1¼″	2½″	3¾″	5″
Width of hind leg at knee	½″	1″	2″	3″	4″
Length of hoof	⁷⁄₁₆″	⅞″	1¾″	2⅝″	3½″
Width of hoof	⅜″	¾″	1½″	2¼″	3″
Width of tail	1″	2″	4″	6″	8″

*Measured perpendicularly from baseline to a horizontal line extended back from top of mane.

that 4⅜″ of the pole extends above the saddle. Glue the pole in place. Add the footrest (Illus. 80) to the pole ¹³⁄₁₆″ below the body. Make a base (see Chapter VI) and glue the pole of the completed carving to it. The approximate carving time is 11 hours; approximately 19 hours are required to carve, sand, and paint the ⅛-scale Flying Tassels.

22. Star Jumper
Circa 1926

Using Illus. 46 as a plan, cut out the thirteen patterns and glue each pattern to wood of the correct thickness, given in Table 43. Refer to Illus. 47 for the complete pattern of the left front and left hind legs. The length of each part should follow the direction of the wood grain. Instructions for large-scale animals are given in chapters VII and VIII. The complete carving block consists of the thirteen parts given in Table 43. For the ⅛-scale horse, drill a ¼″-diameter hole perpendicular through the body for the pole and a ¼″ hole at a 30° angle from the perpendicular for the tail (see Illus. 46). Use the base reference line and drill the holes before the legs are glued in place. Note that the head is at a compound angle. Be certain to add ³⁄₁₆″ to the front neck block and follow the procedure for compound angles as outlined in Chapter II (Illus. 1). Size the end-grain surfaces before gluing the head and legs in place. The head tilts on a vertical axis towards the romance side at approximately a 33° angle.

For the ⅛-scale horse, cut four horseshoes from ³⁄₃₂″ stock and glue one to the bottom of each leg. End-grain gluing is involved, so be certain to "butter" the bottom of each leg with glue. Reduce the middle areas of each horseshoe (Illus. 3) to a thickness of ³⁄₆₄″. Refer to Illus. 46 and 47 to complete the final shapes and details, and to Table 44, which provides the critical dimensions you will need to carve a full-sized jumper or a reduced-scale model.

The tail is only attached at the rump (it does not rest against a leg), so drill a hole on the center line of the dowel end of the tail and insert a 1″ long Number 20 brad to strengthen it. After a final sanding, glue the tail in place in the hole in the body. Use a burning pen to add the hair texture to mane and tail.

Paint the horse in the colors suggested in circles on the illustrations (see color chart in Chapter VI), or in other colors that are pleasing to you. For the ⅛-scale horse, insert a 10½″ length of ¼″-diameter brass pole (Illus. 79), brass tubing, or gold-painted ¼″ dowel

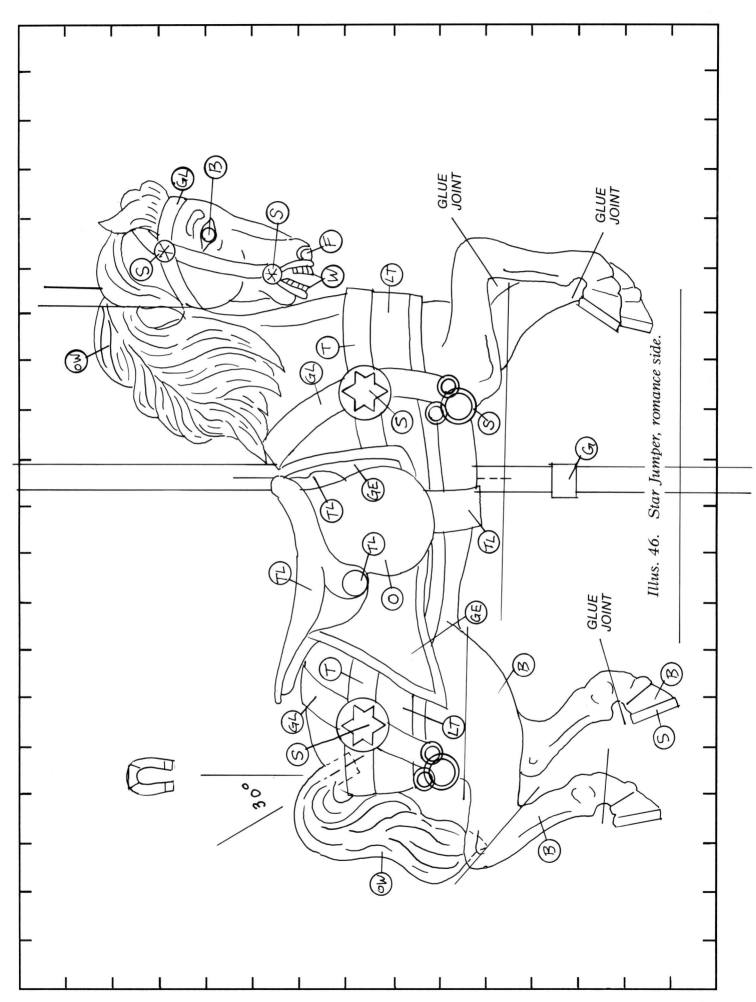

Illus. 46. Star Jumper, romance side.

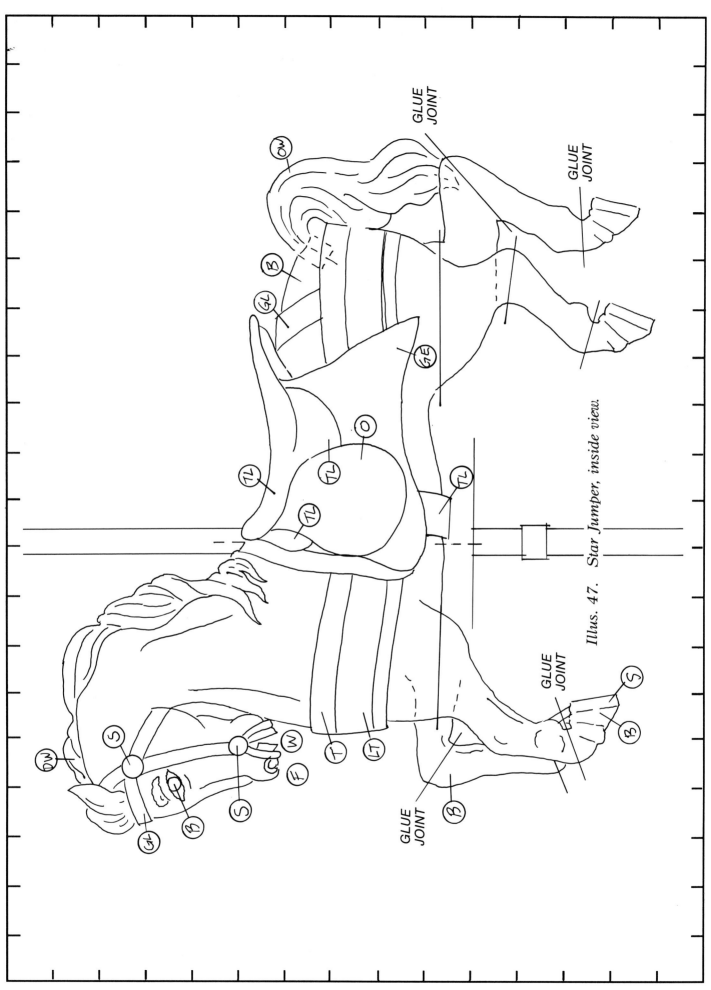

Illus. 47. Star Jumper, inside view.

through the hole in the body of the horse so that 4⅜″ of the pole extends above the saddle. Glue the pole in place. Add the footrest (Illus. 80) to the pole 13/16″ below the body. Make a base (see Chapter VI) and glue the pole of the completed horse to it.

Table 43 Parts List for the Star Jumper (⅛ Scale)

Part	*Length*	*Width*	*Thickness*
Head	2⅜″	1⅜″	¾″
Body and neck	5 11/16″	4⅜″	1⅜″
Right front leg	1⅜″	7/16″	½″
Right front hoof	¾″	7/16″	⅜″
Left front leg	1⅜″	⅞″	½″
Left front hoof	¾″	7/16″	⅜″
Right hind thigh	2⅜″	⅝″	11/16″
Right hind leg	1¾″	½″	½″
Right hind hoof	11/16″	7/16″	⅜″
Left hind thigh	1⅛″	7/16″	11/16″
Left hind leg	1¼″	½″	½″
Left hind hoof	¾″	7/16″	⅜″
Tail	2⅙″	1¼″	¾″

Table 44 Critical Dimensions for the Star Jumper

	Scale				*Full*
	⅛	¼	½	¾	*Size*
From left front hoof to top of mane	6 1/16″	12⅛″	24¼″	36⅜″	48½″
From rump to breast	5 3/16″	10⅜″	20¾″	31⅛″	41½″
From tail to right front knee	5⅝″	11¼″	22½″	33¾″	45″
Width of head	¾″	1½″	3″	4½″	6″
Width of nose	7/16″	⅞″	1¾″	2⅝″	3½″
Distance between tips of ears	7/16″	⅞″	1¾″	2⅝″	3½″
Width of neck at head	11/16″	1⅜″	2¾″	4⅛″	5½″
Width of neck at body	1⅛″	2¼″	4½″	6¾″	9″
Width of body at pole	1⅜″	2¾″	5½″	8¼″	11″
Width of saddle at rear	1 5/16″	2⅝″	5¼″	7⅞″	10½″
Width of rump	1⅜″	2¾″	5½″	8¼″	11″
Width of front leg at body	½″	1″	2″	3″	4″
Width of front leg at knee	7/16″	⅞″	1¾″	2⅝″	3½″
Width of hind leg at body	11/16″	1⅜″	2¾″	4⅛″	5½″
Width of hind leg at knee	7/16″	⅞″	1¾″	2⅝″	3½″
Width of tail	¾″	1½″	3″	4½″	6″
Length of hoof	½″	1″	2″	3″	4″
Width of hoof	⅜″	¾″	1½″	2¼″	3″

23. Flying Mane
Circa 1922

Using Illus. 48 as a plan, cut out the ten patterns and glue each pattern to wood of the correct thickness, given in Table 45. Refer to Illus. 49 for the complete pattern of the left front leg. The length of each part should follow the direction of the wood grain. Instructions for large-scale animals are given in chapters VII and VIII. The complete carving block consists of the ten parts given in Table 45.

For the ⅛-scale horse, drill a ¼″ hole perpendicularly through the body for the pole and a ¼″ hole at a 20° angle from the horizontal for the tail (see Illus. 48). Use the base line provided in Illus. 48 to reference this drilling. Size the end grain of each leg piece and glue the legs in place. There is no sideways tilt to the head of this jumper. The mane flows on the inside of the neck and extends ahead of the breastbone.

For the ⅛-scale horse, cut four horseshoes from ³⁄₃₂″ stock and glue one to the bottom of each hoof. End-grain gluing is involved, so be certain to "butter" the bottom of each leg with glue. Reduce the side sections of each horseshoe (Illus. 3) to a thickness of ³⁄₆₄″. Refer to Illus. 48 and 49 to complete the final shape and details, and to Table 46, which provides the criticial dimensions needed to carve a full-sized horse or a reduced-scale model. After a final sanding, glue the tail into the hole in the body and against the romance side of the hind flank. Use a burning pen to add the hair texture to the mane and tail and to provide the thread texture for the fringe.

After the carving and a final sanding, paint in colors as suggested

by letters in circles on the illustrations (see color chart in Chapter VI), or in other colors that delight your fancy. For the ⅛-scale horse, insert a 10½″ length of ¼″-diameter brass pole (Illus. 79), brass tubing, or gold-painted dowel through the hole in the body so that 4⅜″ of the pole extends above the saddle. Glue the pole to the horse, using household cement. Add the footrest (Illus. 80) to the pole ¹³⁄₁₆″ below the body. Make a base (see Chapter VI) and glue the pole of the completed carving to it. The approximate carving time is 11 hours; approximately 20 hours are needed to carve, sand, and paint the ⅛-scale Flying Mane.

Table 45   Parts List for the Flying Mane (⅛ Scale)

Part	Length	Width	Thickness
Head and body	5⅝″	4⁷⁄₁₆″	1½″
Right front leg	1⅞″	⁹⁄₁₆″	½″
Left front thigh	¹³⁄₁₆″	½″	½″
Left front leg	1³⁄₁₆″	⁷⁄₁₆″	½″
Left front hoof	¾″	⁷⁄₁₆″	⁷⁄₁₆″
Right hind leg	1¼″	⁷⁄₁₆″	¾″
Right hind hoof	¾″	⁷⁄₁₆″	⁷⁄₁₆″
Left hind leg	1⁷⁄₁₆″	½″	¾″
Left hind hoof	¹¹⁄₁₆″	⅜″	⁷⁄₁₆″
Tail	1¹⁵⁄₁₆″	1¹⁄₁₆″	1″

Table 46   Critical Dimensions for the Flying Mane

	Scale				Full Size
	⅛	¼	½	¾	
From left front hoof to top of mane	5⅞″	11¾″	23½″	35¼″	47″
From rump to breast	4⁹⁄₁₆″	9⅛″	18¼″	27⅜″	36½″
From right hind hoof to right front knee	7″	14″	28″	42″	56″
Width of head (with mane)	⅞″	1¾″	3½″	5¼″	7″
Width of nose	⁷⁄₁₆″	⅞″	1¾″	2⅝″	3½″
Distance between tips of ears	⅝″	1¼″	2½″	3¾″	5″
Width of neck at head (with mane)	1¹⁄₁₆″	2⅛″	4¼″	6⅜″	8½″
Width of neck at body	1½″	3″	6″	9″	12″
Width of body at pole	1⅜″	2¾″	5½″	8¼″	11″
Width of saddle at rear	1⅜″	2¾″	5½″	8¼″	11″
Width of rump	1⅜″	2¾″	5½″	8¼″	11″
Width of front leg at body	½″	1″	2″	3″	4″
Width of front leg at knee	⅜″	¾″	1½″	2¼″	3″
Width of hind leg at body	¹¹⁄₁₆″	1⅜″	2¾″	4⅛″	5½″
Width of hind leg at knee	⅜″	¾″	1½″	2¼″	3″
Width of tail	1″	2″	4″	6″	8″
Length of hoof	½″	1″	2″	3″	4″
Width of hoof	⅜″	¾″	1½″	2¼″	3″

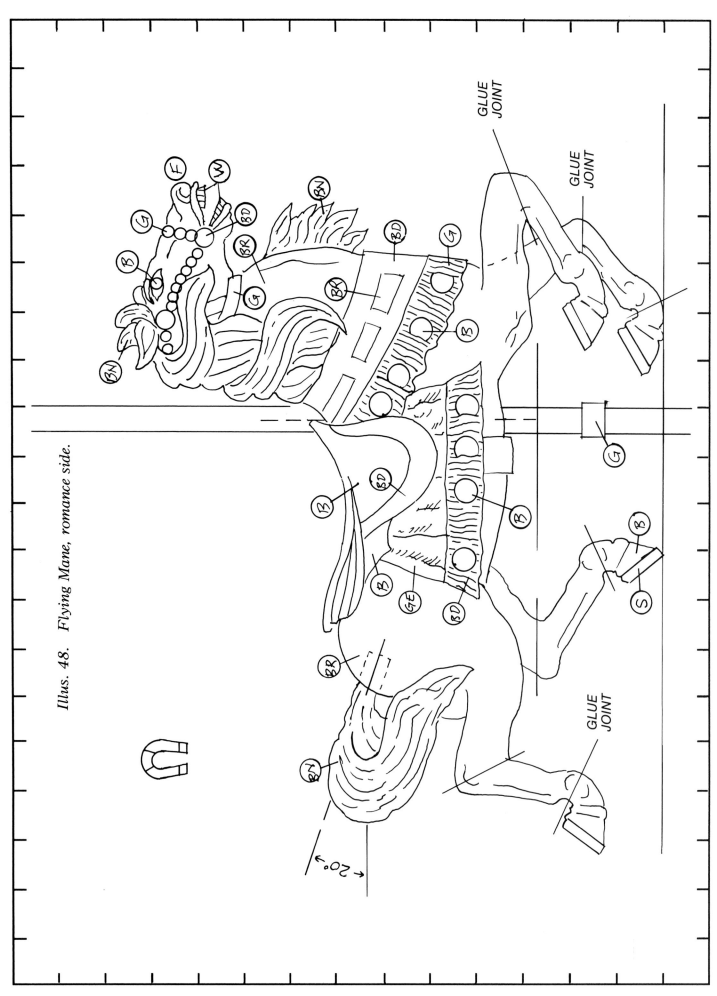

Illus. 48. Flying Mane, romance side.

GLUE JOINT

GLUE JOINT

GLUE JOINT

← 20° →

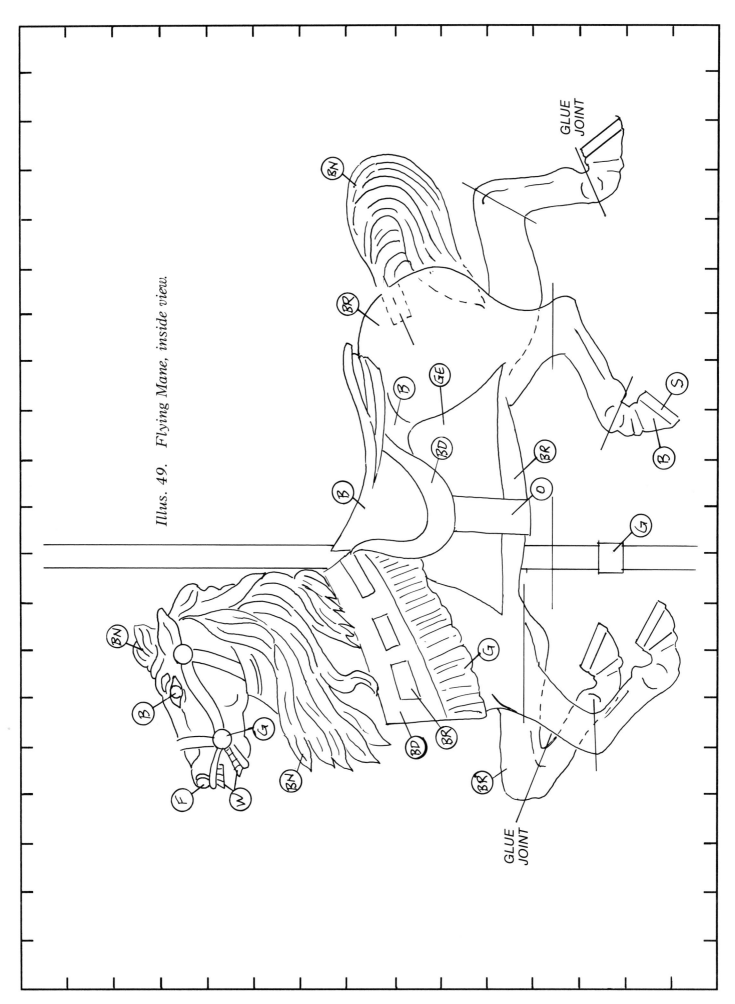

Illus. 49. Flying Mane, inside view.

24. Curly Top

Circa 1922

Using Illus. 50 as a plan, cut out the eight patterns and glue each pattern to wood of the correct thickness as defined in Table 47. Refer to Illus. 51 for the complete patterns of the left front and hind legs. The length of each part should follow the direction of the wood grain. Instructions for large-scale animals are given in chapters VII and VIII. The complete carving block consists of the eight parts listed in Table 47. For the ⅛-scale horse, drill a ¼″-diameter hole perpendicularly through the body for the pole and a ¼″ hole at a 70° angle from the perpendicular for the tail. Use the base reference line in Illus. 50 to locate these holes; drill them before the legs are glued in place. Size all end grain and glue legs in place. There is no tilt to the head; it faces straight ahead.

For the ⅛-scale horse, cut the four horseshoes from ³⁄₃₂″ stock and glue one to the bottom of each leg. End-grain gluing is involved, so be certain to "butter" the bottom of each leg with glue. Reduce the middle areas of each horseshoe (Illus. 3) to a thickness of ³⁄₆₄″. Refer to Illus. 50 and 51 to complete the final shapes and details, and to Table 48, which provides the critical dimensions required when carving a full-sized horse or a reduced-scale model. After a final sanding, glue the tail in the hole in the body and to the romance side of the rump. Use a burning pen to add texture to the mane and tail.

Paint the horse in accordance with the color symbols suggested in circles on the illustrations (see color chart in Chapter VI), or in other colors that are pleasing to you. For the ⅛-scale horse, insert a 10½″ length of a ¼″-diameter brass pole (Illus. 79), brass tubing, or gold-painted dowel through the hole in the body so that 4⅜″ extends above the saddle. Glue the pole in place. Add the footrest (Illus. 80) to the pole ¹³⁄₁₆″ below the body. Make a base (see Chapter VI) and glue the pole of the completed horse to it.

Table 47   Parts List for the Curly Top (⅛ Scale)

Part	Length	Width	Thickness
Head and body	6¾″	4⅝″	1⅜″
Right front leg	1⅞″	⅜″	½″
Left front leg	1⁹⁄₁₆″	⁷⁄₁₆″	½″
Right hind leg	1¼″	⁷⁄₁₆″	½″
Right hind hoof	¾″	½″	⅜″
Left hind leg	1½″	⁷⁄₁₆″	½″
Left hind hoof	⅝″	⁷⁄₁₆″	⅜″
Tail	1⅞″	1⅛″	¾″

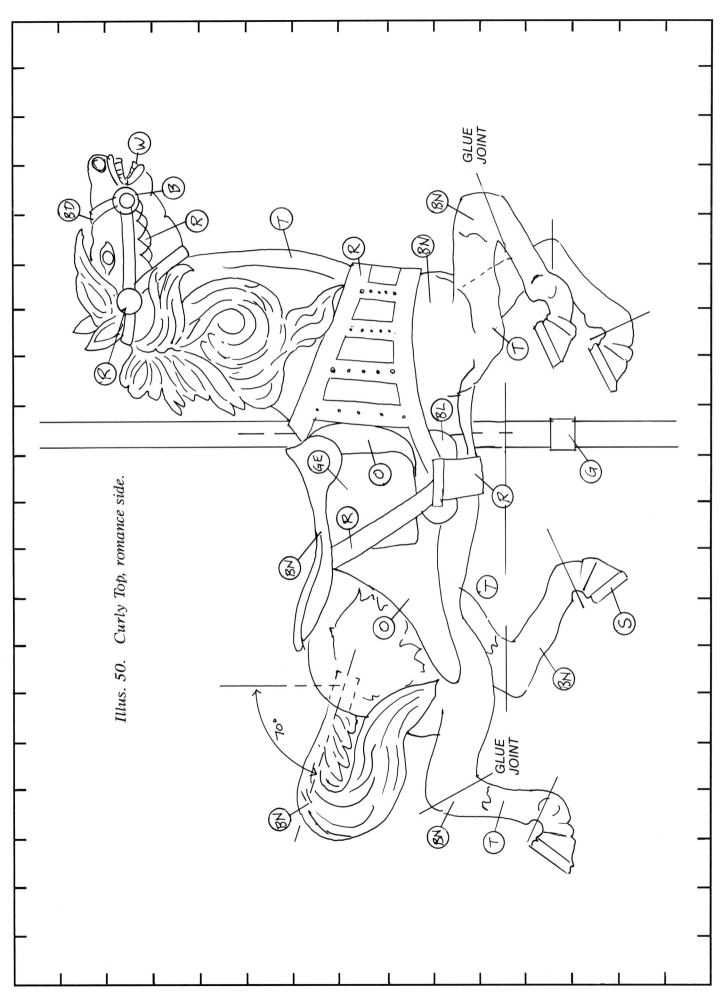

Illus. 50.   Curly Top, romance side.

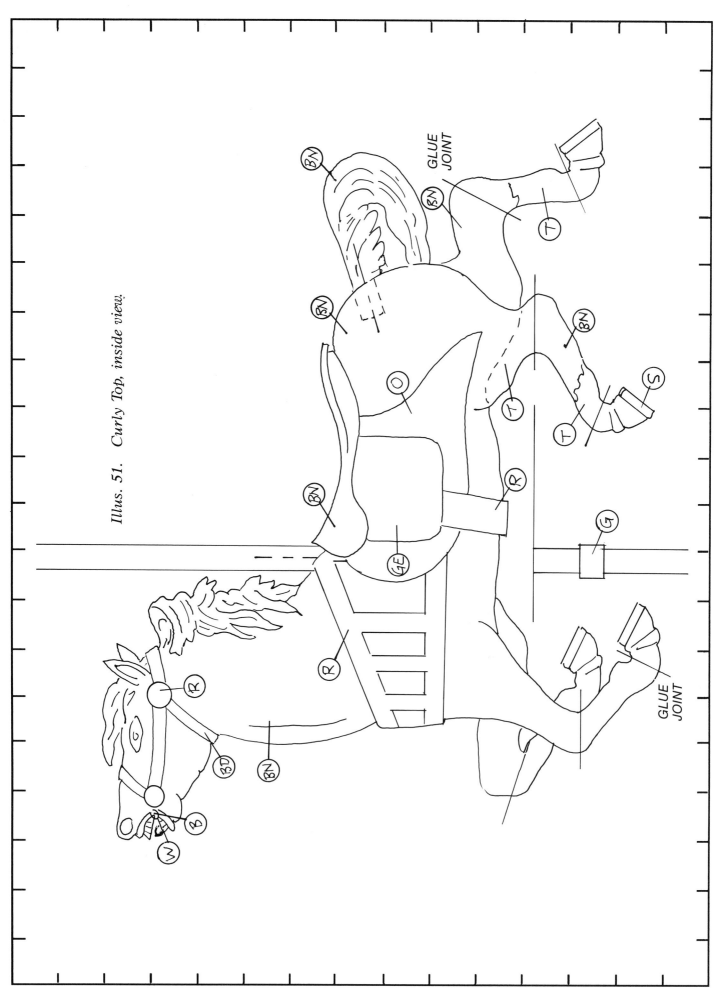

Illus. 51. Curly Top, inside view.

GLUE JOINT

GLUE JOINT

Table 48   Critical Dimensions for the Curly Top

	Scale				Full Size
	1/8	1/4	1/2	3/4	
From front right hoof to top of mane	5¹⁵⁄₁₆″	11⅞″	23¾″	35⅝″	47½″
From rump to breast	4¹³⁄₁₆″	9⅝″	19¼″	28⅞″	38½″
From right hind hoof to right front knee	6¹⁵⁄₁₆″	13⅞″	27¾″	41⅝″	55½″
Width of head	⅞″	1¾″	3½″	5¼″	7″
Width of nose	⁷⁄₁₆″	⅞″	1¾″	2⅝″	3½″
Distance between tips of ears	⅝″	1¼″	2½″	3¾″	5″
Width of neck at head (with mane)	1″	2″	4″	6″	8″
Width of neck at body (with mane)	1⅜″	2¾″	5½″	8¼″	11″
Width of body at pole	1⅜″	2¾″	5½″	8¼″	11″
Width of saddle at rear	1⅜″	2¾″	5½″	8¼″	11″
Width of rump	1¼″	2½″	5″	7½″	10″
Width of front leg at body	½″	1″	2″	3″	4″
Width of front leg at knee	⅜″	¾″	1½″	2¼″	3″
Width of hind leg at body	⅝″	1¼″	2½″	3¾″	5″
Width of hind leg at knee	⅜″	¾″	1½″	2¼″	3″
Length of hoof	½″	1″	2″	3″	4″
Width of hoof	⅜″	¾″	1½″	2¼″	3″

25. Palomino Jumper

Circa 1912

Using Illus. 52 as a plan, cut out the seven patterns and glue each pattern to wood of the proper thickness, given in Table 49. The length of each part should follow the direction of the wood grain. Instructions for large-scale animals are given in chapters VII and VIII. The complete carving block is composed of the seven parts listed in Table 49. For the ⅛-scale horse, drill a ¼″ hole perpendicularly through the body for the pole. The base reference line in Illus. 52 will help in locating this hole. Drill a ⅛″ hole at a 70° angle from the vertical for the tail. Drill the two holes before the legs are glued in place. Size the end grain of each part and glue the legs in their proper alignment. Note that the left and right legs are in the same position. There is no sideways tilt to the head; it is facing straight ahead.

For the ⅛-scale horse, cut four horseshoes from ³⁄₃₂″ stock and glue one to the bottom of each hoof. End-grain gluing is involved, so be certain to "butter" each hoof with glue. Reduce the middle areas of each horseshoe (Illus. 3) to a thickness of ³⁄₆₄″. Refer to Illus. 52 and 53 to complete the final shapes and details, and to Table 50, which provides the critical dimensions that are needed to carve a full-sized horse or a reduced-scale model. Use a burning pen to add the texture to the mane.

Paint the horse in accordance with the colors suggested in circles on the illustrations (see color chart in Chapter VI), or in other colors that suit you. For the ⅛-scale horse, insert a 10½″ length of a ¼″-diameter brass pole (Illus. 79), brass tubing, or gold-painted dowel through the hole in the body of the horse so that 4³⁄₈″ of the pole extends above the saddle. Glue the pole in place. Add the footrest (Illus. 80) to the pole ¹³⁄₁₆″ below the body. Make a base (see Chapter VI) and glue the pole of the completed Jumper to it.

Table 49   Parts List for the Palomino Jumper (⅛ Scale)

Part	Length	Width	Thickness
Head and body	6¾″	4¹⁵⁄₁₆″	1³⁄₈″
Right front leg	1⅞″	⅝″	½″
Left front leg	1⅞″	⅝″	½″
Right hind leg	1³⁄₈″	⁷⁄₁₆″	¹¹⁄₁₆″
Right hind hoof	⅝″	⁷⁄₁₆″	³⁄₈″
Left hind leg	1³⁄₈″	⁷⁄₁₆″	¹¹⁄₁₆″
Left hind hoof	⅝″	⁷⁄₁₆″	³⁄₈″

Table 50   Critical Dimensions for the Palomino Jumper

	Scale				Full Size
	⅛	¼	½	¾	
From hind hoof to tip of ear	6⅛″	12¼″	24½″	36¾″	49″
From rump to breast	4⅞″	9¾″	19½″	29¼″	39″
From hind hoof to front right hoof	7⅝″	15¼″	30½″	45¾″	61″
Width of head	¾″	1½″	3″	4½″	6″
Width of nose	⁷⁄₁₆″	⅞″	1¾″	2⅝″	3½″
Distance between tips of ears	⁷⁄₁₆″	⅞″	1¾″	2⅝″	3½″
Width of neck at head	¹¹⁄₁₆″	1³⁄₈″	2¾″	4⅛″	5½″
Width of neck at body	1⅛″	2¼″	4½″	6¾″	9″
Width of body at pole	1³⁄₈″	2¾″	5½″	8¼″	11″
Width of saddle at rear	1⁵⁄₁₆″	2⅝″	5¼″	7⅞″	10½″
Width of rump	1³⁄₈″	2¾″	5½″	8¼″	11″
Width of front leg at body	½″	1″	2″	3″	4″
Width of front leg at knee	³⁄₈″	¾″	1½″	2¼″	3″
Width of hind leg at body	¹¹⁄₁₆″	1³⁄₈″	2¾″	4⅛″	5½″
Width of hind leg at knee	³⁄₈″	¾″	1½″	2¼″	3″
Length of hoof	⁷⁄₁₆″	⅞″	1¾″	2⅝″	3½″
Width of hoof	³⁄₈″	¾″	1½″	2¼″	3″

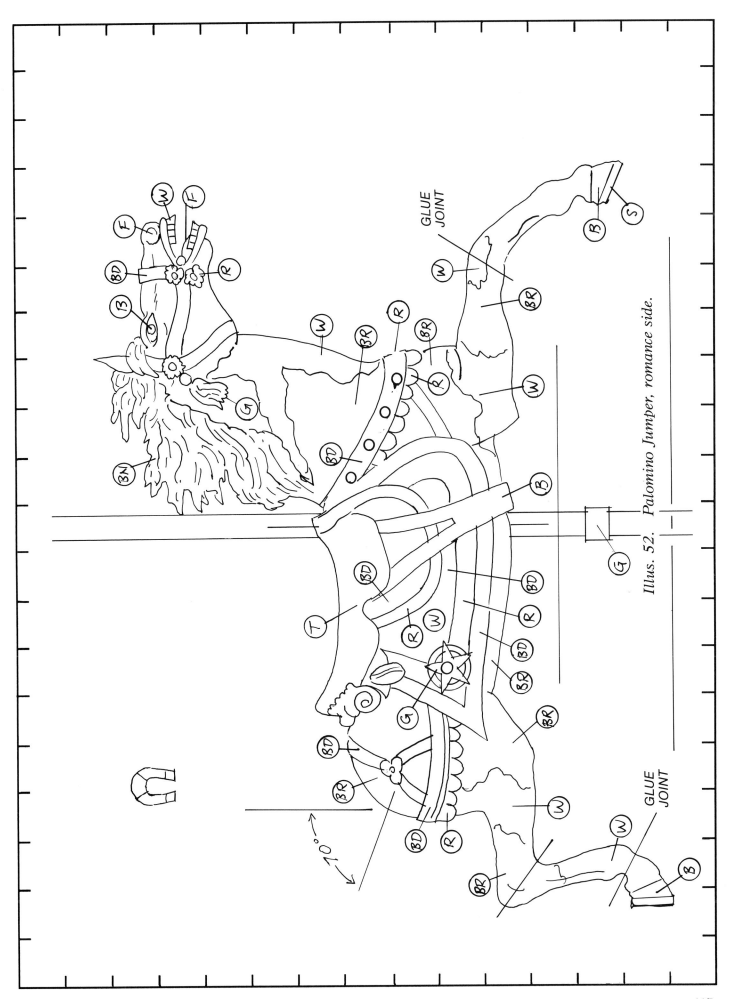

Illus. 52. Palomino Jumper, romance side.

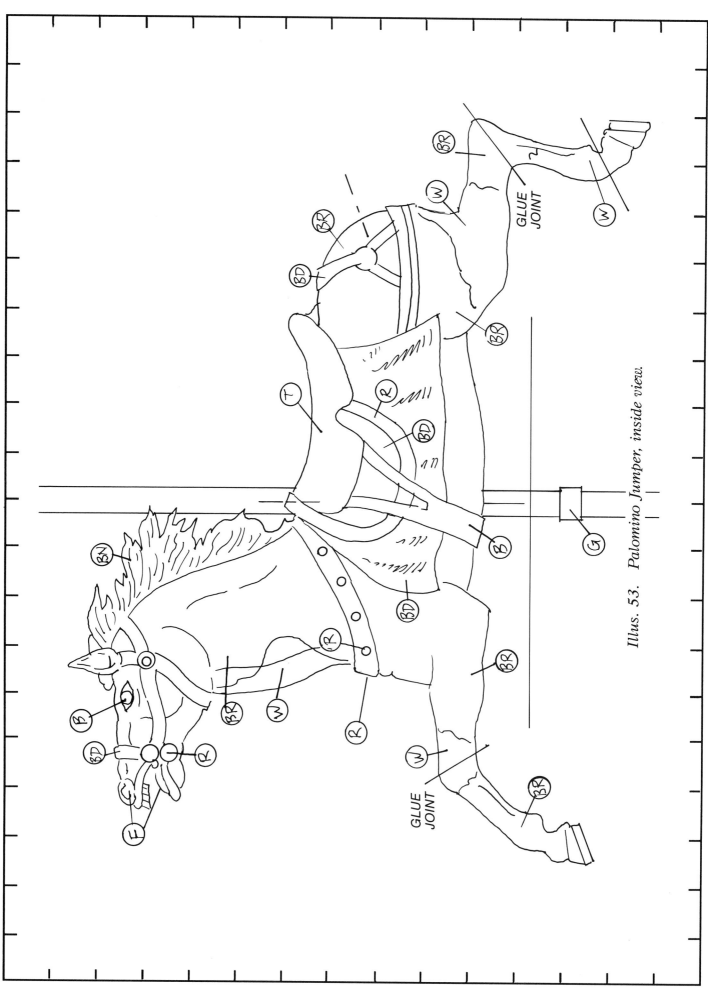

Illus. 53. Palomino Jumper, inside view.

GLUE JOINT

GLUE JOINT

CHAPTER V

Menagerie Animals

his chapter contains both large and small carousel figures, but excludes horses. Some carousel-builders made
only horses; others included other domestic and wild animals, which were referred to as "menagerie animals." The larger
animals—lions, tigers, and deer—were usually on the outside row
and were stationary. The smaller animals—cats, ostriches, rabbits,
and roosters—were on the inside rows and usually moved up and
down while the ride was in progress.

26. Cat

Circa 1905

Using Illus. 54 as a plan, cut out the five patterns and glue each
pattern to wood of the correct thickness, given in Table 52. Refer
to Illus. 55 for the complete patterns of the left front and hind legs.
The length of each part should follow the direction of the wood
grain. Instructions for large-scale animals are given in chapters VII
and VIII. The complete carving block consists of the five parts
given in Table 52. The front legs, with the exception of the right
front paw, are part of the body block. For the ⅛-scale cat, drill a ¼″
hole perpendicularly through the body for the pole. Use the base
reference line given in Illus. 55 to position the hole and drill it before the legs are glued in place. Size the end grain of the front paw
and tail and glue these parts in place. There is no tilt to the head; it
faces straight ahead.

Refer to Illus. 54 and 55 to complete the final shapes and details,
and to Table 53, which provides the critical dimensions that you
will need to carve a full-size cat or a reduced-scale model. Use a
burning pen to add fur texture to the body.

After carving and sanding the cat, paint it in accordance with the
suggested colors in circles on the illustrations (see color chart in
Chapter VI), or use other colors that you like. For the ⅛-scale cat,
insert a 10½″ length of a ¼″-diameter brass pole (Illus. 79), brass
tubing, or gold-painted dowel through the hole in the body so that
4⅜″ of the pole extends above the body. Glue the pole in place. Add
the footrest (Illus. 80) to the pole ¹³⁄₁₆″ below the body. Make a base
(see Chapter VI) and glue the pole of the completed cat to it.

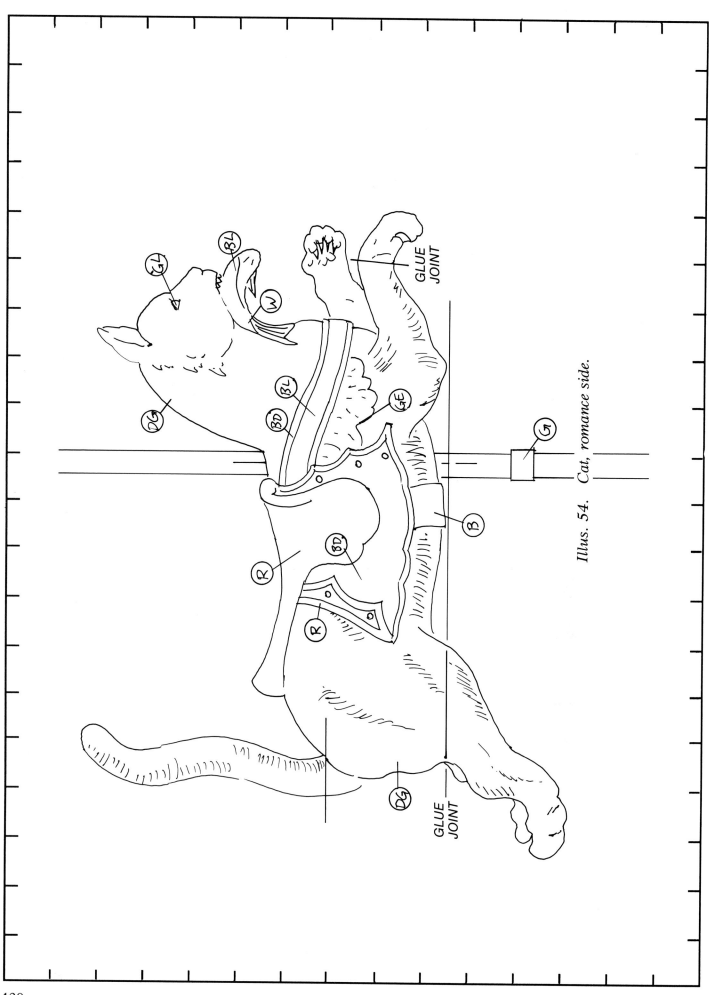

Illus. 54. Cat, romance side.

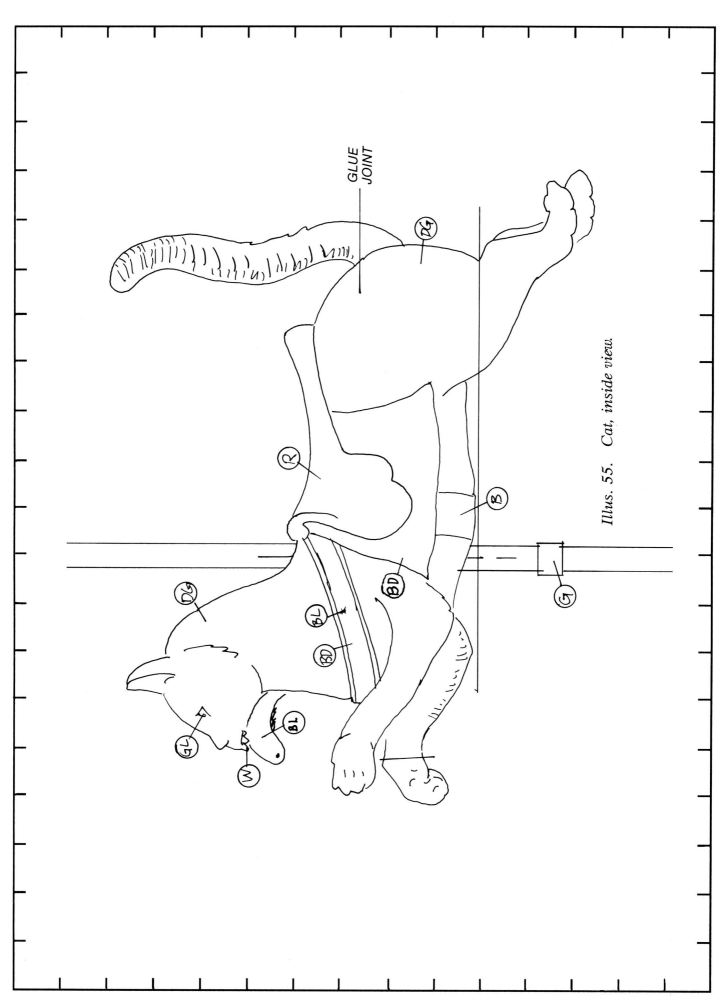

GLUE
JOINT

Illus. 55. Cat, inside view.

Table 52   Parts List for the Cat (⅛ Scale)

Part	Length	Width	Thickness
Head and body	5⅝″	3¾″	1¹⁄₁₆″
Right front paw	¾″	⁷⁄₁₆″	½″
Right hind leg	2⁵⁄₁₆″	⅞″	½″
Left hind leg	2¹⁄₁₆″	⅞″	½″
Tail	2⅝″	¹¹⁄₁₆″	⁵⁄₁₆″

Table 53   Critical Dimensions for the Cat

	Scale				Full Size
	⅛	¼	½	¾	
From rear paw to tip of tail	5⅛″	10¼″	20½″	30¾″	41″
From rump to breast	4¹¹⁄₁₆″	9⅜″	18¾″	28⅛″	37½″
From right hind paw to right front paw	6⅝″	13¼″	26½″	39¾″	53″
Width of head (including fish)	1³⁄₃₂″	2³⁄₁₆″	4⅜″	6⁹⁄₁₆″	8¾″
Width of nose	⅛″	¼″	½″	¾″	1″
Distance between tips of ears	¹³⁄₁₆″	1⅝″	3¼″	4⅞″	6½″
Width of neck at head	⅞″	1¾″	3½″	5¼″	7″
Width of neck at body	¹⁵⁄₁₆″	1⅞″	3¾″	5⅝″	7½″
Width of body at pole	1¹⁄₁₆″	2⅛″	4¼″	6⅜″	8½″
Width of saddle at rear	1″	2″	4″	6″	8″
Width of rump	1″	2″	4″	6″	8″
Width of chest	1¹⁄₁₆″	2⅛″	4¼″	6⅜″	8½″
Width of front leg at body	⅜″	¾″	1½″	2¼″	3″
Width of front leg at knee	¼″	½″	1″	¾″	2″
Width of hind leg at body	½″	1″	2″	3″	4″
Width of hind leg at knee	¼″	½″	1″	¾″	2″
Length of paw	⅝″	1¼″	2½″	3¾″	5″
Width of paw	½″	1″	2″	3″	4″
Width of tail at tip	³⁄₁₆″	⅜″	¾″	1⅛″	1½″
Width of tail at body	⁵⁄₁₆″	⅝″	1¼″	1⅞″	2½″

27. Deer

Circa 1922

Using Illus. 56 as a plan, cut out the ten patterns and glue each pattern to wood of the correct thickness, given in Table 54. Refer to Illus. 57 for the complete patterns of the left front and hind legs. The length of each part should follow the direction of the wood grain. Instructions for large-scale animals are given in chapters VII and VIII. The complete carving block consists of the ten parts given in Table 54. For the ⅛-scale deer, drill a ¼″ hole perpendicularly through the body for the pole before gluing the legs in

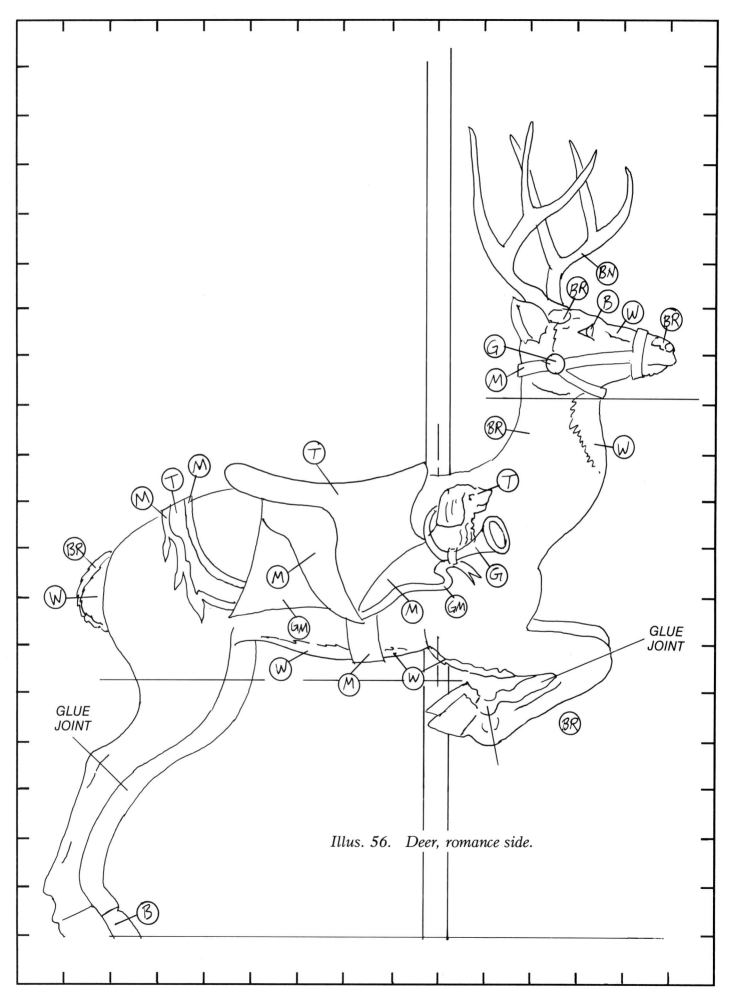

Illus. 56.   Deer, romance side.

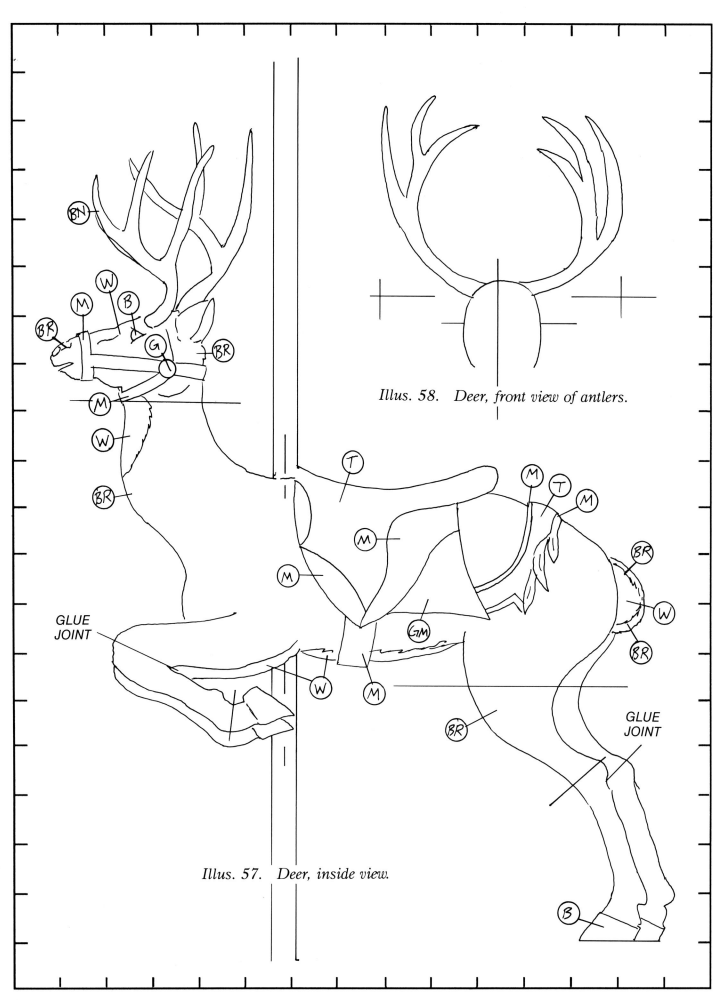

Illus. 58. Deer, front view of antlers.

GLUE JOINT

GLUE JOINT

Illus. 57. Deer, inside view.

place. Use the baseline in Illus. 56 for reference. Size the end grain of the legs and glue the head and legs in place. The head tilts on a horizontal axis 30° towards the romance side. See Illus. 58 for antler details. Table 55 provides the critical dimensions that you will need to carve a full-sized deer or a reduced-scale model.

After carving and sanding, paint the deer in accordance with the suggested colors in circles on the illustrations (see color chart in

Table 54   Parts List for the Deer (⅛ Scale)

Part	Length	Width	Thickness
Head and rack	2¼″	2⅞″	2½″
Body	5⅝″	2⅞″	1⁵⁄₁₆″
Right front leg	1⁹⁄₁₆″	⅜″	⁵⁄₁₆″
Right front hoof	¾″	⁷⁄₁₆″	⁵⁄₁₆″
Left front leg	1⁹⁄₁₆″	⅜″	⁵⁄₁₆″
Left front hoof	¾″	⁷⁄₁₆″	⁵⁄₁₆″
Right hind thigh	1½″	⅞″	⅝″
Right hind leg	1¹⁵⁄₁₆″	⅞″	½″
Left hind thigh	1½″	⅞″	⅝″
Left hind leg	1⅞″	¹³⁄₁₆″	½″

Table 55   Critical Dimensions for the Deer

	Scale				Full Size
	⅛	¼	½	¾	
From hind hoof to top of rack*	8⅜″	16¾″	33½″	50¼″	67″
From rump to breast	4⅝″	9¼″	18½″	27¾″	37″
From right hind hoof to nose	6¾″	13½″	27″	40½″	54″
Width of head	¾″	1½″	3″	4½″	6″
Width of nose	⅜″	¾″	1½″	2¼″	3″
Distance between tips of ears	1¹³⁄₁₆″	3⅝″	7¼″	10⅞″	14½″
Width of neck at head	⅝″	1¼″	2½″	3¾″	5″
Width of neck at body	¹⁵⁄₁₆″	1⅞″	3¾″	5⅝″	7½″
Width of body at pole	1⁵⁄₁₆″	2⅝″	5¼″	7⅞″	10½″
Width of saddle at rear	1⁵⁄₁₆″	2⅝″	5¼″	7⅞″	10½″
Width of rear flank	1¼″	2½″	5″	7½″	10″
Width of rack	2½″	5″	10″	15″	20″
Width of front leg at body	⁵⁄₁₆″	⅝″	1¼″	1⅞″	2½″
Width of front leg at knee	⁵⁄₁₆″	⅝″	1¼″	1⅞″	2½″
Width of hind leg at body	⅝″	1¼″	2½″	3¾″	5″
Width of hind leg at knee	³⁄₁₆″	⅜″	¾″	1⅛″	1½″
Length of hoof	⁹⁄₁₆″	1⅛″	2¼″	3⅜″	4½″
Width of hoof	⁵⁄₁₆″	⅝″	1¼″	1⅞″	2½″

*Vertical distance, perpendicular to baseline, from bottom of hoof to horizontal line extended across from top of rack.

Chapter VI), or in other colors you like. For the ⅛-scale deer, insert a 10½″ length of ¼″-diameter brass pole (Illus. 79), brass tubing, or gold-painted dowel through the hole in the body so that 4⅜″ extends above the body. Glue the pole in place. Add the footrest (Illus. 80) to the pole ¹³⁄₁₆″ below the body. Make a base (see Chapter VI) and glue the pole of the completed deer to it.

28. Giraffe

Circa 1922

Using Illus. 59 as a plan, cut out the nine patterns and glue each pattern to wood of the correct thickness, given in Table 56. Refer to Illus. 60 for the complete patterns of the left front and hind legs and the end of the tail. The length of each part should follow the direction of the wood grain. Instructions for large-scale animals are given in chapters VII and VIII. The complete carving block consists of the nine parts listed in Table 56. For the ⅛-scale giraffe drill a ¼″ hole perpendicularly through the body for the pole. Drill the hole before the neck or legs are glued in place. Size the end grain of each part and glue the neck, head, and legs in place. The head tilts at a 10° angle toward the romance side on a vertical axis.

Refer to Illus. 59 and 60 and to Table 57, which provides the critical dimensions that will be needed to carve a full-sized giraffe or a reduced-scale model, to complete the final shapes and details. After a final sanding, assemble the tail and glue it to the body and to the inside of the right hind leg. Use a burning pen to add texture to the brush on the neck.

After carving and sanding, paint the giraffe as suggested by the color scheme in circles on the illustrations (see color chart in Chapter VI), or in colors natural to this animal. For the ⅛-scale animal,

Part	Length	Width	Thickness
Head	2⅛″	1¹⁄₁₆″	1″
Neck	3⅛″	1¹¹⁄₁₆″	⅞″
Body	4⁹⁄₁₆″	2½″	1½″
Right front leg	3⅛″	⅞″	⅝″
Left front leg	3⅜″	¾″	⅝″
Right hind leg	3³⁄₁₆″	1¼″	¹¹⁄₁₆″
Left hind leg	3¹⁵⁄₁₆″	1⅛″	¹¹⁄₁₆″
Tail, middle section	1¹⁄₁₆″	½″	½″
Tail, end	1½″	⁷⁄₁₆″	½″

Table 56   Parts List for the Giraffe (⅛ Scale)

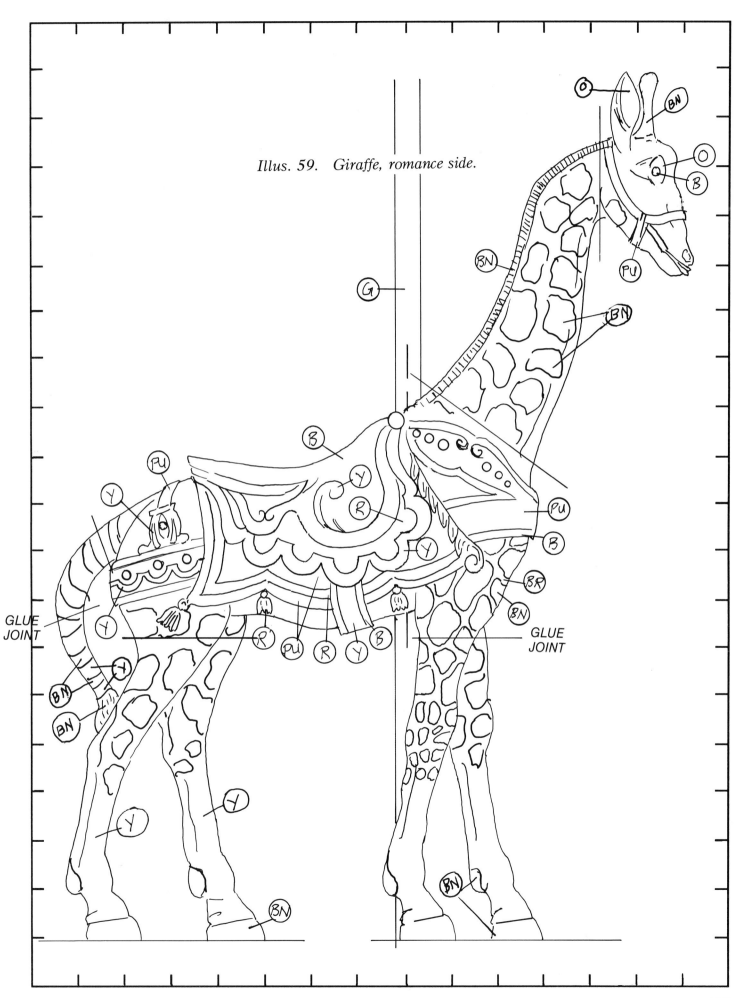

Illus. 59. Giraffe, romance side.

GLUE
JOINT

GLUE
JOINT

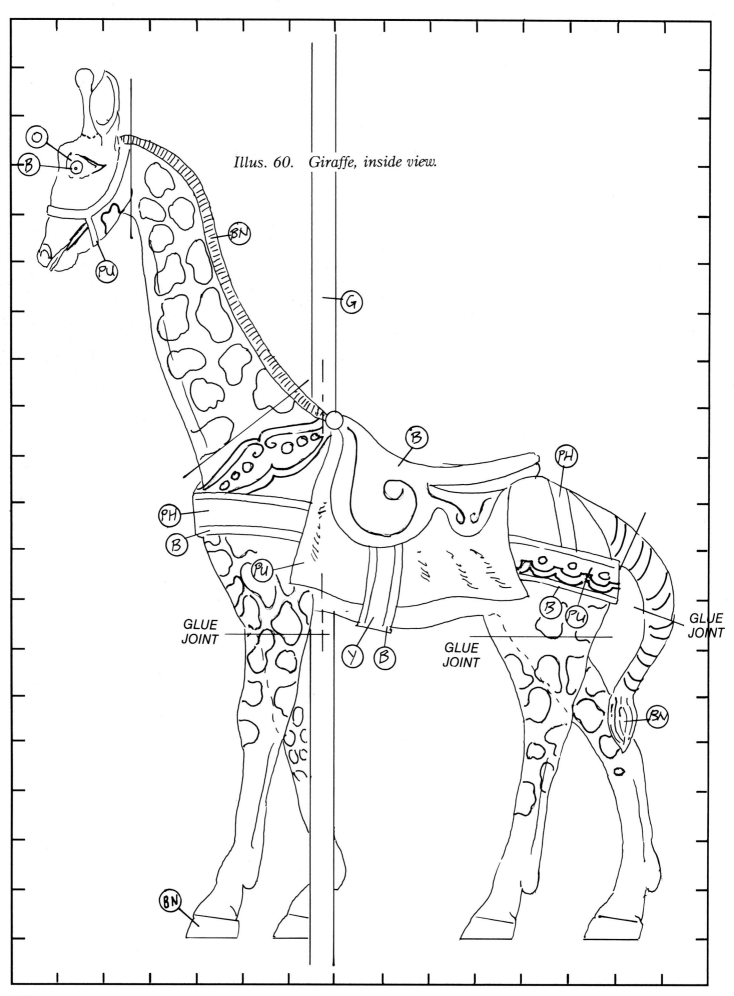

Illus. 60.   Giraffe, inside view.

GLUE JOINT

GLUE JOINT

GLUE JOINT

Table 57 Critical Dimensions for the Giraffe

	Scale				Full Size
	1/8	1/4	1/2	3/4	
From hoof to tip of ear	8⅞"	17¾"	35½"	53¼"	71"
From rump to breast	4⅝"	9¼"	18½"	27¾"	37"
From tail to nose	6¾"	13½"	27"	40½"	54"
Width of head	1"	2"	4"	6"	8"
Width of nose	½"	1"	2"	3"	4"
Distance between tips of ears	1⅜"	2¾"	5½"	8¼"	11"
Width of neck at body	⅞"	1¾"	3½"	5¼"	7"
Width of body at pole	1½"	3"	6"	9"	12"
Width of saddle at rear	1⁷⁄₁₆"	2⅞"	5¾"	8⅝"	11½"
Width of rear flank	1⅜"	2¾"	5½"	8¼"	11"
Width of front leg at body	⅝"	1¼"	2½"	3¾"	5"
Width of front leg at knee	½"	1"	2"	3"	4"
Width of hind leg at body	¹¹⁄₁₆"	1⅜"	2¾"	4⅛"	5½"
Width of hind leg at knee	½"	1"	2"	3"	4"
Width of tail	½"	1"	2"	3"	4"
Length of hoof	⁹⁄₁₆"	1⅛"	2¼"	3⅜"	4½"
Width of hoof	¹³⁄₃₂"	¹³⁄₁₆"	1⅝"	2⁷⁄₁₆"	3¼"

insert a 10½" length of a ¼"-diameter brass pole (Illus. 79), brass tubing, or gold-painted dowel through the hole in the body so that 4⅝" extends above the saddle. Glue the pole in place. There is no footrest on this animal. Make a base (see Chapter VI) and glue the pole of the completed giraffe to it.

29. Hippocampus

Circa 1895

Using Illus. 61 as a plan, cut out the three patterns and glue each pattern to wood of the correct thickness, given in Table 58. Note that the grain runs diagonally for the body and along the length of the front legs. Instructions for large-scale animals are given in Chapters VII and VIII.

The complete carving block consists of the head and body, right front leg, and left front leg. Use the base line given in Illus. 61 for reference and drill a ¼" hole (for ⅛-scale animal) perpendicularly through the body to hold the pole. Size the end grain of the legs and glue them in place. There is no sideways tilt to the head; it faces straight ahead.

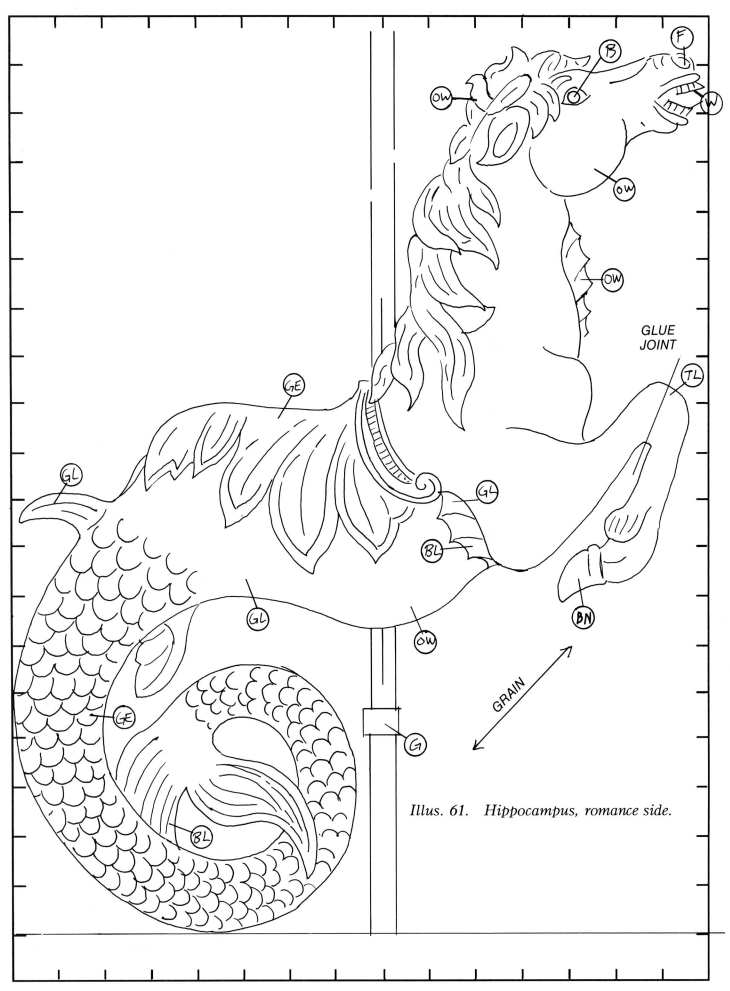

Illus. 61. Hippocampus, romance side.

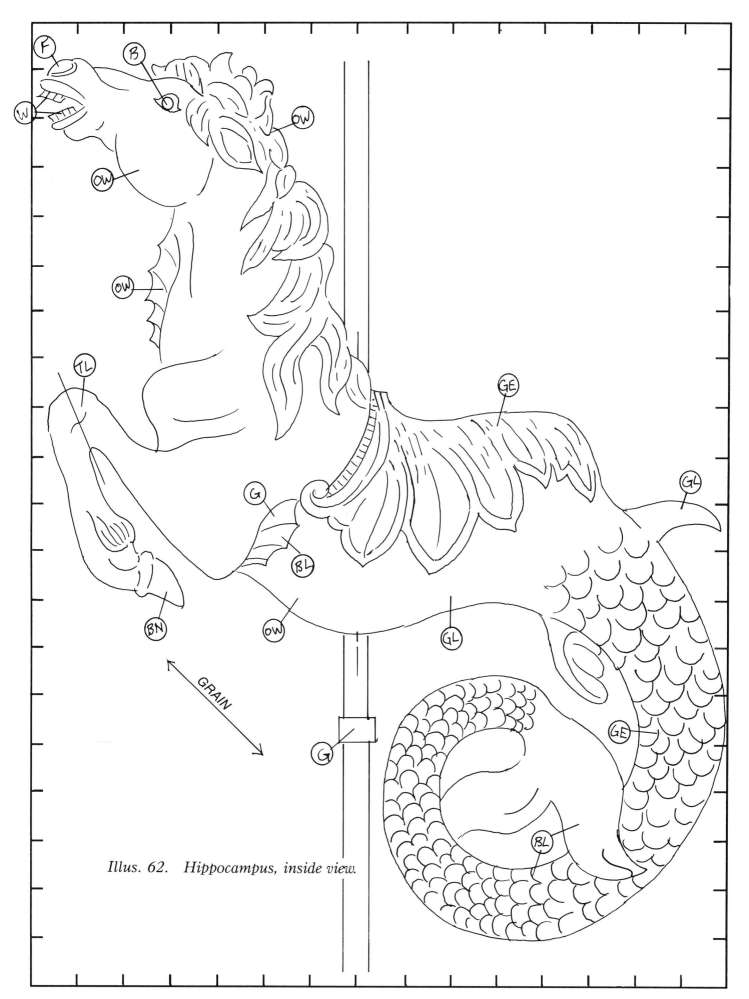

Illus. 62. Hippocampus, inside view.

Refer to Illus. 61 and 62 to complete the final shapes and details, and to Table 59, which provides the critical dimensions that you will need when carving a full-sized animal or a reduced-scale model. The scales may be carved with a knife or with appropriate-sized gouges, or may be burned in with a burning pen. Use a burning pen to add texture to the mane.

After carving and sanding the Hippocampus, paint it in accordance with the color scheme suggested in circles on the illustrations (see color chart in Chapter VI) or in other colors that are pleasing to you. If you want the Hippocampus to have a wet look, you may give it a final coat of gloss varnish. For the ⅛-scale animal, insert a 10½″ length of a ¼″-diameter brass pole (Illus. 79), brass tubing, or gold-painted dowel into the hole in the body so that 4⅜″ extends above the saddle. Glue the pole in place. Add the footrest (Illus. 80) to the pole ¹³⁄₁₆″ below the body. Make a base (see Chapter VI) and glue the pole of the completed Hippocampus to it.

Table 58   Parts List for the Hippocampus (⅛ Scale)

Part	Length	Width	Thickness
Head and body	10½″	5″	1⅛″
Right front leg	2½″	¹³⁄₁₆″	⅜″
Left front leg	2½″	¹³⁄₁₆″	⅜″

Table 59   Critical Dimensions for the Hippocampus

	Scale				Full Size
	⅛	¼	½	¾	
From bottom of tail to top of mane*	9¼″	18½″	37″	55,56″	74″
Horizontal distance from tail to knee	7¼″	14½″	29″	43½″	58″
Width of head	1⅜″	2¾″	5½″	8¼″	11″
Width of nose	¾″	1½″	3″	4½″	6″
Distance between tips of ears	1⅜″	2¾″	5½″	8¼″	11″
Width of neck at body	1⅛″	2¼″	4½″	6¾″	9″
Width of body at pole	1½″	3″	6″	9″	12″
Width of saddle at rear	1¼″	2½″	5″	7½″	10″
Width of rump	1⅜″	2¾″	5½″	8¼″	11″
Width at shoulders	1¾″	3½″	7″	10½″	14″
Width of front at leg	⅜″	¾″	1½″	2¼″	3″

*Measured perpendicular to base line.

30. Lion

Circa 1926

Using Illus. 63 as a plan, cut out the seven patterns and glue each pattern to wood of the correct thickness as defined in Table 60. Refer to Illus. 64 for the complete patterns of the left front and hind legs. The length of each part should follow the direction of the wood grain. Instructions for large-scale animals are given in Chapters VII and VIII. The complete carving block consists of the seven parts given in Table 60. Drill a ¼″ hole (for the ⅛-scale animal) perpendicularly through the body for the pole before the legs are glued in place. Size the end grain of each leg and glue the legs in place. There is no sideways tilt to the head; it faces straight ahead.

Refer to Illus. 63 and 64 and Table 61 to complete the final shapes and details. The mane is quite deep and should be carved. After that, a burning pen can be used to apply and detail the texture. From ⅛″ stock, cut out the lion's head and glue it to the body to provide extra depth for relief. Table 61 provides the critical dimensions that you will need to carve a full-sized lion or a reduced-scale model.

After carving and sanding the lion, paint it in the colors suggested in circles on the plan (see color chart in Chapter VI) or in other colors that are pleasing to you. Insert a 10½″ length of a ¼″ diameter brass pole for the ⅛-scale animal (Illus. 79), brass tubing, or gold-painted dowel through the hole in the body so that ½″ extends below the lion's paws. Glue the pole in place. Add the footrest (Illus. 80) to the pole ¹³⁄₁₆″ below the body. Make a base (see Chapter VI) and glue the pole of the completed lion to it.

Table 60   Parts List for the Lion (⅛ Scale)

Part	Length	Width	Thickness
Head, body and tail	10⅛″	5⅛″	1¾″
Right front leg	2¼″	1⁵⁄₁₆″	¾″
Left front leg	2¼″	1¹⁵⁄₁₆″	¾″
Right hind thigh	2⅜″	1⅜″	⅞″
Right hind leg	1½″	1¼″	⅞″
Left hind thigh	1″	1³⁄₁₆″	⅞″
Left hind leg	2¹⁄₁₆″	1¹⁄₁₆″	⅞″

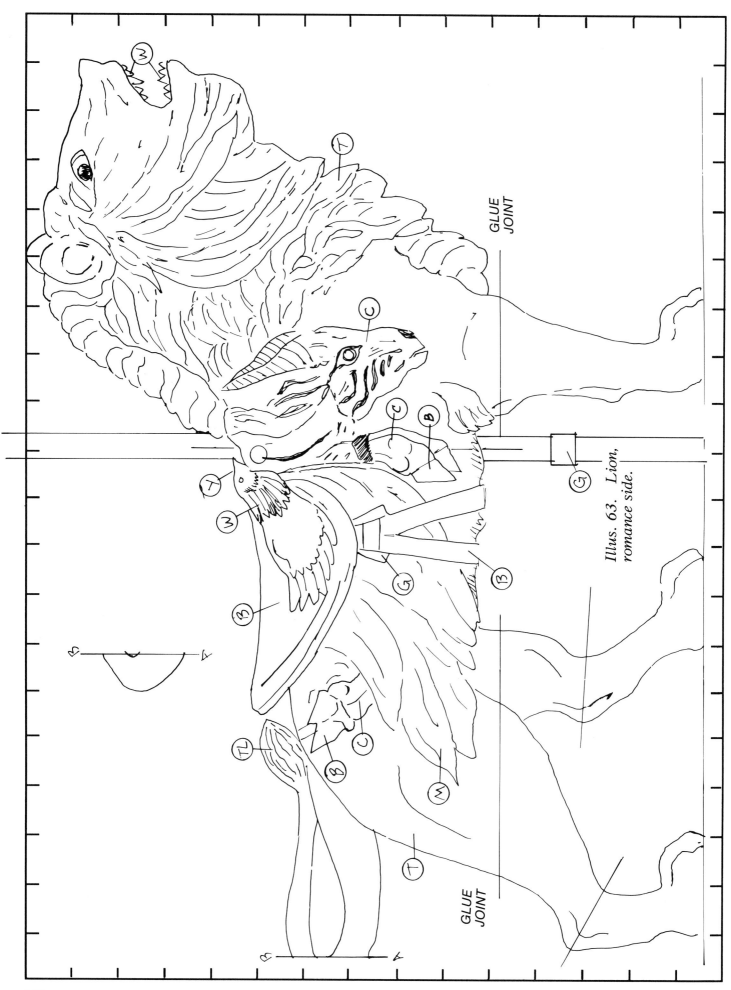

Illus. 63. Lion, romance side.

GLUE JOINT

GLUE JOINT

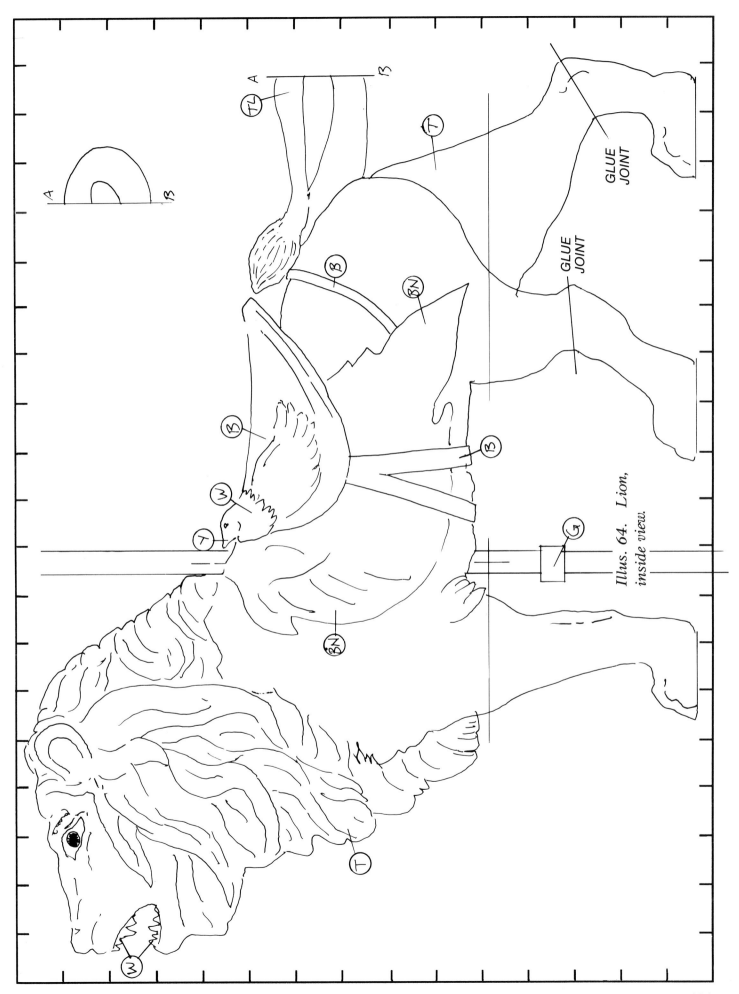

Illus. 64. Lion, inside view.

GLUE JOINT

GLUE JOINT

Table 61   Critical Dimensions for the Lion

	Scale				Full Size
	⅛	¼	½	¾	
From paw to top of mane	7⅜″	14¾″	29½″	44¼″	59″
From rump to breast	6⅞″	13¾″	27½″	41¼″	55″
From tail to nose	9¹⁵⁄₁₆″	19⅞″	39¾″	59⅝″	79½″
Width of head (with mane)	2½″	5″	10″	15″	20″
Width of face	1⅛″	2¼″	4½″	6¾″	9″
Width of nose	¾″	1½″	3″	4½″	6″
Distance between tips of ears	2¹⁄₁₆″	4⅛″	8¼″	12⅜″	16½″
Width of neck at head (with mane)	2¼″	4½″	9″	13½″	18″
Width of neck at body	1¾″	3½″	7″	10½″	14″
Width of body at pole	1¾″	3½″	7″	10½″	14″
Width of saddle at rear	1⁷⁄₁₆″	2⅞″	5¾″	8⅝″	11½″
Width of rump	1¾″	3½″	7″	10½″	14″
Width of front leg at body	¾″	1½″	3″	4½″	6″
Width of front leg at knee	⁷⁄₁₆″	⅞″	1¾″	2⅝″	3½″
Width of hind leg at body	⅞″	1¾″	3½″	5¼″	7″
Width of hind leg at knee	½″	1″	2″	3″	4″
Length of paw	1″	2″	4″	6″	8″
Width of paw	⅞″	1¾″	3½″	5¼″	7″
Width of tail at body	⅜″	¾″	1½″	2¼″	3″
Width of tail at curve	¼″	½″	1″	1½″	2″

31. Ostrich

Circa 1922

Using Illus. 65 as a plan, cut out the five patterns and glue each pattern to wood of the correct thickness, as defined in Table 62. The length of each part should follow the direction of the wood grain. Instructions for large-scale animals are given in Chapters VII and VIII. The complete carving block consists of the five parts listed in Table 62. Use the base reference line and drill a ¼″ hole (for the ⅛-scale ostrich) perpendicularly through the body for the pole. Drill this hole before the legs, neck, and head are glued in place. Size the end grain of the legs and neck and glue the head, neck, and legs in place.

The head tilts on a horizontal axis towards the romance side at approximately a 10° angle. Refer to Illus. 65 and 66 and Table 63 to complete the final shapes and details. Table 63 provides for the crit-

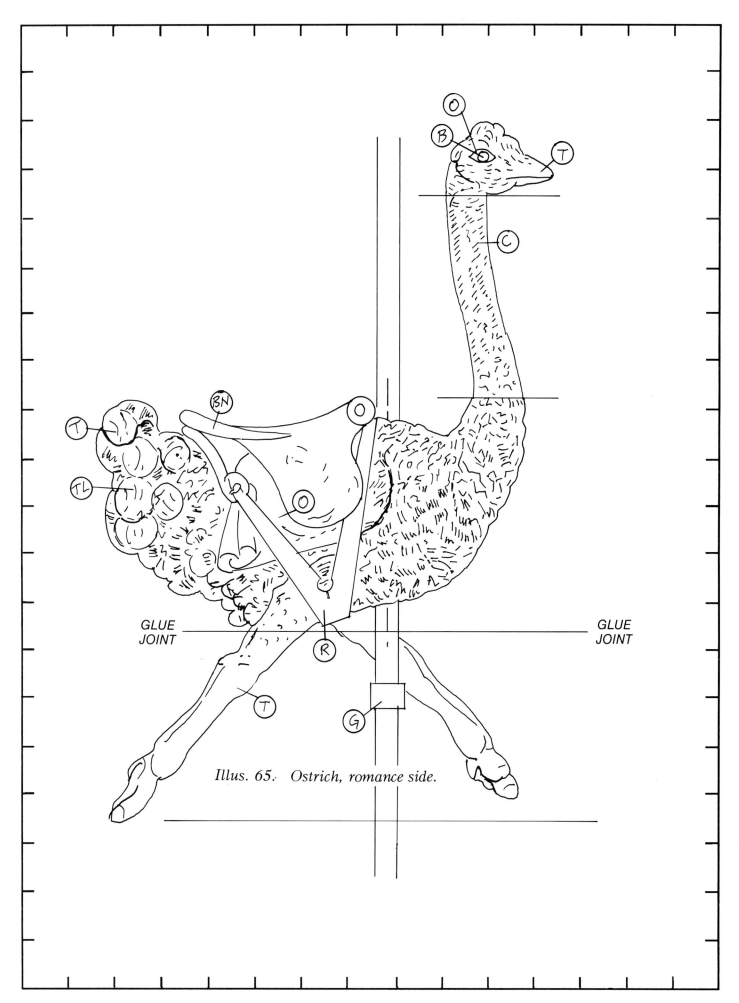

Illus. 65. Ostrich, romance side.

GLUE JOINT

GLUE JOINT

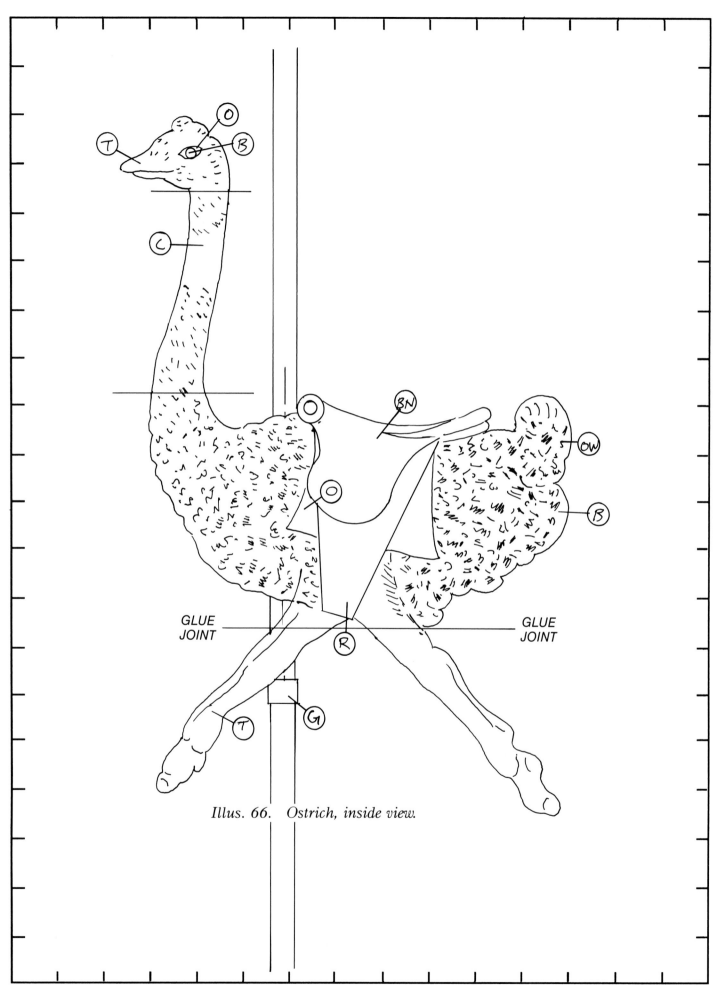

GLUE
JOINT

GLUE
JOINT

Illus. 66.   Ostrich, inside view.

ical dimensions that you will need when carving a full-sized Ostrich or a reduced-scale model. After carving the deep recesses in the feathers, you can use a high-speed triangular cutter in a motor drill to roughen the feather areas.

After carving and sanding the Ostrich, paint it in the colors suggested in circles on the plan (see color chart in Chapter VI) or in colors natural to the bird. For the ⅛-scale bird, insert a 10½″ length of a ¼″-diameter brass pole (Illus. 79), brass tubing, or gold-painted dowel through the hole in the body so that 4⅜″ extends above the saddle. Glue the pole in place. Add the footrest (Illus. 80) to the pole ¹³⁄₁₆″ below the body. Make a base (see Chapter VI) and glue the pole of the completed Ostrich to it.

Table 62   Parts List for the Ostrich (⅛ Scale)

Part	Length	Width	Thickness
Head	¹⁵⁄₁₆″	¾″	⁹⁄₁₆″
Neck	2¹⁄₁₆″	¹³⁄₁₆″	1¼″
Body	4⁹⁄₁₆″	2⅜″	1⅝″
Right leg	2¾″	⅝″	½″
Left leg	2⅜″	½″	½″

Table 63   Critical Dimensions for the Ostrich

	Scale				Full Size
	⅛	¼	½	¾	
From right foot to top of head*	7⅛″	14¼″	28½″	42¾″	57″
From right tail to breast	4½″	9″	18″	27″	36″
Width of head	⁹⁄₁₆″	1⅛″	2¼″	3⅜″	4½″
Width of beak	⅛″	¼″	½″	¾″	1″
Distance between eyes	⁹⁄₁₆″	1⅛″	2¼″	3⅜″	4½″
Width of neck at head	¹³⁄₁₆″**	1⅝″	3¼″	4⅞″	6½″
Width of neck at body	1¼″	2½″	5″	7½″	10″
Width of neck in thin area	⁷⁄₁₆″	⅞″	1¾″	2⅝″	3½″
Width of body at pole	1⅝″	3¼″	6½″	9¾″	13″
Width of saddle at rear	1⅛″	2¼″	4½″	6¾″	9″
Width of rear feathers	1⅝″	3¼″	6½″	9¾″	13″
Width of leg at body	½″	1″	2″	3″	4″
Width of leg at thin area	¼″	½″	1″	1½″	2″
Length of foot	⅝″	1¼″	2½″	3¾″	5″
Width of foot	⅝″	1¼″	2½″	3¾″	5″

*Perpendicular to base line.
**¾″ up from body.

32. Rabbit

Circa 1908

Using Illus. 67 as a plan, cut out the eight patterns and glue each pattern to wood of the correct thickness, given in Table 64. Refer to Illus. 68 for the complete pattern of the left front and hind legs. The length of each part should follow the direction of the wood grain. Instructions for large-scale animals are given in Chapters VII and VIII.

The carving block consists of the eight parts listed in Table 64. Drill a ¼″ hole (for the ⅛-scale rabbit) perpendicularly through the body for the pole, using the base line for reference, before the ears or legs are glued in place. Size the end grain of the ears, legs, and paws and glue each part in place. There is no sideways tilt to the head; it faces straight ahead.

Refer to Illus. 67 and 68 and to Table 65, the critical dimensions that you will need when carving a full-sized Rabbit or a reduced-scale model, to complete the final shapes and details. A high-speed triangular-shaped drill mounted in a motor drill can be used to roughen the body to suggest a fur texture.

After carving and sanding the Rabbit, paint it in the colors suggested in circles on the plans (see color chart in Chapter VI), or select other colors that are pleasing to you. For the ⅛-scale animal, insert a 10½″ length of a ¼″-diameter brass pole (Illus. 79), brass tubing, or gold-painted dowel into the hole in the body so that 4⅜″ of dowel extends above the saddle. Glue the pole in place. Add the footrest (Illus. 80) to the pole ¹³⁄₁₆″ below the body. Make a base (see Chapter VI) and glue the pole of the completed Rabbit to it.

Table 64   Parts List for the Rabbit (⅛ Scale)

Part	Length	Width	Thickness
Ears	2″	1¹³⁄₁₆″	1″
Head and body	6³⁄₁₆″	3¹³⁄₁₆″	1³⁄₈″
Right front paw	1″	⁷⁄₁₆″	⁷⁄₁₆″
Left front paw	¾″	½″	⁷⁄₁₆″
Right hind leg	1″	⁷⁄₁₆″	¹¹⁄₁₆″
Right hind paw	¾″	⁷⁄₁₆″	⁷⁄₁₆″
Left hind leg	1″	⁷⁄₁₆″	¹¹⁄₁₆″
Left hind paw	¾″	⁷⁄₁₆″	⁷⁄₁₆″

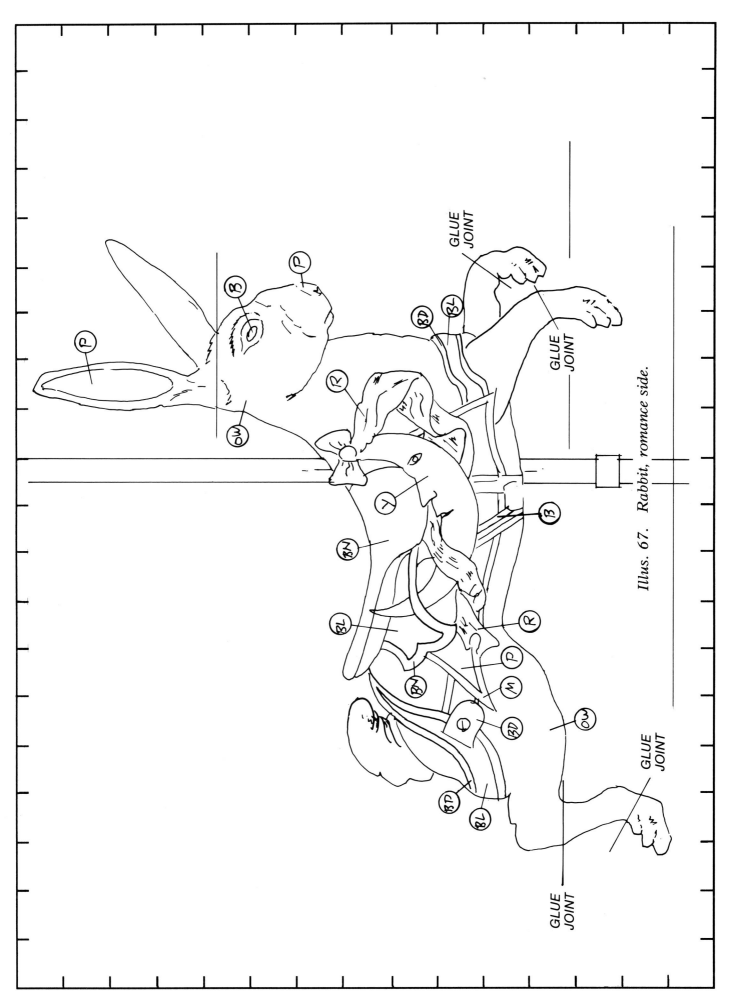

Illus. 67. Rabbit, romance side.

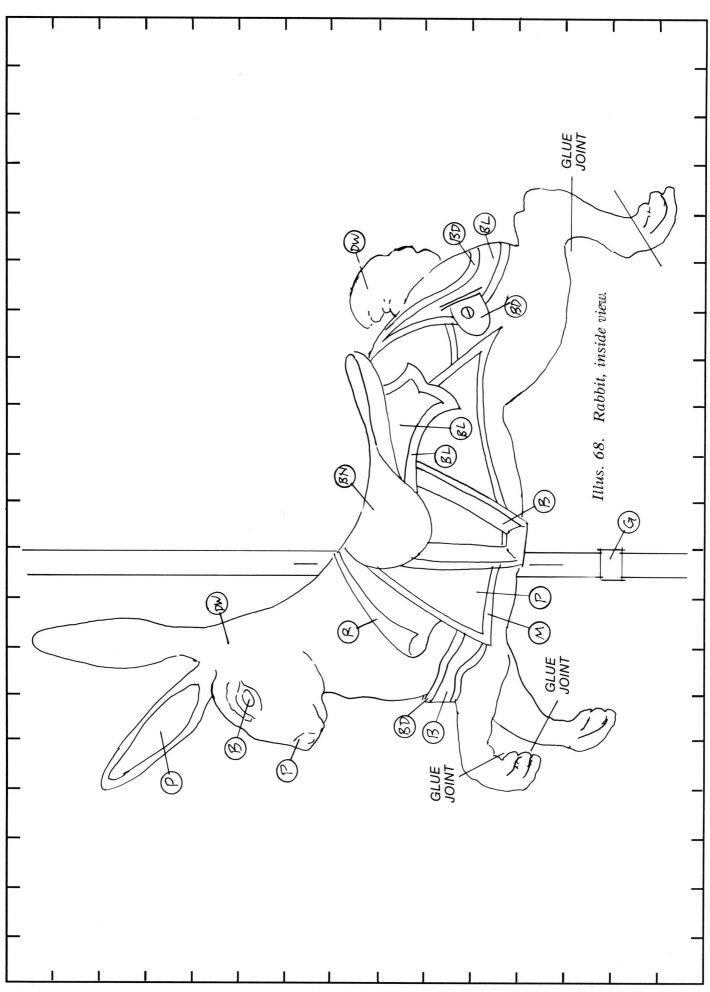

Illus. 68. *Rabbit, inside view.*

Table 65   Critical Dimensions for the Rabbit

	Scale				Full Size
	1/8	1/4	1/2	3/4	
From right hind foot to tip of right ear*	6¹⁵/₁₆"	13⅞"	27¾"	41⅝"	55½"
From rump to breast	4⅝"	9¼"	18½"	27¾"	37"
From left hind foot to left front foot	6⅜"	12¾"	25½"	38¼"	51"
Width of head	1¼"	2½"	5"	7½"	10"
Width of nose	½"	1"	2"	3"	4"
Distance between tips of ears	1"	2"	4"	6"	8"
Width of neck at head	1"	2"	4"	6"	8"
Width of body at pole	1⅜"	2¾"	5½"	8¼"	11"
Width of saddle at rear	1⅜"	2¾"	5½"	8¼"	11"
Width of rump	1⅜"	2¾"	5½"	8¼"	11"
Width of front leg at body	½"	1"	2"	3"	4"
Width of front leg at knee	⅜"	¾"	1½"	2¼"	3"
Width of hind leg at body	¹¹/₁₆"	1⅜"	2¾"	4⅛"	5½"
Width of hind leg at knee	⅜"	¾"	1½"	2¼"	3"
Width of paw	⁷/₁₆"	⅞"	1¾"	2⅝"	3½"

*Perpendicular to base line.

33. Rooster

Circa 1895

Using Illus. 69 as a plan, cut out the seven patterns and glue each pattern to wood of the correct thickness, given in Table 67. The length of each part should follow the direction of the grain. Instructions for large-scale animals are given in Chapters VII and VIII. The complete carving block consists of the seven parts listed in Table 66. Use the base line for reference and drill a ¼" hole (for the ⅛-scale Rooster) perpendicularly through the body for the pole. Size the end grain for the legs and feet and glue them in place. There is no sideways tilt to the head—it faces straight ahead. Refer to Illus. 69 and 70 and to Table 67, the critical dimensions needed to carve the full-size Rooster or a reduced-scale model, to complete the final shapes and details. Use a burning pen to add texture to the feathers.

After carving and sanding the Rooster, paint it in accordance with the suggested color symbols in circles on the plans (see color chart

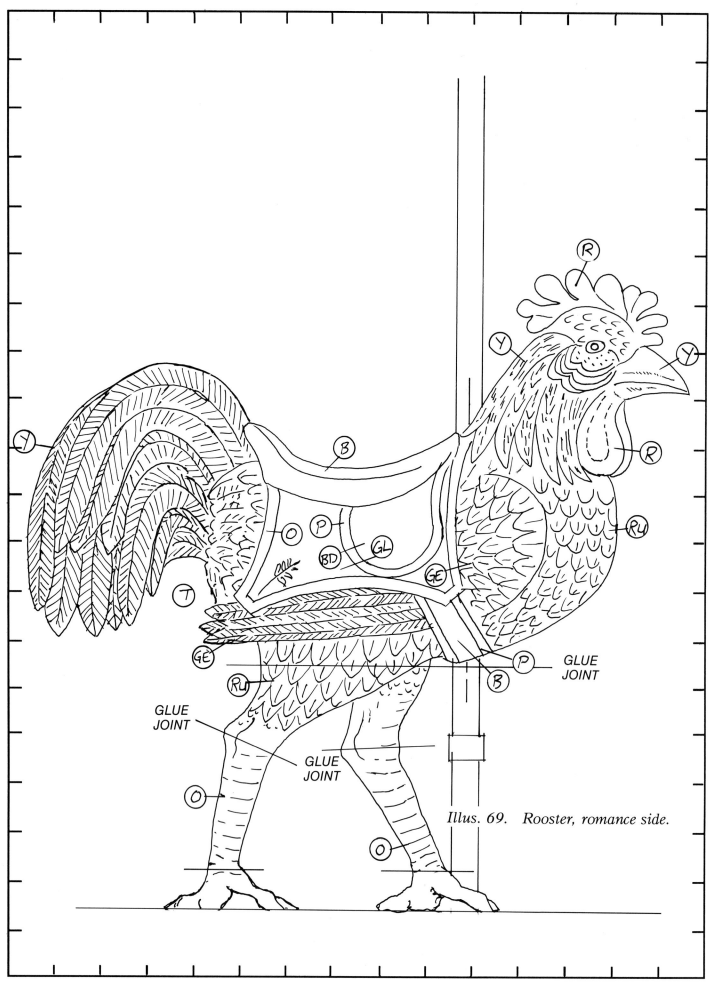

GLUE
JOINT

GLUE
JOINT

GLUE
JOINT

Illus. 69.   Rooster, romance side.

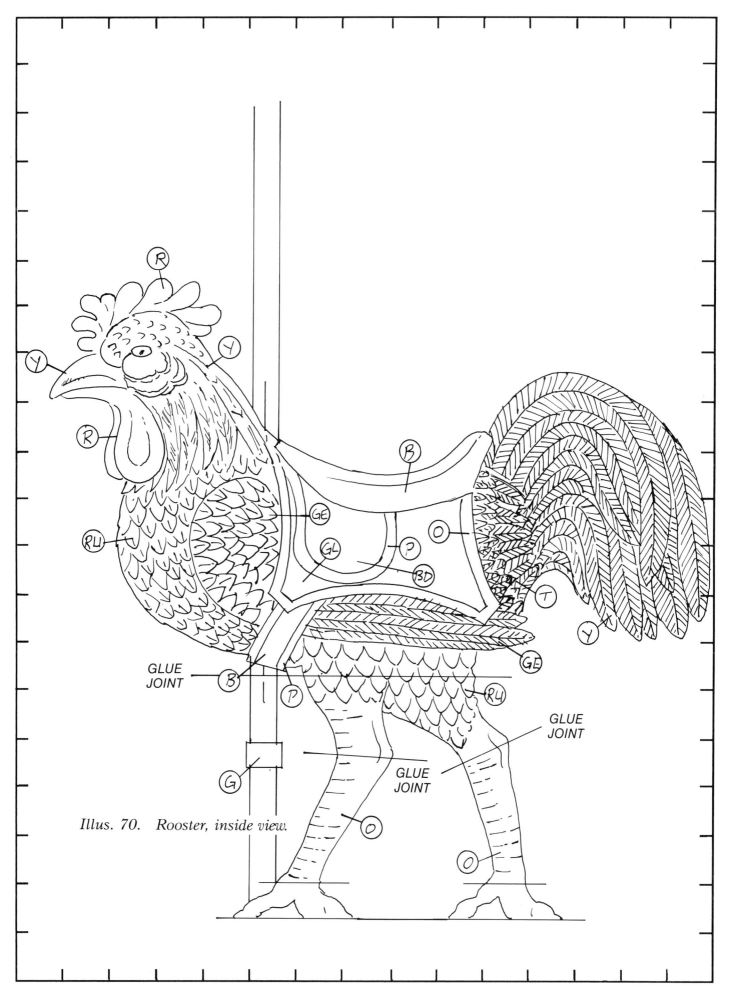

GLUE JOINT

GLUE JOINT

GLUE JOINT

Illus. 70.   Rooster, inside view.

in Chapter VI) or according to your own taste. Since this is a reproduction of an earlier carving, you may want to thin the enamels so that you achieve an antique rather than a glossy finish. For the ⅛-scale Rooster, insert a 10½″ length of a ¼″-diameter brass pole (Illus. 79), brass tubing, or gold-painted dowel into the hole in the body so that 5⅛″ extends above the saddle. Glue the pole in place. Add the footrest (Illus. 79) to the pole ¹³⁄₁₆″ below the body. Make a base (see Chapter VI) and glue the pole of the completed Rooster to it.

Table 66 Parts List for the Rooster (⅛ Scale)

Part	Length	Width	Thickness
Head and body	7″	4″	1½″
Right thigh	1⅞″	1″	¾″
Right leg	1⁷⁄₁₆″	⁹⁄₁₆″	½″
Right foot	1¼″	⅜″	⁹⁄₁₆″
Left thigh	1″	1″	¾″
Left leg	1¹¹⁄₁₆″	⅝″	½″
Left foot	1¼″	⅜″	⁹⁄₁₆″

Table 67 Critical Dimensions for the Rooster

	Scale				Full Size
	⅛	¼	½	¾	
From foot to tip of comb*	6⁹⁄₁₆″	13⅛″	26¼″	29⅜″	52½″
From tail to breast	6¼″	12½″	25″	37½″	50″
Width of head	⅝″	1¼″	2½″	3¾″	5″
Width of neck at head	⅝″	1¼″	2½″	3¾″	5″
Width of neck at body	⅞″	1¾″	3½″	5¼″	7″
Width of body at pole	1½″	3″	6″	9″	12″
Width of saddle at rear	1½″	3″	6″	9″	12″
Width of comb on body	⁵⁄₁₆″	⅝″	1¼″	1⅞″	2½″
Width of body at breast	⅞″	1¾″	3½″	5¼″	7″
Width of leg at body	½″	1″	2″	3″	4″
Width of leg at knee	⅜″	¾″	1½″	2¼″	3″
Width of leg at foot	¼″	½″	1″	1½″	2″
Length of foot	1¼″	2½″	5″	7½″	10″
Width of foot	⁹⁄₁₆″	1⅛″	2¼″	3⅜″	4½″

*Perpendicular to base line.

34. Tiger
Circa 1926

Using Illus. 71 as a plan, cut out the ten patterns for the Tiger and glue each pattern to wood of the correct thickness, as defined in Table 68. Refer to Illus. 72 for complete patterns of the left front and hind legs. The length of each part should follow the direction of the wood grain. The complete carving block consists of the ten parts given in Table 68. Use the base reference line to drill a ¼″ hole (for the ⅛-scale Tiger) perpendicularly through the body for the pole. Drill the hole before the legs are glued in place. Size the end-grain surfaces of all leg parts and glue them in place. There is no sideways tilt to the head; it faces straight ahead. Refer to Illus. 71 and 72 to complete the final shapes and details, and to Table 69, which provides the critical dimensions needed to carve a full-size Tiger or a reduced-scale model.

After carving and a final sanding, assemble the three tail parts and glue the tail to the body and to the inside of the left leg. Paint the Tiger in its natural colors, orange and black. For the ⅛-scale Tiger, insert a 10½″ length of a ¼″-diameter brass pole (Illus. 79), brass tubing, or gold-painted dowel into the body so that ½″ of the pole extends below the paws. Glue the pole in place. There is no footrest on this animal. Make a base (see Chapter VI) and glue the pole of the completed Tiger to it.

Table 68   Parts List for the Tiger (⅛ Scale)

Part	Length	Width	Thickness
Head and body	7¹⁵⁄₁₆″	4¼″	1¹¹⁄₁₆″
Right front leg	3″	1″	⅝″
Left front leg	2⅛″	1¹⁵⁄₁₆″	⅝″
Right hind thigh	2⅜″	1½″	¹¹⁄₁₆″
Right hind leg	1⅜″	1³⁄₁₆″	⅝″
Left hind thigh	1¾″	1⁷⁄₁₆″	¹¹⁄₁₆″
Left hind leg	1¹³⁄₁₆″	⅞″	⅝″
Tail, top section	1⁵⁄₁₆″	¹¹⁄₁₆″	½″
Tail, middle section	1¹⁵⁄₁₆″	⁷⁄₁₆″	⅜″
Tail, end	2⅜″	⅜″	¼″

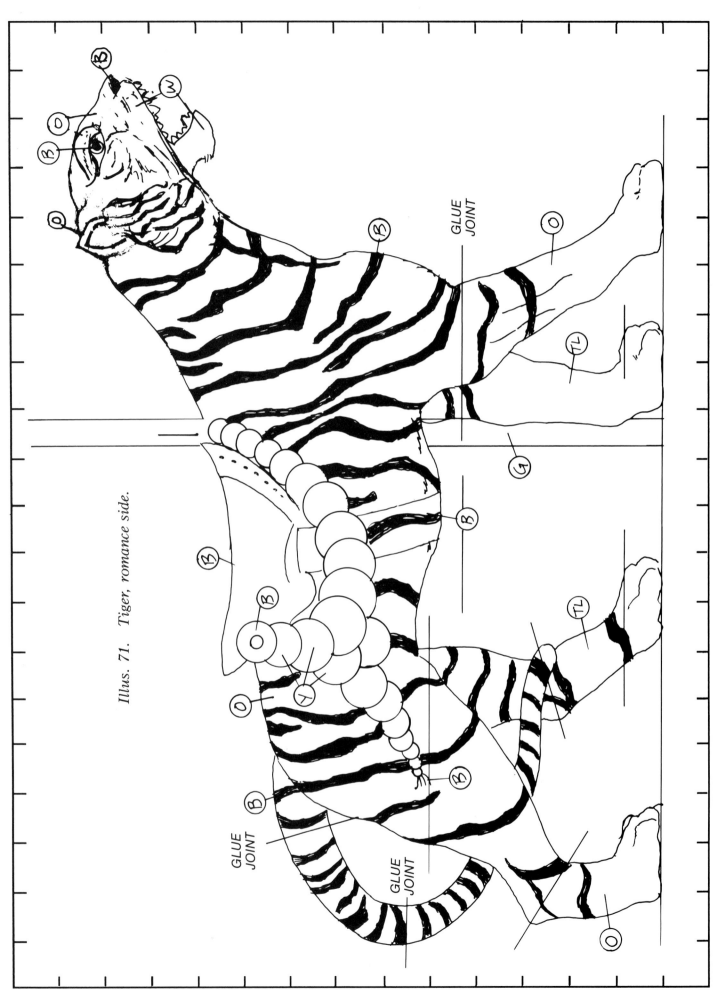

Illus. 71. Tiger, romance side.

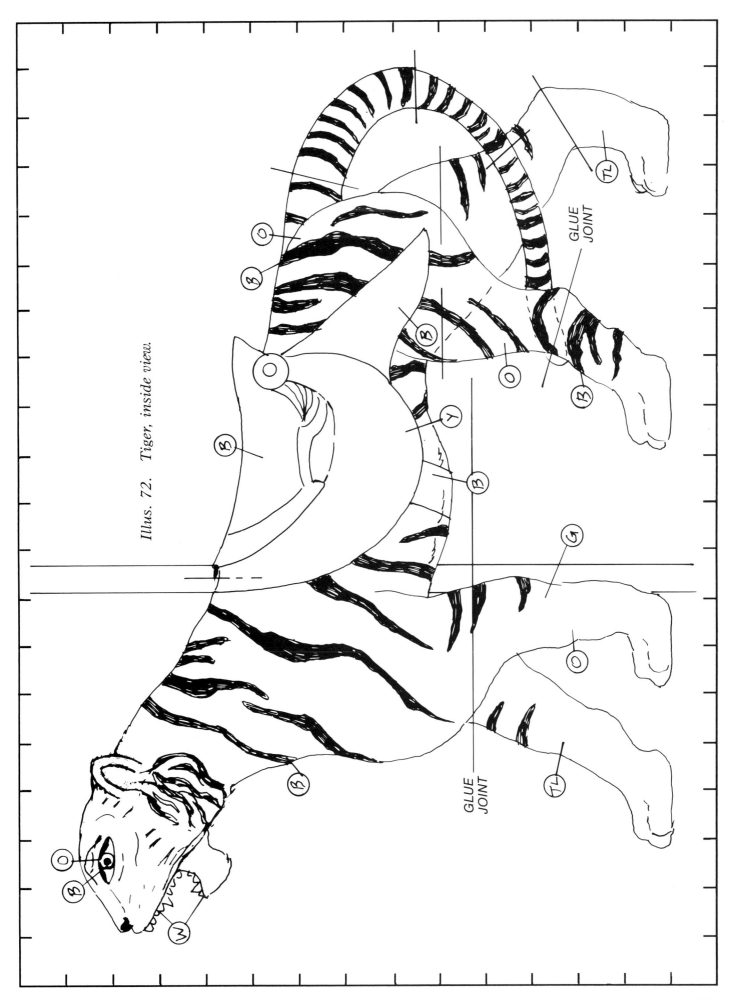

Illus. 72. Tiger, inside view.

GLUE JOINT

GLUE JOINT

Table 69   Critical Dimensions for the Tiger

	Scale				Full Size
	⅛	¼	½	¾	
From foot to top of head	6⅜"	12¾"	25½"	38¼"	51"
From rump to breast	5⅞"	11¾"	23½"	35¼"	47"
From tail to nose	8¹⁵⁄₁₆"	17⅞"	35¾"	53⅝"	71½"
Width of head	1¼"	2½"	5"	7½"	10"
Width of nose	¹¹⁄₁₆"	1⅜"	2¾"	4⅛"	5½"
Distance between tips of ears	1¼"	2½"	5"	7½"	10"
Width of neck at head	1¼"	2½"	5"	7½"	10"
Width of body at pole	1¹¹⁄₁₆"	3⅜"	6¾"	10⅛"	13½"
Width of saddle at rear	1¹¹⁄₁₆"	3⅜"	6¾"	10⅛"	13½"
Width of rear flank	1⅜"	2¾"	5½"	8¼"	11"
Width of front leg at body	⅝"	1¼"	2½"	3¾"	5"
Width of front leg at knee	⁹⁄₁₆"	1⅛"	2¼"	3⅜"	4½"
Width of hind leg at body	¹¹⁄₁₆"	1⅜"	2¾"	4⅛"	5½"
Width of hind leg at knee	⁹⁄₁₆"	1⅛"	2¼"	3⅜"	4½"
Length of foot	⅞"	1¾"	3½"	5¼"	7"
Width of foot	⅝"	1¼"	2½"	3¾"	5"
Width of tail, top section	½"	1"	2"	3"	4"
Width of tail, middle section	⅜"	¾"	1½"	2¼"	3"
Width of tail, end section	¼"	½"	1"	1½"	2"

Finishing Touches

his chapter presents ideas, techniques, and suggestions that will add some niceties to the ⅛-scale carving. A rare number of carousel animal collectors like to leave the carving unfinished. This is especially true if the carving is made from wood with a beautiful grain or if the owner wants to show off the laminated construction. Under these conditions, a sealer of some type—varnish, oil, or wax—should be applied to seal the pores of the wood and to minimize soiling.

COLOR SCHEME

For most carousel carvings, bright colors are desired. It is almost impossible to positively know the exact colors of the original paint on carousel animals. The carousel was usually given a new coat of bright paint at the beginning of each new fair season. The painting was done by roustabouts, who were more interested in making the carousel look clean and bright than they were in the history of the animals as objects of art. It is not uncommon to find antique carousel animals covered by thirty layers of paint, which often obscure some of the fine carving details.

The decision as to what type of paint is to be used is entirely up to you. The animals shown in the color section were finished with oil-based gloss enamels, which are readily available at any hardware store. These paints are ideal to use on the carousel figures for the following reasons: (1) they come in brilliant colors; (2) they can be easily mixed to desired shades; (3) the paints do not dry too rapidly, permitting the blending of some colors, especially on the horses where a gradation of color is desired; (4) they provide a durable finish; (5) they are safe; and, (6) you do not have to be a skilled color mixer to achieve outstanding results. Acrylic or latex paints also may be used. However, the water base may cause the grain to rise and then additional sanding will be required. Acrylic and latex paints have a big advantage—the speed with which they dry, which enables you to paint the carving in less time than is required for painting with oil-base paints. The brushes used for acrylic and latex painting may be cleaned in warm water, another advantage.

I have found it helpful to start the painting process by applying a base coat to the entire carving. This initial coat should be "cut" (diluted) by about 30%, helping it to penetrate farther into the wood. This initial coat will also show the carver any rough places, cuts, or dents. A good final sanding is recommended when the initial coat is thoroughly dry. It will generally be helpful if the initial base coat is the color of the body of the animal.

In the illustrations in this book, a suggested color scheme is offered for each animal. The meanings of the symbols on all of the plans are shown in Table 70. The final color selection should be yours; the carving should be painted in colors that you find pleasing, harmonious, and satisfying. When a fine line is desired, a draftsman's ruling pen (Illus. 73) may be used. This can be used not only for

Illus. 73. Draftsman's ruling pen.

straight lines; if a pattern is cut from 1/16″ thick wood, plastic, or cardboard, the ruling pen will help the painter to produce a very professional finish. A draftsman's french curve can also be used successfully to guide the ruling pen. The paint should be thinned slightly and a supply placed in the pen's nib. Wipe off any excess paint, hold the pen upright, and trace along a straight edge or along a pattern. The Indian Stander (Illus. 14) is a good example of what can be accomplished with a ruling pen.

Table 70   Colors and Their Abbreviations

(A)	Aqua		(GR)	Grey (dark)
(B)	Black (gloss)		(GS)	Green stain
(BA)	Blue/grey		(J)	Jonquil (Bright yellow)
(BB)	Black/brown		(M)	Maroon
(BD)	Blue (dark)		(O)	Orange
(BG)	Brown/grey		(OL)	Olive
(BK)	Blue/black		(OW)	Off-white
(BL)	Blue (light)		(P)	Pink
(BN)	Brown (dark)		(PU)	Purple
(BR)	Brown (light)		(R)	Red
(C)	Cream		(RU)	Rust
(DG)	Dapple grey		(S)	Silver
(F)	Flesh		(T)	Tan
(G)	Gold		(TL)	Tan (light)
(GE)	Green (dark)		(W)	White
(GL)	Green (light)		(Y)	Yellow
(GM)	Grey (light)		(YL)	Yellow (light)

MAKING BASES

A stand or base is needed to keep the carving in an upright position. For the ⅛-scale animal this may be a simple block of wood with a ¼″ hole drilled in it, or it may be a more artistic base. The seven base designs that follow provide a wide variety of options for the carver. (See Chapter VII for a base for the large-scale animal.)

Rectangular Base

One simple base is a rectangular block, 1″ longer than the length of the carving × 4″ wide × ½″ thick (Illus. 74, top). Any kind of wood may be used. If you plan to paint the base, pine, poplar, or basswood will work nicely. If you want to finish the base with oil or varnish, a wood with a definite grain, such as walnut or mahogany, should be used. This block may be improved slightly by chamfering the edges, as shown. Drill a ¼″ hole in the base to receive the pole. The base dimensions are not critical and may be adjusted depending upon the size of the carving and the carver's preference. This base may be used to support any ⅛-scale carousel horse or menagerie animal.

Oval Base

The oval is a more pleasing variation of the rectangular base. It can be laid out using a 30°–60° triangle and a compass. Start by drawing perpendicular lines AB and CD (Illus. 75). On line AB measure 3″ above and below line CD. From these points on line AB, draw four lines at a base angle of 30° until they intersect line CD (Step 2). From point A draw a line on the right at a 30° angle to AB until it intersects line CD. This will be line AE. From point B draw a line to the left at a 60° angle to your base line until it intersects line CD at F. This will make line BF.

Set the compass point at point F and set the radius so that it is tangent to line AC. Draw an arc from line AC to line BC. Move the compass point to E and draw an arc from line AC to line BD. Place the compass point at B and adjust the radius so that it meets smoothly the first arc drawn. Draw an arc from line AC to AD. Move the compass point to point A and draw an arc from BC to BD. You have now constructed an oval. By varying the base angle, you can develop a narrower or fatter oval. The dimensions and angle may be varied to suit your needs, but the procedure remains the same.

Turned Base

The turned base (Illus. 74, bottom) provides a good option for supporting prancers and jumpers, although it could be used for any

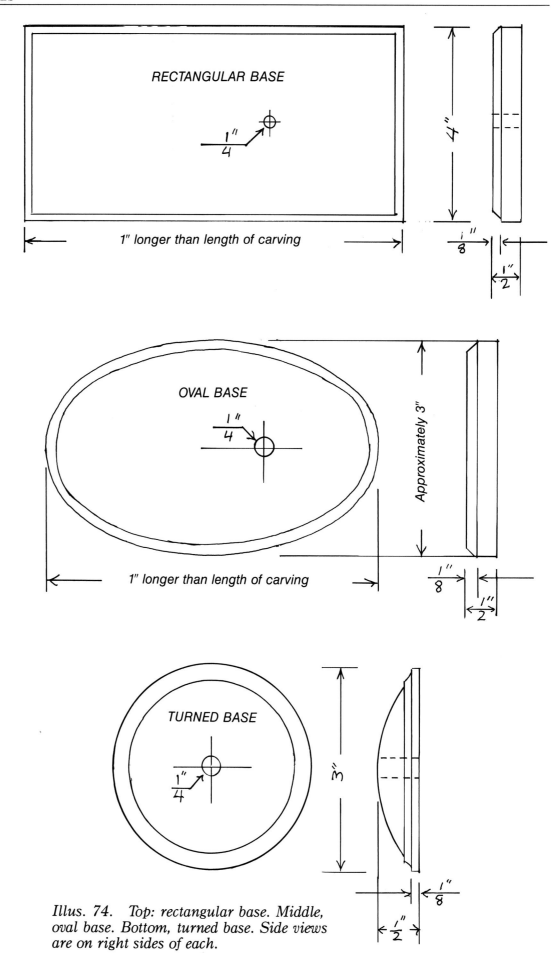

RECTANGULAR BASE

1"/4

4"

1" longer than length of carving

1"/8

1"/2

OVAL BASE

1"/4

Approximately 3"

1" longer than length of carving

1"/8

1"/2

TURNED BASE

1"/4

3"

1"/8

1"/2

Illus. 74.   Top: rectangular base. Middle, oval base. Bottom, turned base. Side views are on right sides of each.

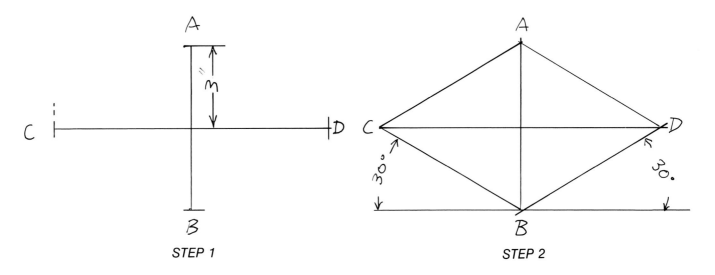

STEP 1   STEP 2

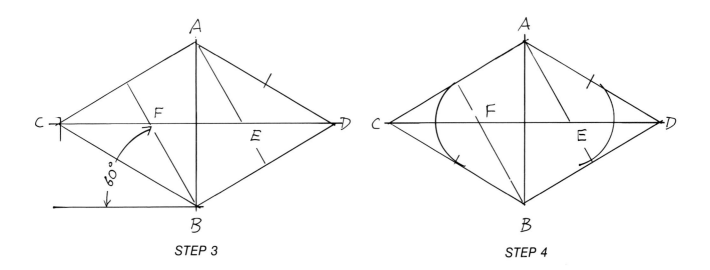

STEP 3   STEP 4

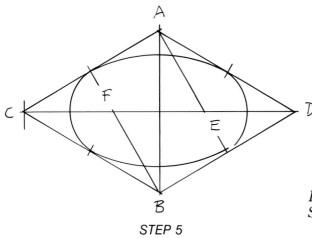

STEP 5

Illus. 75.   Steps in laying out an oval base.
See text (page 153) for details.

SINGLE SUPPORT

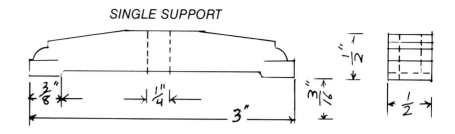

CROSSOVER

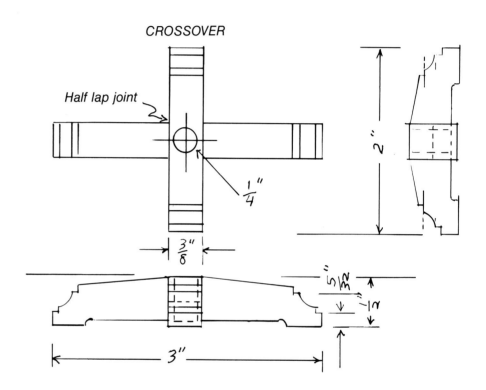

Half lap joint

MODIFIED CROSSOVER

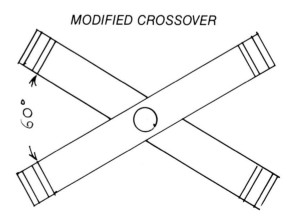

Illus. 76.   Top: single support base. Middle: crossover base. Bottom: modified crossover base.

carving. The shape and dimensions are not critical, but are offered only as suggestions. You may vary the design and dimensions to suit your preference. When this base is used with standers or prancers, the bottom half of the pole should be shortened by ½″ from the dimensions given in the instructions with each project.

Single Support Base

This is the smallest and simplest of the suggested bases. It consists of only one piece of wood, approximately 3″ × ½″ × ½″ (Illus. 76, top). The size and dimensions can vary to suit the carver's taste. This base can be used for any ⅛-scale carving except for a jumper. When used with standers, prancers, or menagerie animals, the pole should be reduced in height by ½″ from the dimension suggested in the projects.

Crossover Base

The crossover base consists of two pieces of the single-support base fastened together with a half-lap joint (Illus. 76, middle). It may be used with any of the ⅛-scale carvings. The pole will have to be shortened by ½″ when crossover bases are used for any carvings other than jumpers.

Modified Crossover Bases

In some cases the carver finds a modified crossover design more pleasing (Illus. 76, bottom). Use the side view of the 3″ member of the crossover (Illus. 76, middle) as a pattern and cut out a pair. Change the 90° half lap joint of the usual crossover to an angle of 60°, or to one that is acceptable to you. With both crossover bases, the carving may be more susceptible to a sideways fall and may not be as stable as the other bases. Once again the pole will have to be shortened by ½″ when this base is used with any carving other than a jumper.

Platform Base

The platform base represents a segment of a circular carousel platform. It is perhaps the most realistic of all the bases. For the ⅛-scale animal, the base is made up of a ½″-thick solid curved bottom covered by 1⁄16″ thick flooring and facing boards. The size of the base ranges from 10¹⁵⁄₁₆″ for the lion to 6⅝″ for the smaller animals. The length of each base is determined by the length of each animal, as suggested in Table 71. Using Illus. 77 as a reference, start at the extreme right point on the long latitudinal center line (℄) and draw a line equal to the length of chord A (given in Table 71) for the selected animal. (For some of the longer animals it will be necessary to glue together two copies of Illus. 77.) Draw a radial line through

Table 71   Base Dimensions

Animal	Length of Base (Chord A)	Pole Location (Chord B)
Patriotic Horse	8½″	4⅞″
Dapple White with Flowers	8⅞″	5³⁄₁₆″
Armored Horse	8¾″	4⅞″
Stander with Bells	8¹³⁄₁₆″	5¼″
Military Horse	8¹⁄₁₆″	4⁵⁄₁₆″
Indian Stander	8⅜″	4¹¹⁄₁₆″
Stander with Garlands	8⅞″	5¼″
Cerni's Figure	8⅞″	4¹⁵⁄₁₆″
Roached Stander	8⅜″	4⅝″
Tassels and Disks	8¹³⁄₁₆″	5¼″
Orange Blanket Stander	8″	4½″
Lead Horse	8″	4½″
Red Blanket Prancer	7¼″	4¼″
Indian Prancer	7¼″	4⁹⁄₁₆″
Buccaneer	6⅝″	4⅜″
Yellow Fringe Prancer	9⅛″	5¹⁄₁₆″
Prancer with Brown Saddle	8¾″	4¹³⁄₁₆″
Western Prancer	9¹⁄₁₆″	4¹⁵⁄₁₆″
Red Stripe Jumper	7¾″	4¹³⁄₁₆″
Diamond Light	7⅞″	4½″
Flying Tassels	7½″	4⅝″
Star Jumper	6⅝″	4¹¹⁄₁₆″
Flying Mane	8″	4⅝″
Curly Top	8″	4⅜″
Palomino Jumper	8⅝″	4⁷⁄₁₆″
Cat	7⅝″	4⁹⁄₁₆″
Deer	7¾″	4¹¹⁄₁₆″
Giraffe	7¾″	4¼″
Hippocampus	8¼″	4⅜″
Lion	10¹⁵⁄₁₆″	6⁵⁄₁₆″
Ostrich	5⅞″	3⅝″
Rabbit	7⅜″	4½″
Rooster	7⅞″	5¼″
Tiger	9¹⁵⁄₁₆″	5¾″

the point where chord A intersects the center line so that the radial line intersects the front and back edges of the drawing. This determines the width of the stand.

The location of the ¼″ hole for the pole is determined in a similar manner. The position for the hole is on the longitudinal center line and is located so that there will be approximately ½″ in front and behind the figure, measured on the longitudinal center line. This is

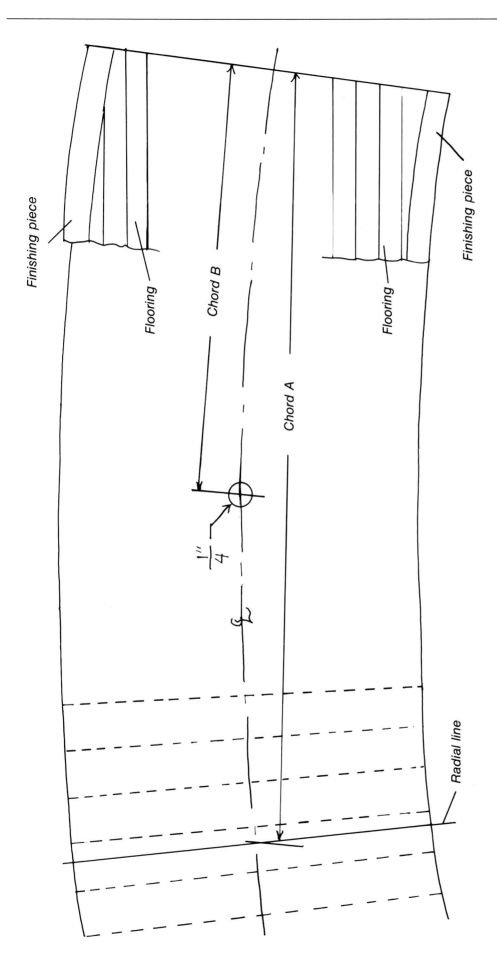

Illus. 77. Pattern for platform base. See text and Table 71 for sizes.

an arbitrary decision; you can change the dimensions to suit your taste. Again, starting at the extreme right point on the longitudinal center line, measure the distance of Chord B (given in Table 71). This will determine the location of the pole hole.

Using Illus. 77 as a pattern and with Chord A determining the length, cut the base from ½" stock. Glue flooring fashioned from ⅟16" thick × ⅛" wide × random lengths on the top of the base. Most of the floorboards run parallel to each other, but there should be a curved finishing piece on the front and back. The front curved finishing piece should overhang the base by ⅟16". It will be necessary to shape the floorboards where they meet the finishing pieces. The edges of each piece of flooring should be bevelled slightly so that the floorboard effect will be obvious in the finished base. One way to bevel the edges of the flooring is to use a stop block, as suggested in Illus. 78. A piece of ⅟16" × ⅜" stock is glued to a base, ¼" in from the edge. Place a piece of flooring (⅟16" × ¼" stock) and use a small hand plane to bevel one edge. When one side is bevelled, turn the flooring board around and bevel the other edge. Sand it lightly and glue the piece in place on the base.

If you do not want to go to the extra trouble of "laying the floor," the base may be left plain (with no overhang) and painted or stained to your desire. An alternative method is to scribe the flooring on the solid stock using a knife or awl.

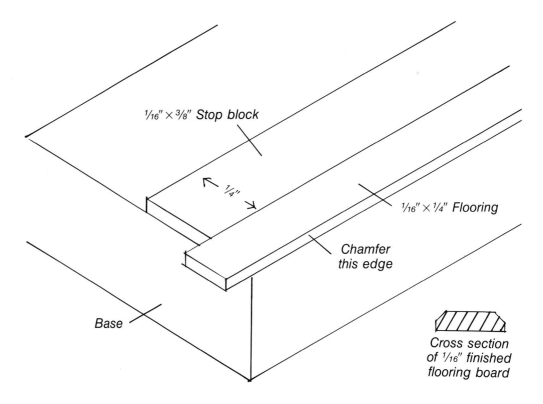

Illus. 78. Detail of base for ⅛-scale animal.

One suggestion for the finish of the platform base is to use mahogany stain under a satin varnish. This contrasts with the brightly painted carving and shows it to its best advantage. The base is further enhanced when the vertical surface of the leading edge is painted a bright color. Some carousels have a plain painted floor; you may want to forget the flooring pattern and merely paint the base. In this situation, select a color that will complement and not distract attention from the carving.

POLE AND FOOTREST

There are several things you can do to create the pole for a ⅛-scale carving. The most impressive is to have a ¼″-diameter brass rod turned with a spiral effect, as shown in Illus. 79. Check with a local machine shop to have them do this work for you. If you don't want to go to the trouble of having the pole turned, a good substitute is to use ¼″-diameter brass rod or tubing. If none of these are possible, then a gold-painted ¼″ dowel will work. In any case, the suggested length of the pole is 10½″. Additional realism can be achieved by adding a footrest to the pole. A suggested footrest design is shown in Illus. 80. This drawing shows an exploded view, the dimensions of the parts, and gives full-sized patterns for the parts.

The sleeve is the central part of each footrest. It is a hollowed-out ¼″ segment of a ⁵⁄₁₆″ dowel, to which parts A and B are glued. The sleeve has fairly close tolerance for woodworking, but it can be successfully made by the following procedure: Clamp a piece of ¾″ scrap stock on the drill press table. Drill a ⁵⁄₁₆″ perpendicular hole into the scrap. Do not move the scrap wood or change the drill press setting. Replace the ⁵⁄₁₆″ drill with a ¼″ drill. Cut a segment approximately 1⅛″ long from a ⁵⁄₁₆″-diameter dowel. Insert this dowel segment into one end of a ⁵⁄₁₆″ dowelling jig sleeve (Illus. 81). Insert a ⁵⁄₁₆″ brad point drill into the other end of the sleeve. Rotate the drill against the dowel. The brad point will mark a center indentation in the dowel. Place the dowel segment in the hole in the scrap wood. Drill a ¼″ hole into the dowel, using the center indication as a starting point. Since the setup has not changed, the ¼″ hole will be centered in the ⁵⁄₁₆″ dowel. Use a very fine blade (30 teeth to the inch, .018″ thick and .042″ wide) in the scroll saw and

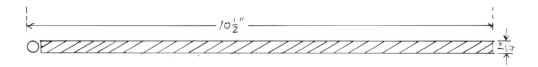

Illus. 79. Reduced sketch of brass carousel pole, ¼″ diameter, for ⅛-scale animal.

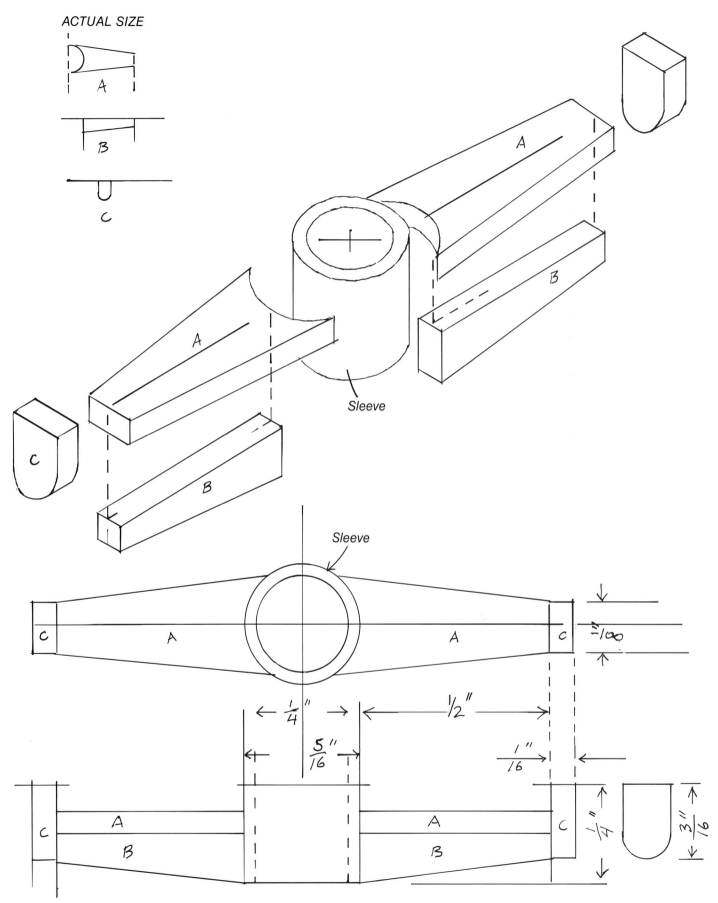

ACTUAL SIZE

Illus. 80. Footrest. Upper left: actual size patterns. Middle: exploded view of parts of footrest. Bottom: top and side views.

cut the hollow dowel into ¼" lengths. To minimize breakage, insert a ¼" dowel in the hole while cutting the sleeve to length.

Using the actual size drawings in Illus. 80 as a pattern, cut out of ¹⁄₁₆" stock two each of parts A, B, and C. Glue Part B perpendicular to A (see Illus. 80, top). Glue Part C to the narrow end of A and B, as shown (Illus. 80, top). Wrap sandpaper around a ⁵⁄₁₆" dowel and shape the wide end of A/B in an arc to conform to the circumference of the sleeve. Glue the assembled parts (A, B, and C) to each side of the sleeve. Slide the completed footrest onto the pole and glue it approximately ¹³⁄₁₆" below the belly of the animal. If the footrest is being glued to a brass rod or metal tubing, clear household cement or epoxy cement should be used. If the footrest is glued to a wooden dowel, carpenters glue should be used.

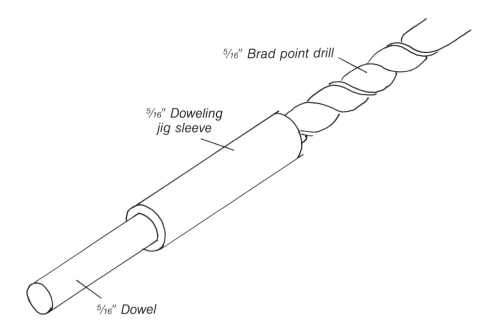

Illus. 81. Doweling jig and dowel segment.

CHAPTER VII

Preparing to Carve a Large Animal

oday, with many people living in small houses, apartments, and condos, it may not be possible for lovers of carousel animals to have a full-sized horse in their homes. An exact replica on a reduced scale may be just the right answer. The scale can be adjusted so that the carving will optimize the available space. This chapter presents all the information needed to carve a large horse or other animal. You can determine the actual size to meet your needs. The procedures remain the same, only the dimensions, amount of basswood, and carving time are changed. The basic steps for carving a small-scale model, outlined in the previous chapters, apply equally well to carving a large animal. The major differences are the size of the carving blocks, the carving tools (gouges rather than knives), and the amount of time required to complete the carving.

ENLARGING THE PLAN

The first step is to decide upon the animal to be carved. If a plan must be developed, review the suggestions offered in Chapter I. Next determine the desired scale. How much smaller than full size is desirable? For the purpose of illustrating the principle of enlargement by the square method, let's decide upon a ⅞th-scale animal (this will be in keeping with the horse to be carved in the next chapter) and select the Horse with Tassels (Illus. 86).

Using the plan presented in Illus. 86, draw parallel lines between the topmost and lowest grid points the horse touches. Do the same between the leftmost and rightmost grid points. The plan will now be covered with a grid; each square measures ½″ on a side. Each square would be equal to 4″ for a full-sized horse. However, since we will be constructing a reduced-size horse (⅞ scale), each square will represent 3½″ on a side (7 × ½″). Start at the lower left corner and designate each line with a number, (as shown in Illus. 82 for the head only). Let the lower left corner represent 0 (zero) and number the vertical lines 1 to 17 on the horizontal axis. Letter the horizontal lines A to P on the vertical axis.

Next, secure large sheets of white paper from an art or stationery store and glue them together using rubber cement until you have a sheet measuring at least 56″ × 56″. Rule the paper into 3½″ squares.

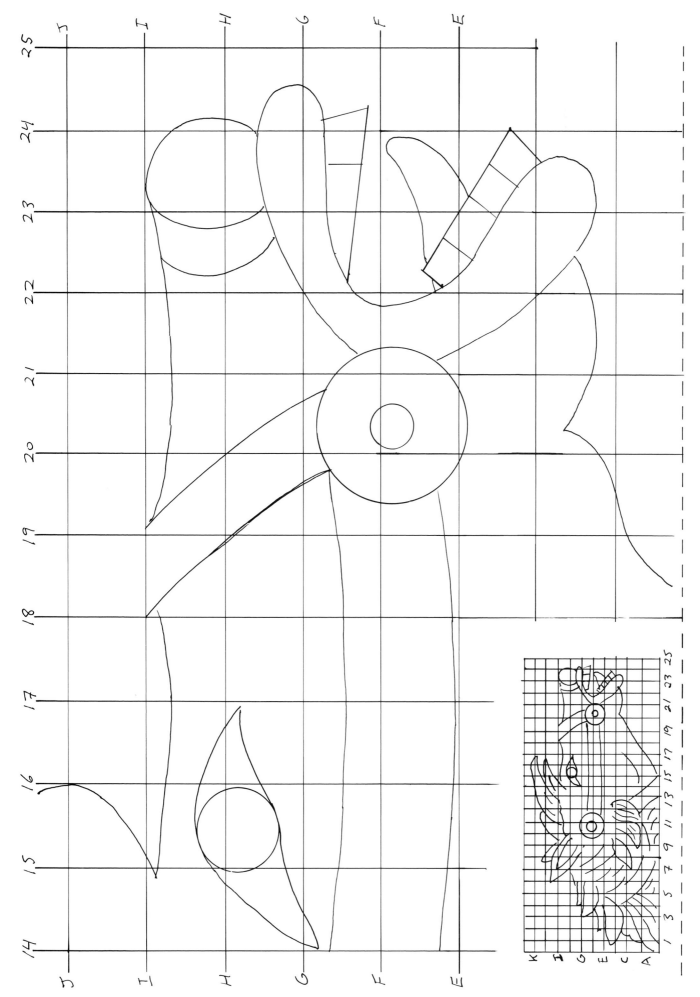

Illus. 82. Enlarging by the "square" (or grid) method. Detail of Horse with Tassels (Illus. 91).

Number and letter the lines on the large sheet with exactly the same letters and numbers as you used on the ⅛-scale plan.

To make the ⅞-scale pattern, follow the grid on the small plan and transfer each line to the same relative position on the larger sheet. This procedure is commonly known as enlarging by the square method, and is illustrated in Illus. 82. For example, upper lip meets the nostril on line 24 about halfway between lines G and H. From there the lip line proceeds to the right, curves in mid square and crosses line G about midpoint between lines 24 and 25. From there it curves back to the left and crosses line 24 slightly less than ⅓ the length of a square below line G. The lip line continues almost horizontally, crossing line 23 and curving downward as it approaches line 22. It then continues on in an arc, crossing line F about ⅐ of the square to the left of line 22. This is only an example showing the head. Follow this procedure until the entire small plan of the whole horse has been transferred and enlarged on the large sheet.

Scale plans can be enlarged commercially, but care must be exercised to see that exactly the desired ratio is maintained. It is also possible to enlarge the plan with a pantograph. The size of the enlargement will be limited by the length of the arms on the pantograph. It is also possible to make the enlargement in a series of steps, using a photocopier machine, as also could be done with the pantograph. Such step-by-step enlargement is a time-consuming process and has built into it the possibility of a cumulative error. For the large-sized plans, the square method is the best.

MAKING THE TEMPLATES

Since the large carving blocks are made up of many pieces of wood laminated together, it is often necessary to repeat a particular shape. Although this can be done from the plan you just drew, it is more convenient and accurate to use templates. A template is merely a cardboard pattern of each part that will constitute the carving block, with added provision for the desired mortise or tenon attachment that is needed in larger animals. Using the full-sized plan, note the desired number of carving blocks. Trace the pattern of each carving block onto approximately 1⁄16″-thick noncorrugated cardboard. The backing from charts used in seminars is a good source for this material. Since this backing is discarded when the pad of paper is used, ask your local motel or conference center to save the material for you. Where appropriate, add the tenon to each pattern or mark the mortise area (See Illus. 88. This is discussed in more detail in Chapter VII). Cut out the outline of each part to form the template, which will be used to transfer the pattern to the basswood.

LAMINATING THE CARVING BLOCKS

To carve a large carousel animal from a single block of wood is not a good idea for three reasons: (1) it would be almost impossible to prevent it from checking and cracking; (2) it would be extremely heavy and hard to manipulate while the carving is being done; and, (3) at some point on the carving, cross grain would become involved. These disadvantages can be overcome by laminating—gluing several thin pieces together—to form each carving block. Illus. 83 shows a laminate part for the head being roughed out. Large carousel animals have hollow bodies to reduce their weight and to save lumber. The carving blocks should each be prepared following the plans given in Chapter VIII. Be certain that the template is laid out on the wood so that the length of each part follows the grain of the wood. When laminating, lay out each part so that the annual rings alternate, as shown in Illus. 84. The gluing suggestions provided in Chapter I also apply here. You will need a supply of large C-clamps, furniture bar clamps, clamping straps, or very heavy weights to hold each laminate as it is being glued (see Illus. 85). Do not attempt to glue all of the laminates together at one time.

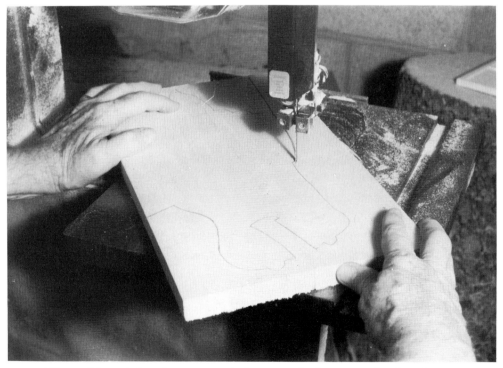

Illus. 83.   A laminate part being roughed out on the band saw.

After you have laminated all the blocks, each block should be carved separately and sanded. The blocks should then be assembled together to insure the proper fit. Do not glue the blocks together at this time. It may be necessary to slightly rework the area

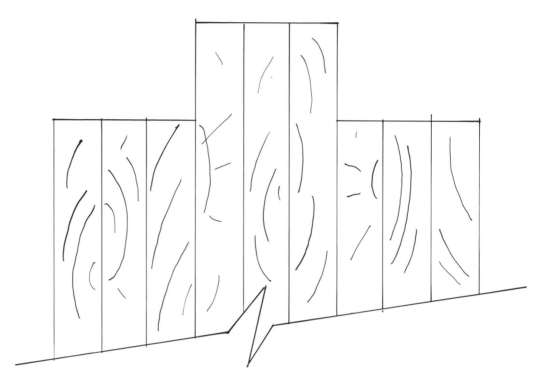

Illus. 84.   Direction of annual rings in laminated block.

Illus. 85.   Laminated parts held in place by a pipe clamp during gluing.

where the separate blocks are joined. It is best to minimize the amount of work required as the carving becomes larger and larger. Then glue the blocks together to make a completed figure. A good rule to follow is to attach the various completed carving blocks in this order: (1) glue head to neck and rework, if necessary, the area where these two pieces come together; (2) glue neck/head unit to the body (Illus. 86); (3) glue the bent legs; (4) add the other legs; and, (5) if there is a carved tail, glue it in place last.

It is extremely important to seal the finished carving to prevent it from absorbing moisture. Household enamel works very well. Paint the body of the horse with four coats of a semigloss enamel. Cut (dilute) the first coat by ⅓ with thinner, and lightly sand the horse between each coat. The final color selections should be of your choice and should harmonize with the horse's surroundings. It is almost impossible to accurately determine the original colors that were used on the Dentzel horses, so don't be limited by the color guides in the book.

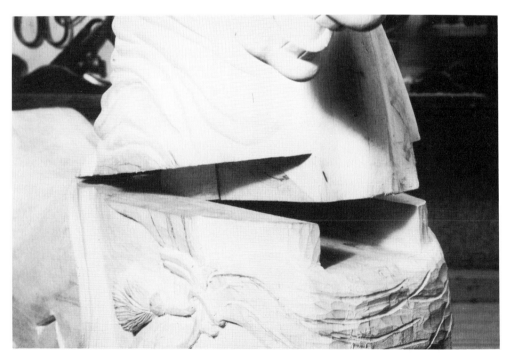

Illus. 86. Mortise and tenon method of joining the neck to the body of a large horse.

HORSESHOES

Just as the romance side plan and inside plan have to be enlarged for the larger animals, so must the horseshoe pattern. Illustration 87 provides a suggested pattern for a ⅞-scale horse. Each shoe is cut from a block of basswood 3¹⁵⁄₁₆″ long, 3″ wide, and ⁹⁄₁₆″ thick. All horseshoes are not a standard design, so the actual style may be adjusted to your likes. Using a band saw, cut out the outline of each shoe. Size or "butter" the end grain at the bottom of each hoof with glue and glue one shoe to each hoof. After the glue is dry, reduce the middle of each side by ⁵⁄₃₂″ as shown (Illus. 87, right). Use a round file or coarse sandpaper wrapped around a ⁵⁄₁₆″ dowel to make a smooth edge between the wearing surface and the reduced area. Use a 2-mm #11 veiner to cut the six indentations in shoe.

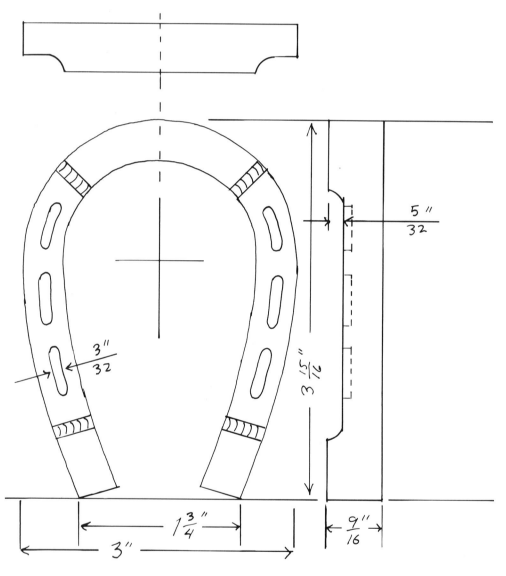

Illus. 87. Horseshoe pattern for ⅞-scale horse.

THE POLE

Commercially available brass sleeves to cover the support pole are available in two popular dimensions, 1″ and 2″ in diameter. It is necessary to select the pole size while the larger animal is being planned. A thin-wall 1¾″ outside diameter pipe that can be purchased from an electrical supply store makes a good support pole.

Illus. 88. Hole saw, for cutting a hole in the body for the support pole.

The pipe goes through the body of the horse and into the stand. The holes can be made using a hole saw (Illus. 88). A 5″-long cross support is inserted perpendicularly into the pole at the point where it will just fit into the underbelly of the horse. A ½″ × 5″ recess is carved in the underside of the body to accept the cross support (Illus. 89). The cross support may be made from a ½″-diameter piece of rod or pipe, or from a large bolt. After the hole is drilled into the support pole, the cross support is inserted and held in place with epoxy glue. The pole is covered by two pieces of the 2″ diameter brass sleeve—one under the horse and the other above the saddle. The pole is topped off with a finial. Several different styles and sizes are commercially available.

The one-inch diameter sleeve and correspondingly smaller pole should be used with the smaller of the large animals (¼ scale and ½ scale). The procedure described above will apply, but the pole openings in the horse and base must be reduced. Depending upon the style of the animal, a cross support may not be necessary for the smaller-scale animals.

Illus. 89.   The support pole inserted into the body. Note the cross-support rod and corresponding carved recess in the underside of the body.

MAKING THE BASE

The large carousel animal when completed will weigh several hundred pounds and will possess a relatively high center of gravity. In order to avoid damaging the carving and to protect individuals from injury from a falling animal, it is important that a sturdy base be selected or constructed. Several different kinds of bases are available commercially; you may want to investigate these possibilities.

I tend to feel that greater realism is achieved using a base that resembles a segment of a carousel platform; it seems more natural to mount the carving this way. The base should be scaled to fit the carving. A full-sized carousel animal will need a base measuring approximately 62″ in length and 24″ in width. Illustration 90 shows the suggested dimensions for a ⅞-scale base. These dimensions can be scaled down or up to suit the larger carving.

This platform segment stand is made from 2 × 4's (which actually measure 1⅝″ × 3⅝″) covered with 3″ tongue-and-groove flooring. In order to achieve uniform bending in the facing board, it will be necessary to cut a series of ⅜″-deep saw kerfs approximately every 6 inches. When the facing is in place, these kerfs can be filled with strips 3⅝″ long and ⅜″ deep, with a thickness slightly less than the saw kerf. This operation is not required, but will make the facing board stronger, and better able to withstand a hard knock.

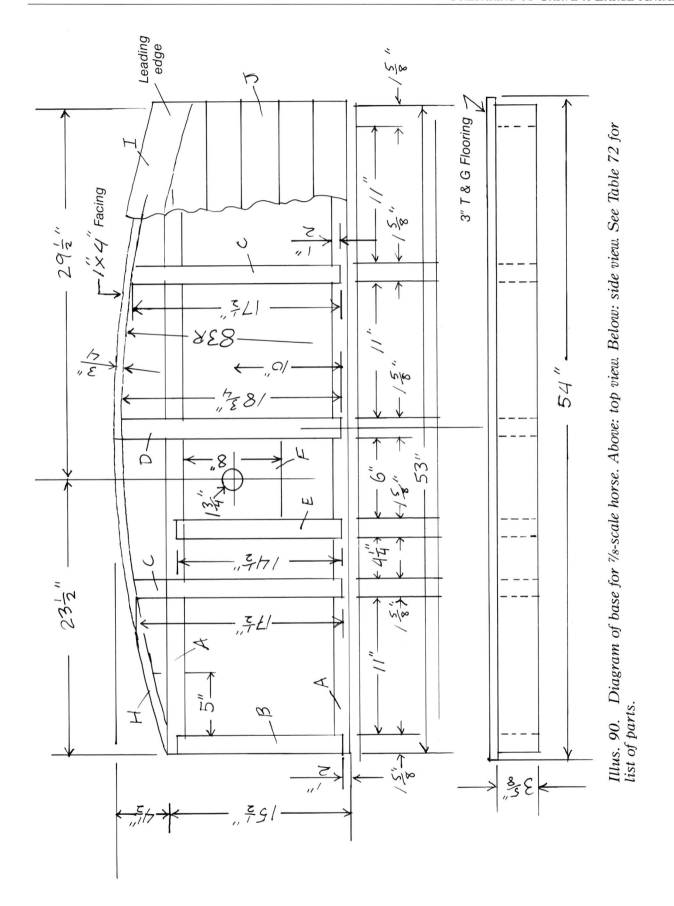

Illus. 90. Diagram of base for ⅞-scale horse. Above: top view. Below: side view. See Table 72 for list of parts.

After the framework is constructed, drill a hole 1¾″ in diameter in a piece of wood (Part F in Illus. 90) that measures 8″ long × 6″ wide × 3½″ thick. If you do not have an extended hole saw, it will be necessary to laminate this block from several pieces after the hole is drilled. Glue a piece of ⅛″ hardboard to the bottom of Part F and glue Part F in place between the studs, as shown. The hardboard will prevent the support pole from scratching the floor.

When the 2 × 4 framework is completed, make the leading edge from three pieces of ¾″ stock. This edge overlaps the facing board by ½″. Cover the framework with 3″ tongue-and-groove flooring. If it is necessary to piece any of the floorboards together, the joint should occur on the center line of a cross member. Cut the front section of the flooring to fit the curve of the leading edge. Table 72 provides a parts list for making the ⅞-scale stand. The stand should be stained or painted to harmonize with its surroundings; it can be highlighted by painting the leading edge a bright color. It will take approximately 24 hours to construct, sand, and finish the stand.

Table 72   Parts List for a ⅞-Scale Horse Stand

	Part	Dimension	Number or Amount Required
A.	Longitudinal member	1⅝″ × 3⅝″ × 53″	2
B.	Cross member	1⅝″ × 3⅝″ × 14½″	2
C.	Cross member	1⅝″ × 3⅝″ × 17½″	2
D.	Cross member	1⅝″ × 3⅝″ × 18¾″	1
E.	Cross member	1⅝″ × 3⅝″ × 14½″	1
F.	Pole support	3½″ × 6″ × 8″	1
G.	Hardboard	⅛″ × 6″ × 8″	1
H.	Facing	¾″ × 3⅝″ × 55″	1
I.	Leading edge	¾″ × 3″ × 20″	3
J.	Flooring	¾″ × 3″	Approx. 7 sq. feet

*See Illus. 90 for diagram of parts.

Carving a Large Horse

he previous chapter presented the basic overview of carving a large-sized carousel animal. Chapter VIII presents specific details, plans, templates, and specifications for carving a ⅞-scale stander, the Horse with Tassels. The horse is a replica of a Dentzel Stander; the trappings were designed for a specific individual.

PLANS AND TEMPLATES

The horse consists of eight carving blocks: head, neck, body, four legs, and tail. Illustrations 91 and 92 present plan views for the romance side and inside of the horse. Each carving block is made up of four or more laminates, to give the correct thickness. Each laminate is made from a template to which a mortise, tenon or both have been added. Illustration 93 shows the location of each carving block in the complete horse. See Illus. 94 through 98 to get plans of pieces, including mortises. Make the templates by enlarging Illus. 94–98 700% (7×), and follow the procedures presented in Chapter VII.

STEP-BY-STEP ASSEMBLY OF LAMINATES

Approximately 100 board feet of basswood having a finished thickness of ⅞″ will be required to construct the eight carving blocks. Because of the size and weight of each part, each carving block should be laminated, carved, and sanded before the horse is assembled.

The parts to be cut out and the order of laminates for each block are presented in Illus. 94–98 and Illus. 99 and 100. As noted previously, the blocks are held together by mortise-and-tenon joints. Dowels may be inserted through these joints if desired, but they will not be necessary if proper care is taken in making the mortise-and-tenon joints. Some carvers may prefer butt joints held together with dowels; however, I would not recommend this. If this is your choice, each template will need to be modified to reflect this decision.

Plan the work so that as you use the templates to mark the laminates, the annual growth rings in the adjacent laminates will be alternated (Illus. 84). The length of each laminate should follow the wood grain. The gluing suggestions provided in Chapter I also apply here. You will need a supply of large C-clamps, furniture clamps, clamping straps, or very heavy weights to hold each lami-

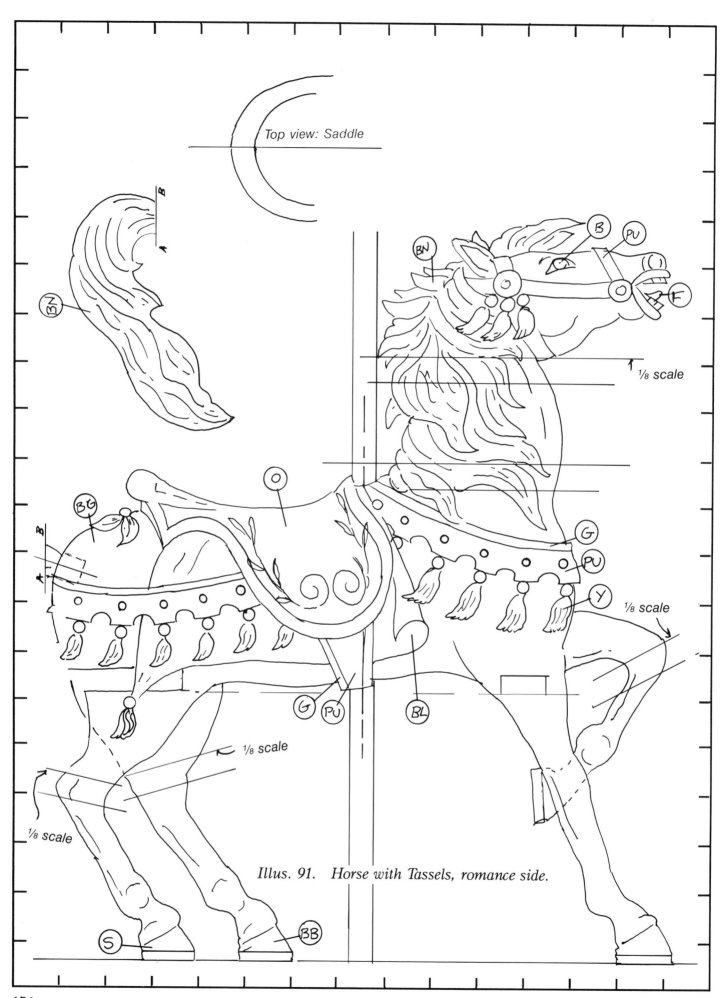

Top view: Saddle

¹/₈ scale

¹/₈ scale

¹/₈ scale

¹/₈ scale

Illus. 91.   Horse with Tassels, romance side.

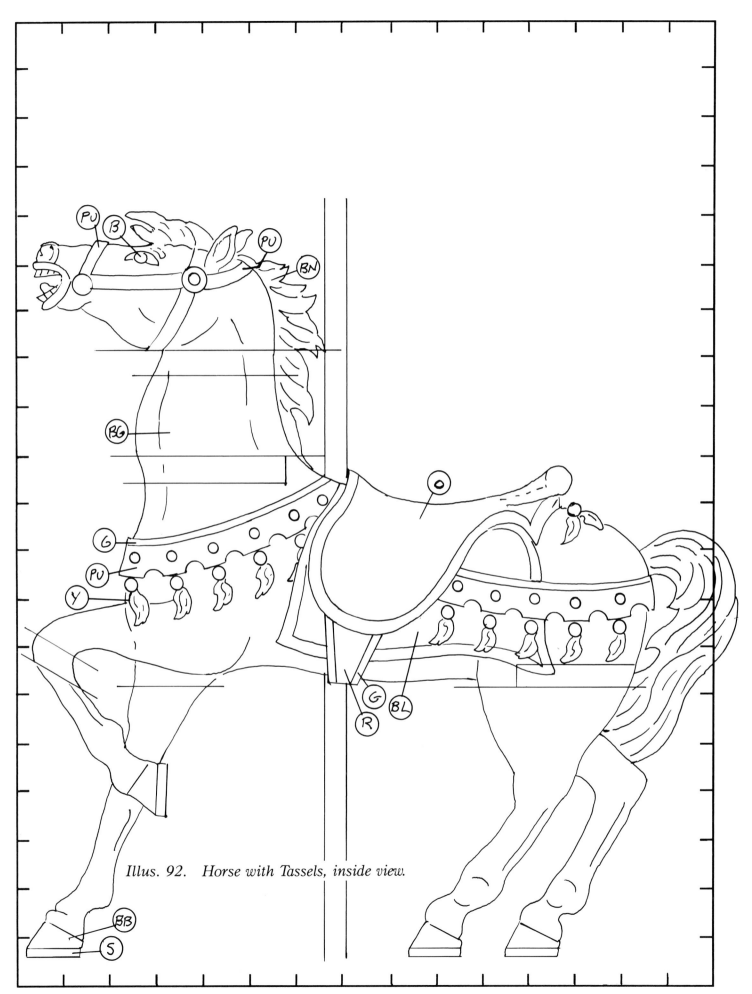

Illus. 92. Horse with Tassels, inside view.

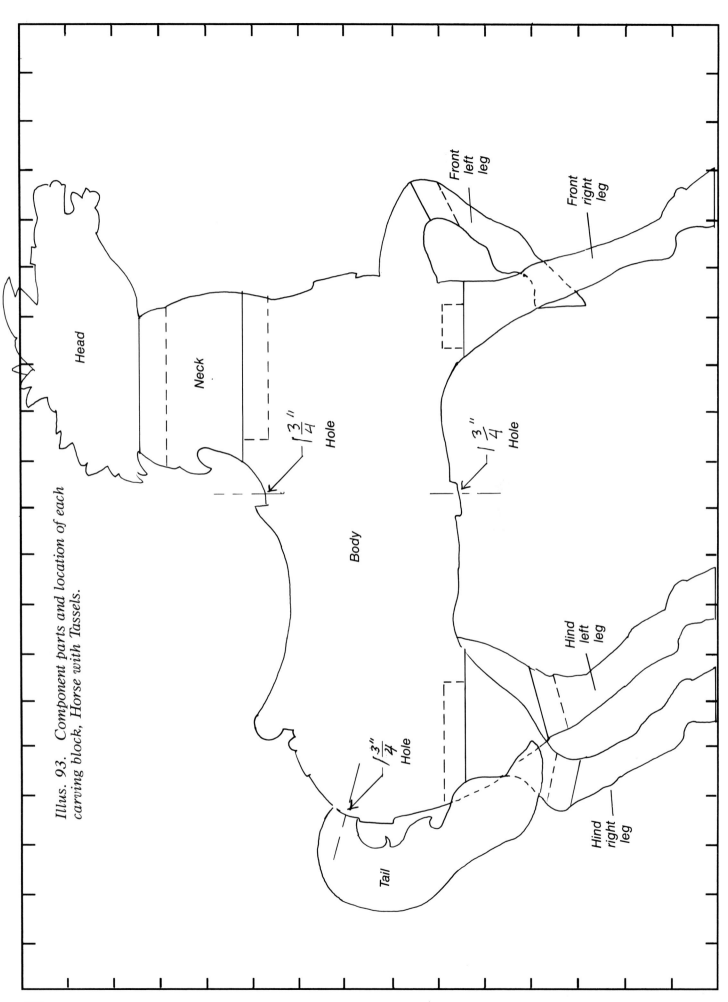

Illus. 93. Component parts and location of each carving block, Horse with Tassels.

Head

Neck

$1\frac{3}{4}''$
Hole

$1\frac{3}{4}''$
Hole

Body

$1\frac{3}{4}''$
Hole

Front left leg

Front right leg

Hind left leg

Hind right leg

Tail

nate until the glue dries. Do not attempt to glue all of the laminates together at one time.

Head

The head is composed of nine pieces and requires seven templates (Illus. 94). Cut out the pieces using a band saw. Imagine that you are standing in front of and facing the horse. Assemble the pieces in the following order: A, B, C, D, D, D, E, F, G. Piece A will be on your left and piece G will be on your right (see Illus. 94, bottom).

Neck

The neck is made up of twelve pieces and uses seven templates (Illus. 95). Cut out the pieces using a band saw. Imagine yourself in the same position as previously described for the head, and assemble the pieces in the following order: H, I, I, J, K, K, K, K, L, M, M, N. Piece H will be on your left and piece N on the extreme right (see Illus. 95, bottom). After the entire neck carving block has been assembled and the glue has dried, the diagonal mortise is cut. On the front, top edge of the mortise (K pieces) measure ⅞″ to the left of the center line. From that point, draw a line through the center line and the midpoint of the top of K. This will give you a new center line running approximately at an 8° angle to the initial center line. Measure 1¾″ on each side of this new center line and draw parallel lines (Illus. 95, bottom right). Where these lines will appear on J and L will determine the new sides for the neck mortise. Using a back saw, cut out the wedge pieces and glue them on the opposite side of the mortise. The piece cut from J, for example, will be put on top of the right-hand K and glued against L. This procedure will restore the 3½″ wide by 2″ deep mortise, but now it will be angled slightly towards the romance side of the horse.

Body

The body is made up of twelve pieces and requires nine templates (Illus. 96–98). The body carving block is hollow and constitutes the largest block. Cut out all of the pieces with the band saw. Assemble the body in two halves. Working in the same position as explained for assembling the head and neck, assemble the romance side half in this order: O, P, Q, R, S, S, Ϙ. Piece O will be on the left and piece S on the right. Assemble the inside view half in this order: Ϙ, S, S, T, U, V, W. The S pieces will meet at the longitudinal center line.

After the glue on both halves has dried, mark the center line for the pole hole (top and bottom) and for the tail. Cut a ⅛″-wide V groove on these center lines in both halves. Put the two halves together and hold them in place with bar clamps. Do not glue them together at this time. Using the V grooves carved in pieces S as a center, and with a hole saw (Illus. 88) set at 2″ diameter make a cut ¼″

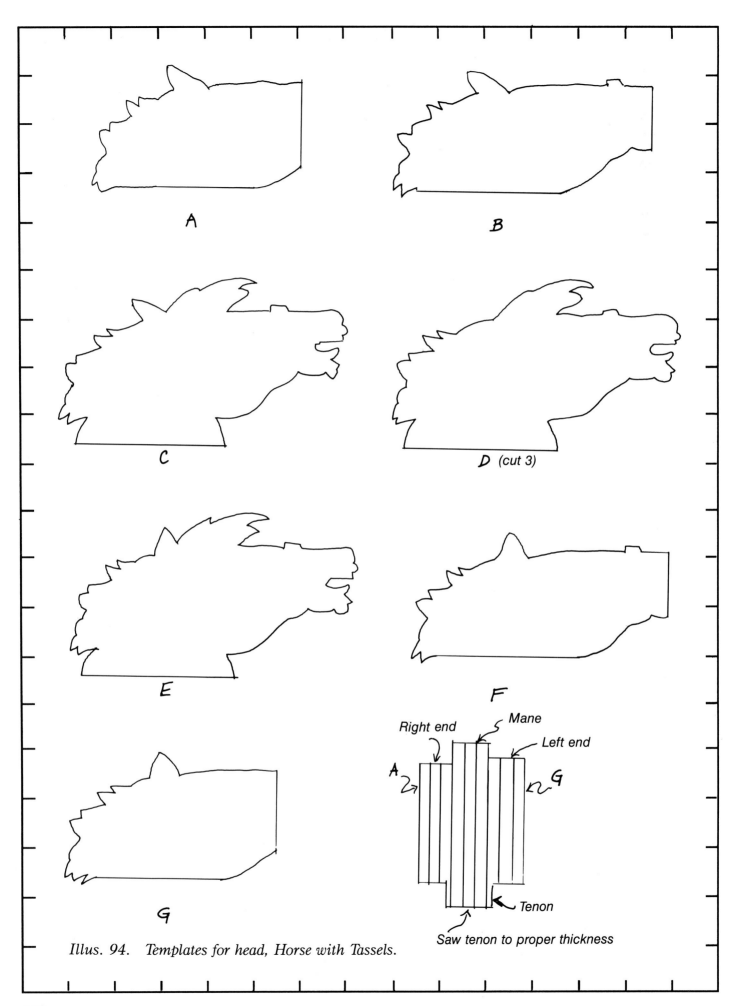

A

B

C

D (cut 3)

E

F

G

Right end

Mane

Left end

A

G

Tenon

Saw tenon to proper thickness

Illus. 94.   Templates for head, Horse with Tassels.

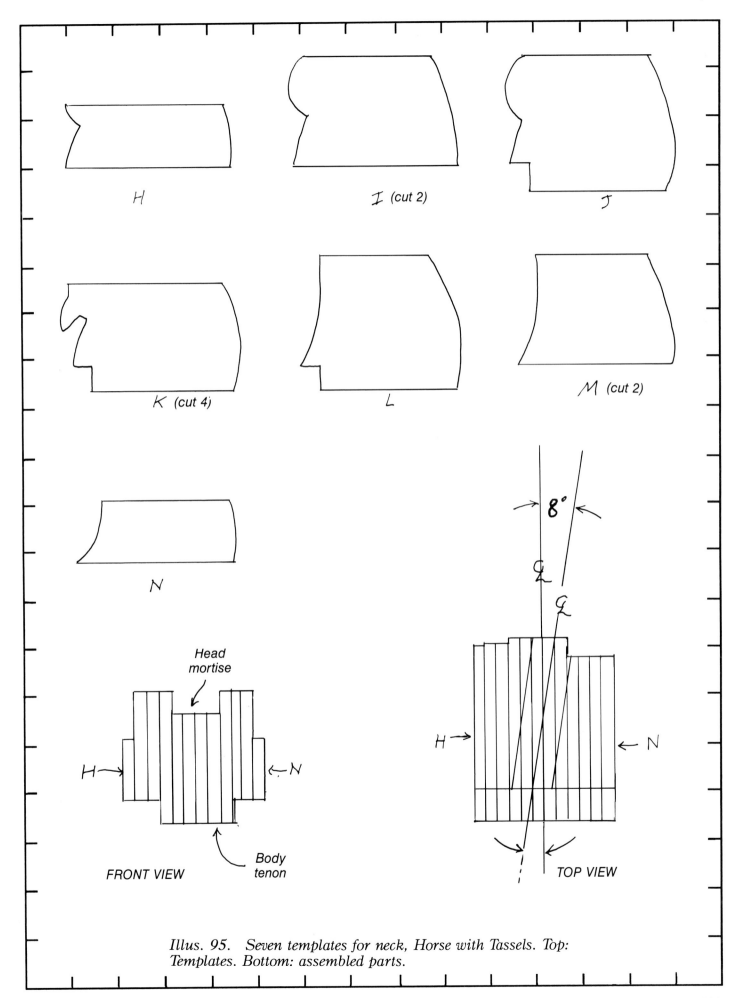

H

I (cut 2)

J

K (cut 4)

L

M (cut 2)

N

8°

℄

℄

Head
mortise

H → ← N

Body
tenon

FRONT VIEW

H → ← N

TOP VIEW

*Illus. 95. Seven templates for neck, Horse with Tassels. Top:
Templates. Bottom: assembled parts.*

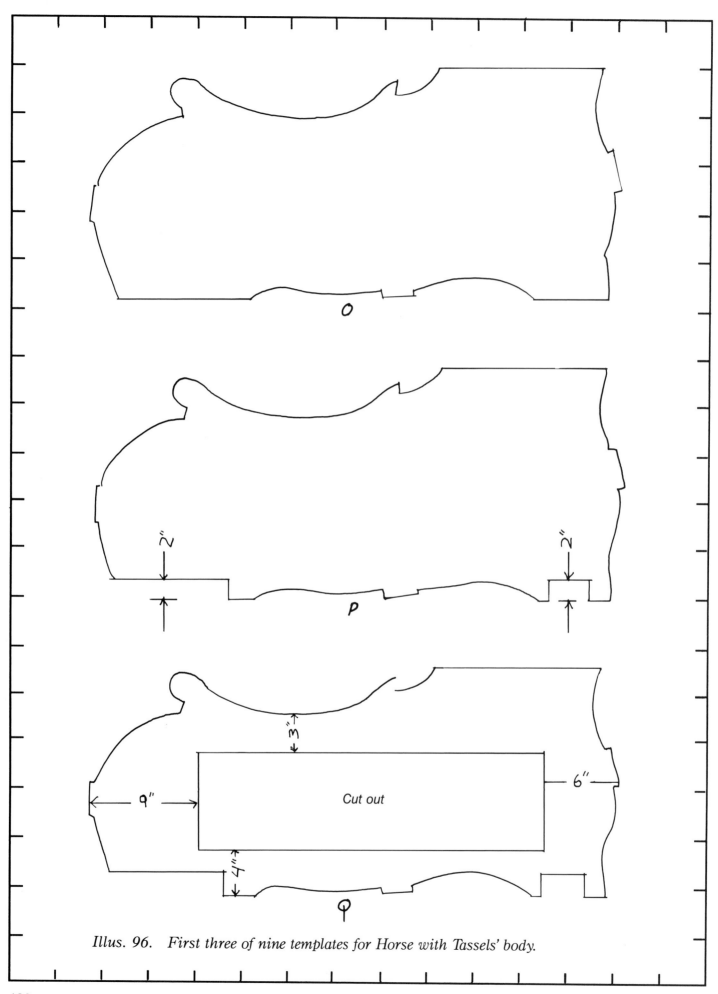

Illus. 96.   First three of nine templates for Horse with Tassels' body.

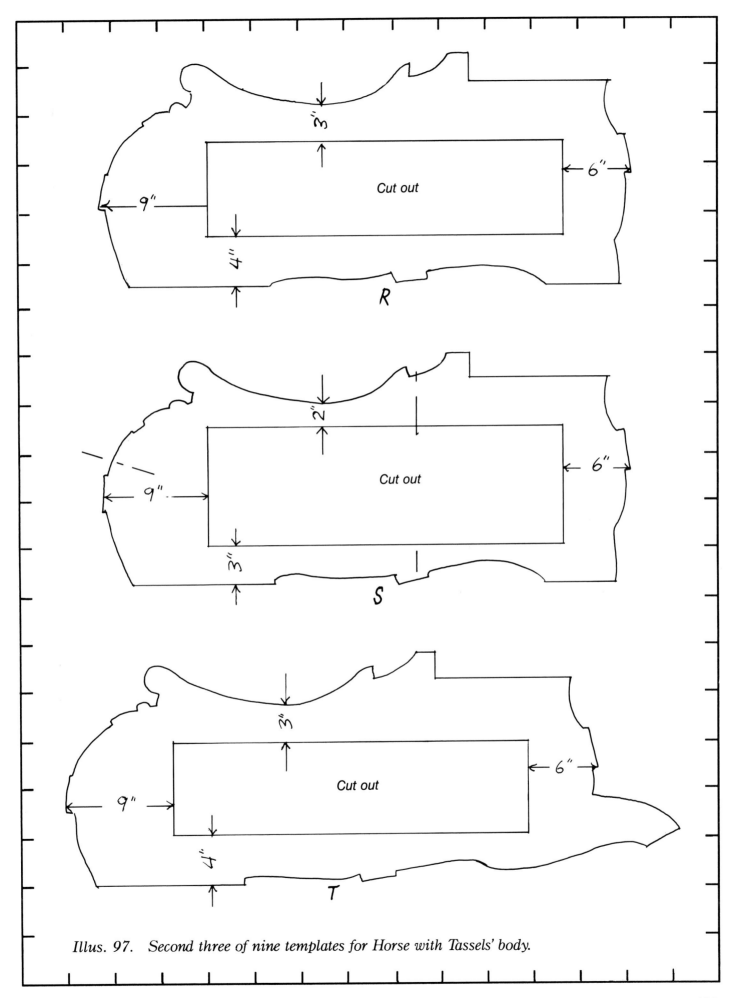

Cut out

Cut out

Cut out

Illus. 97. Second three of nine templates for Horse with Tassels' body.

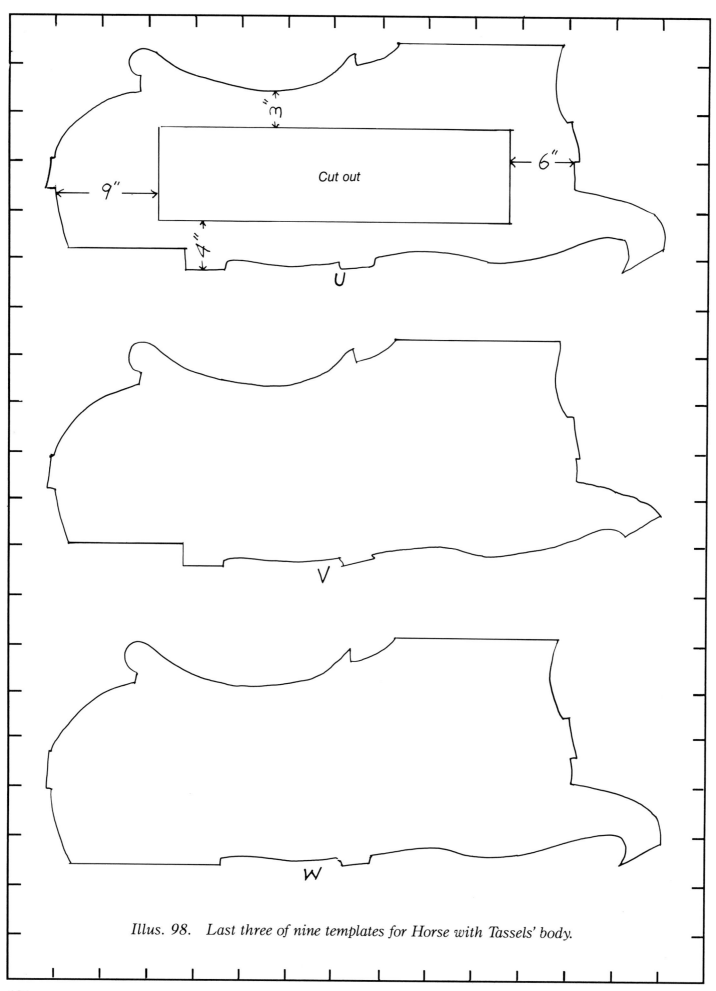

Illus. 98. Last three of nine templates for Horse with Tassels' body.

deep at the top and bottom of the body to cut the recess for the brass sleeve that holds the pole. Reset the hole saw to 1¾" diameter and make a cut in the top and bottom of the body for the pole and in the rump for the tail. Make these cuts as deep as the hole saw will permit. Separate the body into the two halves. Using a straight edge, connect the hole-saw cuts at the top and bottom of each half. With a gouge, such as a #9 35 mm, channel out this area until you have a groove 1¾" wide by ⅞" deep running from top to bottom. This groove will form the opening for the support pole. Using a chisel or knife, cut a ¼" chamfer on the bottom edge of the top semicircles. When the horse is completely assembled, the support pole will be inserted from underneath and this chamfer will assist in guiding the pole into the top hole. Using the same technique, extend the hole saw cut for the tail to a depth of 2½". Glue the two halves together.

Cut a groove ½" deep and 5" long into the underside of the body perpendicular to the length of the animal where the pole will exit, to receive the cross support rod. From ⅝" stock cut out the 22 tassels for the romance and inside of the horse and glue each in on the sides. This will provide added carving depth for the tassels.

Right Front Leg

The right front leg is made of 4 pieces and requires two templates (Illus. 99, top left). Cut out the pieces and assemble them in this order: X, Y, Y, X.

Left Front Leg

The left front leg is partly carved on the body block and partly on four more pieces. Two templates are needed for the additional leg pieces. They are assembled in this order: a, Z, a, Z. (See Illus. 99, top, for templates.)

Right Hind Leg

The right hind leg is composed of ten pieces. It requires six templates and is assembled in two parts—the thigh and leg (see Illus. 99). Cut the ten pieces to shape. Standing in front of and facing the horse, assemble the right hind thigh pieces in the following order: b, c, d, e, e, e, ɕ. Assemble the right hind leg pieces in the following order: j, k, j, k. Join the thigh and leg together to form the complete carving block for the leg.

Left Hind Leg

The left hind leg is also made up of ten pieces, from six templates. It is assembled in two parts—the thigh and leg (see Illus. 95). Cut the pieces to shape. Standing in the same position relative to your work as for the right hind leg, assemble the left hind thigh in the following order: ɕ, i, i, i, h, g, f. Assemble the left hind leg in the

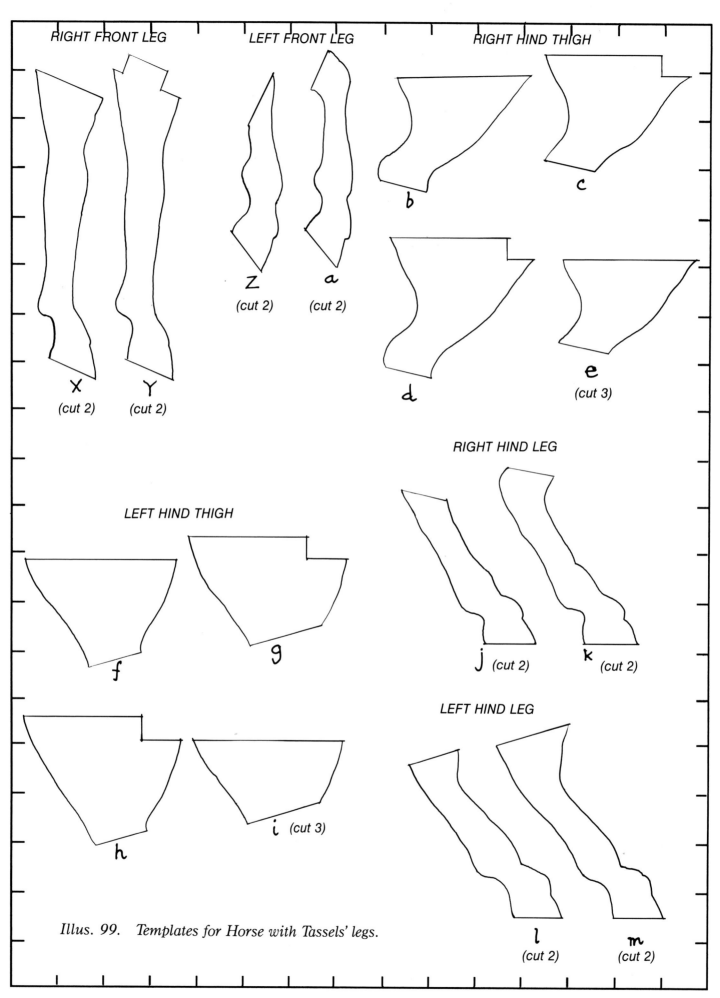

RIGHT FRONT LEG

LEFT FRONT LEG

RIGHT HIND THIGH

b

c

Z
(cut 2)

a
(cut 2)

X
(cut 2)

Y
(cut 2)

d

e
(cut 3)

RIGHT HIND LEG

LEFT HIND THIGH

f

g

j (cut 2)

k (cut 2)

LEFT HIND LEG

h

i (cut 3)

l
(cut 2)

m
(cut 2)

Illus. 99.   *Templates for Horse with Tassels' legs.*

following order: m, l, m, l. Join the thigh and leg together to form the complete carving block for the left hind leg.

Tail

The tail (Illus. 100) is made of six pieces and requires two templates. Cut out the pieces and assemble them in this order: n, n, o, o, n, n. If you desire a less full tail, this block could be made by eliminating one n piece on each end. When the glue is dry, refer to Illus. 3. Starting approximately 8″ from the bottom of the tail, on the inside, draw a sweeping curve across to the bottom and going toward the romance side edge. Follow this line and cut off the triangular segment drawn. Reglue the segment to the romance side of the tail (see Illus. 3). This will enable the tail to curve around the flank and rest on the top of the horse's right hind thigh.

HORSESHOES

Using Illus. 87 as a pattern, cut out four horseshoes from 9/16″ stock and shape as explained in the illustration. Glue one shoe to the bottom of each leg. End-grain gluing is involved, so be certain to "butter" each leg with glue before gluing the shoes in place.

BLOCK CARVING AND ASSEMBLY

Carve each block of the horse separately. Refer to Table 73 for the critical dimensions needed to complete the carving. After all the blocks are carved and sanded, start the assembly by gluing the neck to the head. Attach the carved blocks to the body in this order: left front leg, neck/head, right front leg, right hind leg, left hind leg, and tail. Smooth the joint between carving blocks as they are assembled. Do a final sanding of the entire horse.

The actual carving time will vary with the speed and experience of the carver. In general, a full-sized animal will require 10 to 15 times longer to carve than a 1/8-scale figure. It will take approximately 15 hours to develop the plans and templates, 62 hours to cut and laminate the carving blocks, 195 hours to actually carve and assemble the blocks, 50 hours to sand the animal, and 31 hours to paint it, a total construction time of approximately 353 hours.

FINISHING DETAILS

The thread texture for the tassels and the hair texture of the mane and tail can be created using a burning pen. This will darken the wood, but will not affect the final color, as you can lightly sand after the burning operation. The front of the horse may be embellished with a shield or oval. This provides an opportunity to personalize the horse. A family crest, shown in Illus. 101, was used to add some detail to the Horse with Tassels. The painting suggestions presented in Chapter VI also apply here. The color symbols shown in

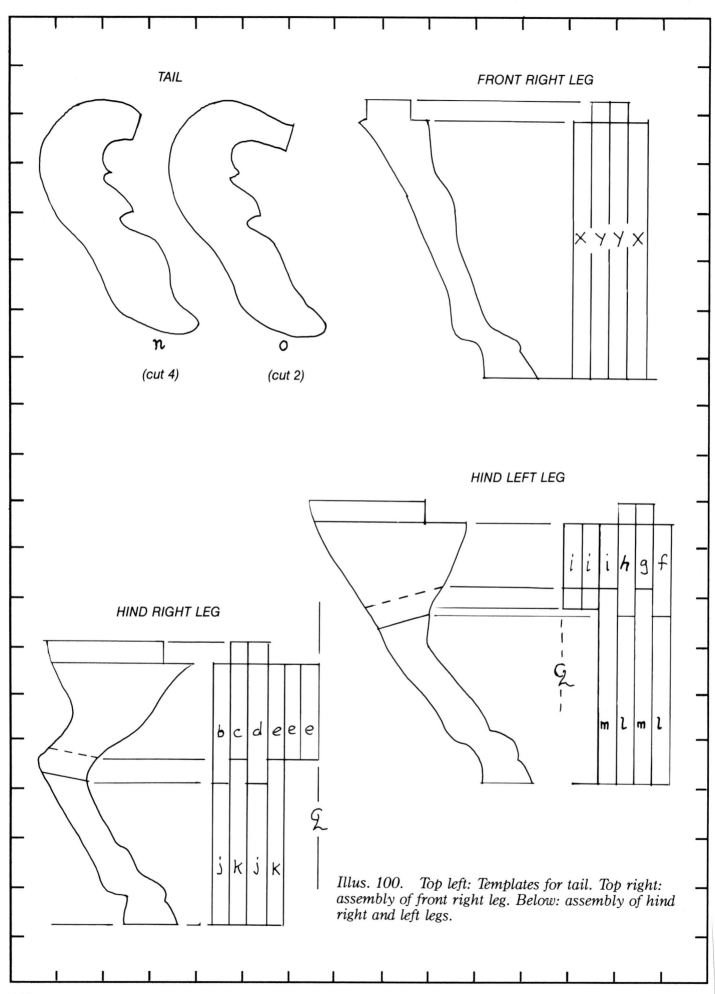

TAIL

FRONT RIGHT LEG

n

(cut 4)

o

(cut 2)

HIND LEFT LEG

x y y x

i i i h g f

HIND RIGHT LEG

b c d e e e

m l m l

j k j k

Illus. 100. Top left: Templates for tail. Top right: assembly of front right leg. Below: assembly of hind right and left legs.

Table 73   Critical Dimensions for the
⅞ Scale Horse

From hoof to tip of ear	52½″
From rump to breast	39⅜″
From tail to front right knee	53⅜″
Width of head	6⅛″
Width of nose	3¹⁄₁₆″
Distance between tips of ears	4¹⁄₃₂″
Width of neck at head	5¼″
Width of neck at body	7⅞″
Width of body at pole	10½″
Width of saddle at rear	10½″
Width of rump	9⅝″
Width of mouth	2³⁄₁₆″
Distance between eyes	5¼″
Width of front leg at body	3½″
Width of front leg at knee	2⅝″
Width of hind leg at body	4⅜″
Width of hind leg at knee	2⅝″
Width of leg below knee	2″
Length of hoof	3¹⁵⁄₁₆″
Width of hoof	3″

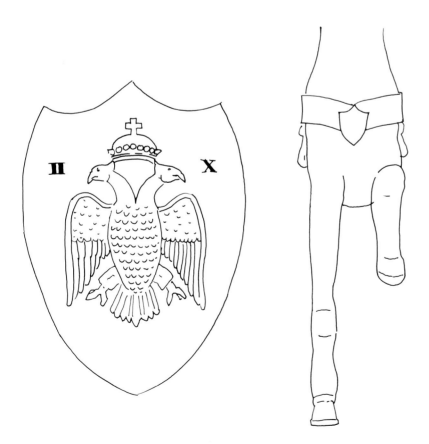

Illus. 101.   Family crest (left); in place on horse (right).

circles in Illus. 91 and 92 were followed in the large Horse with Tassels. A slight deviation from most Dentzel animals was made in that fourteen 18-mm ruby jewels were added in our model.

The pole and base suggestions made in Chapter VII were followed for the ⅞-scale Horse with Tassels. The 1¾″ support pole, which was one piece that went through the horse into the stand, was covered by two segments of a 2″-diameter brass spiral sleeve. The bottom section of the sleeve was 20⅛″ long and the top was 35⅞″. The pole was capped with a global finial.

ASSEMBLING AND DISASSEMBLING A LARGE CAROUSEL ANIMAL

Assembling

1. Lay the animal flat with the romance side up.
2. Insert the support pole from the underside of the belly and position the 5″ long cross support (see Chapter VII).
3. Insert a pin into a hole in the support pole at front of saddle.
4. Place the top and bottom brass sleeves on support pole.
5. Tie the bottom brass sleeve to the animal (this will keep the sleeve in place during the lifting).
6. Lift the animal and place the support pole in the hole in the base.
7. Untie the bottom brass sleeve.
8. Raise the top brass sleeve high enough to remove the pin. Lower the top brass sleeve.
9. Place the finial on top of pole.
10. Insert horsehair tail (if appropriate). (In the Horse with Tassels a carved tail was used.)

Disassembling

1. Remove the finial and horsehair tail (if there is one).
2. Raise the top brass sleeve high enough to insert a pin into the hole in the support pole at the front of saddle.
3. Lower the top brass sleeve.
4. Tie the bottom brass sleeve to the animal (this will keep the sleeve in place during the lifting).
5. Lift animal straight up to remove the pole from the base and lay the animal flat, with the romance side up.
6. Untie the bottom brass sleeve and remove the top and bottom brass sleeves.
7. Remove the pin from support pole.
8. Remove the support pole.

Index

Metric Conversion Table

INCHES TO MILLIMETRES AND CENTIMETRES

MM—millimetres   CM—centimetres

Inches	MM	CM	Inches	CM	Inches	CM
⅛	3	0.3	9	22.9	30	76.2
¼	6	0.6	10	25.4	31	78.7
⅜	10	1.0	11	27.9	32	81.3
½	13	1.3	12	30.5	33	83.8
⅝	16	1.6	13	33.0	34	86.4
¾	19	1.9	14	35.6	35	88.9
⅞	22	2.2	15	38.1	36	91.4
1	25	2.5	16	40.6	37	94.0
1¼	32	3.2	17	43.2	38	96.5
1½	38	3.8	18	45.7	39	99.1
1¾	44	4.4	19	48.3	40	101.6
2	51	5.1	20	50.8	41	104.1
2½	64	6.4	21	53.3	42	106.7
3	76	7.6	22	55.9	43	109.2
3½	89	8.9	23	58.4	44	111.8
4	102	10.2	24	61.0	45	114.3
4½	114	11.4	25	63.5	46	116.8
5	127	12.7	26	66.0	47	119.4
6	152	15.2	27	68.6	48	121.9
7	178	17.8	28	71.1	49	124.5
8	203	20.3	29	73.7	50	127.0